LAURENCE STERNE AND THE ARGUMENT ABOUT DESIGN

LAURENCE STERNE AND THE ARGUMENT ABOUT DESIGN

Mark Loveridge

BARNES & NOBLE BOOKS
TOTOWA, NEW JERSEY

First Published in the U.S.A. 1982 by
BARNES & NOBLE BOOKS
81, Adams Drive, Totowa,
New Jersey, 07512

ISBN 0-389-20106-5

Printed in Hong Kong

To Olive and Basil

Contents

Preface

A number of studies have been of particular help in the construction of this book. Martin Battestin's article '*Tom Jones*: The Argument of Design' suggested a banner under which various aspects of the work could be brought together. The most useful general studies were John Traugott's *Tristram Shandy's World: Sterne's Philosophical Rhetoric*, R. F. Brissenden's *Virtue in Distress*, the chapter on Sterne in A. D. McKillop's *The Early Masters of English Fiction*, and Gabriel Josipovici's *The World and the Book.* Victor Erlich's *Russian Formalism: History–Doctrine* provided the starting-point for the first chapter, and helped to show me an approach to the other materials of the book. The other work which helped to suggest an approach was Ronald Paulson's *Theme and Structure in Swift's 'A Tale of a Tub'*. The chapter on *A Sentimental Journey* has benefited from having to disagree with Arthur Cash's *Sterne's Comedy of Moral Sentiments: The Ethical Dimension of the Journey*.

Rather late in the day, I read Eric Rothstein's *Systems of Order and Enquiry in Later Eighteenth-Century Fiction*, and found it highly interesting on the subjects of system and analogy, and on their prevalcnce in eighteenth-century thought and art. It also has a stimulating chapter on Sterne's methods of construction and control in *Tristram Shandy.*

In the endnotes and bibliography, provenance of sources is London where not otherwise specified.

I should like to record my gratitude for the constant encouragement and stimulation offered by Dr Howard Erskine-Hill of Pembroke College, Cambridge, who supervised the work for the thesis from which this study is adapted. And to Kate, who typed it.

January 1980 *Mark Loveridge*

Acknowledgements

The author and publishers wish to thank the following, who have kindly given permission for the use of copyright material: Oxford University Press for extracts from *An Essay Concerning Human Understanding* by John Locke edited by P. H. Nidditch (1975); and Ram's Horn Music for two lines from *Idiot Wind* by Bob Dylan, copyright © 1974, 1975, all rights reserved.

Abbreviations

TS	Laurence Sterne, *The Life and Opinions of Tristram Shandy, Gentleman* (1760–67), ed. J. A. Work (New York: Odyssey Press, 1940), 4th printing 1960.
SJ	Laurence Sterne, *A Sentimental Journey through France and Italy* (1768), ed. Ian Jack (London: OUP, 1968).
ELH	*Journal of English Literary History*
PMLA	*Publications of the Modern Language Association of America*
MLQ	*Modern Language Quarterly*
EC	*Essays in Criticism*
PQ	*Philological Quarterly*

Introduction

This study is an enquiry into Laurence Sterne's uses of the concepts of pattern, design and form. It examines Sterne's literary applications of these concepts in his two novels, *Tristram Shandy* and *A Sentimental Journey*, and seeks to relate this aspect of his art to elements in the general cultural background to the works, as well as to their specifically literary background.

The original argument about design alluded to in the title is the same argument as is discussed in relation to Fielding's *Tom Jones* in an article by Martin Battestin.[1] Battestin's article is one of the latest works in a long tradition of analysis of the plot of *Tom Jones*. Critics have always been aware that there is something special about the construction of Fielding's book: Coleridge thought that the plot was one of 'the three most perfect ever planned'.[2] More recently, Dorothy Van Ghent described the book as 'a complex architectural figure, a Palladian palace perhaps';[3] and William Empson talks of the received opinion of Fielding having invented 'the clockwork plot'.[4]

What Battestin does is (roughly speaking) to take such words as 'plot' and 'structure', and to put them all on one side in favour of the word 'design'. He advances the theory that the perfection in the design of *Tom Jones* is the perfection of the ultimate neo-classical, Augustan art object. In support of this argument he quotes widely from background sources to show that the attitude of early-eighteenth-century writers to the principles of order, design and symmetry in the work of art grows out of their attitude to the physical and moral cosmos:

> For Fielding, as for Pope and a hundred philosophers and divines of the eighteenth century, Nature was 'the Art of God'; its characteristics were Order and Design, symmetry and proportion.[5]

The evidence of design in the physical universe is used as evidence of moral direction. 'The metaphor of the universe as a vast and intricate machine implying the existence of God, the supreme artificer, was a commonplace in the period.'[6] As indeed it was, and in many periods before this. The argument from design is one of the most ancient and most respected arguments for belief in a deity.

Battestin treats the plot of *Tom Jones* in terms of this argument. In particular he makes an analogy between Fielding's attitude to chance or coincidence in the book, and the attitude of the thought of the age to the same things. The argument is that the apparent coincidences through the novel all tend to promote the happy ending, and that this creates a feeling that even those events which are sensed by the reader as random or casual are in fact under the control of a higher power, 'Fortune', or the more Christian 'Providence'. Battestin quotes from William Sherlock's *Discourse Concerning the Divine Providence* (1694), which refers to 'God's Government of accidental Causes'.[7] He goes on to infer that

> On one level, the design of *Tom Jones* *is* the argument of the novel; and this argument is, in sum, the affirmation of Providence—a just and benign, all-knowing and all-Powerful Intelligence which orders and directs the affairs of men towards a last, just close. . . .
>
> Form *is* meaning . . .'.[8]

Battestin describes the relation between text and background in terms of 'ulteriority'; the novel will deal with 'certain extrinsic, non-organic principles which may generally be termed *figurative* or *analogical*'.[9] The present study attempts to do for Sterne what Battestin did for Fielding. Sterne, though, is a very different kind of artist, and in one sense *Tristram Shandy* is clearly the opposite of *Tom Jones*. Fielding's book is hailed as a conscious masterpiece of design, Sterne's as a conscious masterpiece of undesign. If Sterne's novels are satiric about proportion, decorum and design in the literary sense, they may well betray a sceptical or derogatory attitude towards the manifestations of those same qualities in the background. (To tell the truth, so may *Tom Jones*: it depends whether the reader feels that the coincidences actually disvalue the happy ending.)

One of the features of Sterne's writing is a great skill in creating and playing with correspondences between the world of fiction and the world of his own general cultural and intellectual inheritance. It is often said that his art involves an extensive use of *literary* correspondences of many kinds: pun, double entendre, ambiguity or ambiguousness of meaning, metaphor, analogy, association and so on: it does not seem too far-fetched to extend this concept a little further, and to say that the texts are actually metaphors, literary renderings of their background. And to describe the relation between text and background in terms of a literary process (metaphor) is to admit the very real difficulty of arguing such a claim at any length. It rules out the possibility of pointing to a body of material, or a doctrine, which can be described as 'ulterior'. The 'non-organic principles' are only interesting when the novelist's skill makes them appear to be intrinsic to his work. The interest lies in the manifestations of the artist's talent, not in the objective character or qualities of the background, which can only have the character that the novelist gives it in the course of his work as novelist. Books are not built like the world, but built so as to make the world appear to be like the book.

Structuralist critics in particular complain about the 'myth of the origin',[10] the common idea that novels and other literary works are written in response to a more or less specific stimulus hailing from some department of the 'real', i.e. non-literary world. They do not, I think, complain because such an attitude is entirely false, but because it is limiting. To claim a strong causal relationship between background and text can easily trivialise and systematise the novelist's intentions.

There do seem to be quite genuine temperamental differences between the two types of commentary, formal-intrinsic and background-extrinsic. Critics who explain literature look down on those who merely describe it: those who describe inveigh against those who are so presumptuous as to think literature can be explained, or described by explanation. It may be wise to state at the outset that this is so, and that one is at least going to try to remember it. To state in the same article both that 'form is meaning' and that a novel is designed to reflect certain 'extrinsic, non-organic principles' is only to reveal a dualism, without really adopting a definite position relative to it. Possibly the most profitable attitude in such circumstances is simply to say that it is interesting that the relation between text and background has to be expressed in vocabulary so strongly allusive of literary technique—that it is a 'figurative' relationship, and so cannot be external. The power of literary illusion leads the reader to credit the real world with literary qualities. This happened particularly forcefully to me when I tried to read in the history of ideas in the early eighteenth century after reading Sterne. The peculiar filter of Sterne's fiction coloured the most serious thought of his age—the age of his youth—and persuaded me to see it as comedy, or as conspiracies, forces which his characters had to respond to in comic and obsessive ways. So the background of thought itself was made to take on a dual nature, at once comic and rather sinister, and this in turn seemed to bring out the nature of the novels themselves. The particular tone of Sterne's novels is, I think, achieved through blending comedy of several kinds with a genuine sense of psychological danger and instability which comes partly from the strength of the influence that the world outside has on the characters.

With these qualifications in mind, the following chapters will argue between texts and background by presenting two or three different cases, each concerned with a particular aspect of form and design. The overall argument is really no more than that these several arguments are all consistent with each other, and tend to demonstrate the same thing.

The first of these cases is a short consideration of *Tristram Shandy* and *A Sentimental Journey* in relation to The Novel—are they representative of the form in general, or are they extreme and eccentric?

Here a paradox begins to emerge. Sterne's intention in *Tristram Shandy* appears to be satiric or destructive of 'form' in this general sense of conventionality. Sterne's novel seems like a shantytown alongside Fielding's palace. Yet it is *Tristram Shandy*, and not *Tom Jones*, which has been referred to as 'the most typical novel in world literature'[11] by a critic using a formalist approach. The paradox is that to break design and pattern is to be expressive of form, or to be seen to be expressive of it. A possible explanation of this paradox will be sought through an examination of the state and the reception of the English novel in the 1760s, and through an examination of some reactions to Sterne's novels from literary artists who have found Sterne of relevance to their own efforts to understand and effect changes in the form of the novel.

Those chapters which deal with the wider background to the novels will discuss some of the uses, applications and perversions of the idea of design in the religious, scientific and moral thought of the late seventeenth and early eighteenth centuries. They will also try to establish that the scepticism about the concept of pattern that Sterne exhibits in his novels is in part a result of—or a corollary of—his contemplation of this background. Sterne, in his modern, anti-classical, indecorous, disproportionate novels, breaks up the old ground and thus breaks new. But are his reasons merely negative, or are they also positive? Are his novels in fact expressive of what he sees as true values under attack from a perversion of the old, outdated values? Are they even great defensive humanist statements?

Such questions are, of course, much too serious to be applied to Sterne—akin to the present overvaluation of Sterne as a serious thinker, a miraculous precursor of moderns. They also seem to be leading the discussion away from an examination of Sterne's art as a novelist towards 'ulteriority'. But I hope that the close reading of the novels which is attempted in the remaining chapters will reinforce the character claimed for the background, and will lead the reader to wonder whether such large and portentous questions do not, after all, have some validity. 'Is there any great novelist', asks F. R. Leavis —thirty pages after a description of Sterne's writing as 'irresponsible (and nasty) trifling'—'whose preoccupation with "form" is not a matter of his responsibility towards a rich human interest, or complexity of interests, profoundly realised?'[12] This question seems to me to be as applicable to Sterne as to anyone else. The diversity and precision of Sterne's manipulations of 'form', once recognised, allow an approach to his work which can acknowledge that his awareness of his 'responsibility' may well originate in his peculiar consciousness of form.

1 Sterne and the Form of the Novel

I STERNE AND THE ENGLISH NOVEL

Sterne's novels occupy a curious and quite specific position in English literary history. They were published in a period when prose fiction was entering upon a difficult time.

> During the years that follow the death of Smollett . . . the two chief facts about the novel are its popularity as a form of entertainment and its inferiority as a form of art.[1]

People thought that the novel was dying, and they noted its imminent demise regretfully. As early as the 1760s the critical periodicals begin to deplore the low achievement of the contemporary novel, and to lament the fall of the form from its past greatness. John Northouck, for instance, is already complaining about the lack of any originality in 'the common race of novels' in 1768. He particularly complains about

> the machinery by which they are all conducted, as hard-hearted, avaricious fathers, proud mothers, base, abandoned, libertine lovers, stolen or pretended marriages, sham arrests, the usual workings of the tender passions, rivals, exalted double-refined love, heroic fortitude, poverty and distress, unexampled generosity, unexpected good fortune, and improbable coincidences of events; all these constitute a general sameness as will . . . render them at length tiresome.[2]

His acquaintance with a 'common stock of foolish incident' in a tradition of conventional sub-Richardsonian novels is clearly of long standing. But the other classic writers of the time—

Fielding, Smollett and Sterne—were also treated as models, as patterns to be followed. 'Close imitations of Fielding, Richardson and Smollett were stock lines.'[3] By 1822 these writers were being seen (by Charles Lamb) as 'Great Nature's Stereotypes',[4] seen as novelists having the stature of absolutes or epitomes, defining the forms inside which later writers were to have their being, and from which no evolution was possible.

But though no real progress was made, there was a kind of devolution from the forms of the novel that the early masters had set up—a nominal devolution. Novelists began to see themselves not as writing A Novel so much as a particular kind of novel, which usually had a particular name to it. The 'Sentimental' and 'Gothic' schools are the two best-known ones, but there are others: for example, between 1760 and 1800 there was a large number of publications of imitation 'Quixote'-novels, most of which derive in part from Fielding's use of the Cervantic character, notably that in *Joseph Andrews*. There were City and Female Quixotes, Quixotes Spiritual, Philosophical, Amicable, Benevolent, Political and Infernal.[5] There was also a long run of 'Cottage' novels, a domestic-romantic-sentimental genre (Miss Sterling's choice remark in *The Clandestine Marriage*—'Love and a cottage!—Eh, Fanny—Ah, give me indifference and a coach and six!—'[6] is made with half an eye on this tradition). The genre took upon itself the job of blending the idylls of the Romance with the sense of interchangeable experience to which Richardson had accustomed readers. But these forms were still mainly dependent on the earlier models.

With their relevant conventions so clear that they could be easily listed by a contemporary observer such as Northouck, these new forms of the novel existed in high definition. The most representative works of each genre tended to be those in which the conventions were most closely or most wholeheartedly followed. This makes for a rather curious situation, in that it is sometimes very difficult to distinguish between representative works and eccentric works. It is hard to tell genuine, seriously-intended novels from parodies: the genres seem quite capable of burlesquing themselves with no outside interference. This creates retrospective critical astonishment—for instance, Archibald Shepperson, talking about a novel published in 1802 called *The Slave of Passion; or, The Fruits of Werther*, says, 'Incredible as it may seem, *The Slave of Passion* appears to have been intended and received as a serious novel and not as a burlesque'.[7] Occasionally the introductory remarks to a novel will express this awareness of confusion: at the beginning of *Family Secrets* (1797), the 'librarian' requests that the author should provide 'fine light tragical reading', not 'one of your heavy merry books'.[8]

With the drama the situation is a little clearer, in that the best works—the only works that have lasted to be regularly performed in the twentieth century—are the sentimental comedies of Sheridan and Goldsmith and one or two others, all of which were produced, in part at least, in conscious reaction to the genre of 'serious' sentimental plays. The tenth-night prologue to *The Rivals* again shows the writer's awareness of the contemporary heightening and muddling of genre. Three figures are described: firstly, Comedy; secondly

> The Goddess of the woeful countenance,
> The sentimental Muse;[9]

and thirdly, Tragedy. Of these, Tragedy fulfils her conventional function, Comedy is 'humorous', good-humoured, and the 'sentimental muse' is the spirit of high camp and histrionics:

> She'll snatch the dagger from her sister's hand;
> And having made her votaries *weep a flood*,
> Good Heav'n! She'll end her Comedies in blood.[10]

And in the first scene of *The Critic*, Sir Fretful Plagiary (a dramatic travesty of Richard Cumberland, author of sentimental plays such as *The Brothers* and *The West Indian*—this last was also the stimulus to Goldsmith's writing *She Stoops to Conquer*) complains to Sneer that

> 'a dext'rous plagiarist might do any thing.—Why, sir, for ought I know, he might take out some of the best things in my tragedy, and put them into his own comedy.'
>
> 'That might be done, I dare be sworn,'[11]

sneers back Sneer.

It is curious that no novel of the period displays quite so light and sure a touch on such questions as do these plays. No novel illustrates quite so well the taste of a late-eighteenth-century audience which is sophisticated and aware of questions of literary form and genre.

There is, however, a course of action open to the novel in such circumstances which is not available to the drama. A novel, much more readily than a play, may burlesque or make fun of its own potential audience. In particular, it may try to draw from its readers a conventional response to material which has been designed to be ambiguous as to the conventions of the form (rather than completely ludicrous). In this way, the particular form within which the novelist appears to work will be left ostensibly untouched, even enriched, but the propriety of the audience's response to that form will be called into question. The enthusiastic response to the work of art becomes, unconsciously, an ironic object. So by establishing a complicated and ambiguous relationship with the audience, a novelist may implicitly provide a formal commentary: as the taste of the audience is defined and played upon, so the favourite fare of that taste is judged. A dramatist cannot take such liberties, because he cannot reserve to himself the tool with which it is accomplished: rhetoric.

One could not wish for a novel in which the relationship between writer and reader is more complicated than *Tristram Shandy*, nor for a more comprehensive parody of the conventional novel. Tristram is the opposite of a dramatist, in that he reserves most of his powers of rhetoric for himself, and only sparingly delegates them among his characters. Walter Shandy would be eloquent, but most of the time he lacks that most basic of requirements for a rhetor, a naturally responsive audience. Tristram takes the presence and involvement of his own audience very much for granted, and plays up to it.

This is of course partly due to Sterne's choice of form, which is what Wayne Booth calls the 'self-conscious narrator'[12]—not a new form, in fact 'almost hackneyed'[13] by the time Sterne wrote *Tristram Shandy*. But Tristram does not talk to the audience simply as a representative of a tradition of self-conscious narration. It is highly directional rhetoric: he talks from one tradition to another, to readers who read conventional novels and who bring some of their values along with them to this eccentric work. Rhetorical devices which appear purely conventional inside the book take on other implications when they are considered in their wider eighteenth-century context.

To take an obvious instance: one of the readers that Tristram conjures up is a being addressed as 'Madam'—a conventional enough premise from which to start. But as he uses the convention he also makes a larger point, a point invisible in the book as it stands but which becomes clearly visible in the context of the contemporary audience. *Tristram Shandy* is the devil's work.[14] It is obscene, nasty and lewd, and to be kept at all costs from the decent and virtuous members of the weaker sex. So 'Madam', the 'gentle reader' ('Fy! Mr. *Shandy*:—'[15]) that Tristram puts forward as his idea of who is reading his book is violently at odds with the idea his audience has of who should be allowed to read it, or who would enjoy it. It is a typical joke for *Tristram Shandy*, in that it does not exist in the book so much as in the situation of its being read in the late eighteenth century, in the context of an audience more female than male, and much more middle-class than otherwise: the audience, in fact, whose craving for conventional fiction was to lead to the decay of the novel as an art form at this time.

Rhetoric is so much Tristram's natural mode of expression that it has even been claimed as a Structural Principle of the book. Ian Watt asserts[16] that the arrangement of chapters is based on units of rhetoric, not of narrative—that the conversational period determines the length of the chapter: and John Traugott's pioneering study, *Tristram Shandy's World*,[17] is, in part, a demonstration of Tristram's purpose as being to describe the mental processes of the characters and the readers through the forms of rhetoric.

Yet if we suppose that the most important function of Sterne's rhetoric is to further his discussion of questions of literary form and genre, it becomes clear that *Tristram Shandy* is in fact the less rhetorical *in form* of Sterne's novels. The work alluded to in the paragraph about the burlesquing of the audience is *A Sentimental Journey*. This involves a particular kind of rhetoric, one which is also found in *Tristram Shandy* but which is central to the *Journey*. Rhetoric poses questions, creates dualisms which appear to demand answers, demand that the auditor commit himself and adopt a particular stance in relation to the subject under discussion. The ambiguity in the relationship between the text and the readers of the *Journey* is primarily of one type. The book forces a single question on the reader. Are the events and their presentation by Yorick genuinely sentimental, or do they satirise sentiment? Readers find themselves faced with one continual choice of interpretation, a choice which determines whether the book is seen as the epitome of the sentimental genre or a parody of it.

The history of criticism of the *Journey* is largely a history of attitudes to this particular question. At first the work was accepted as genuine: the sentimental response took place. When enthusiasm for naked sentiment in literature waned, the book was regarded as an interesting oddity. More recently, the other side of the case has been popular: works such as those by Dilworth[18] and New[19] have argued for a satirical interpretation, a kitsch *Journey*, emphasising that there is a sentimental 'trap' in the book.

In between these extremes is much sensible criticism which finds it has to deal with both sides of a question. Gardner Stout says that the *Journey* embodies 'a double awareness, combining the subjective experience of the "man of feeling" and the objective vision of the man of infinite jest'.[20] R. F. Brissenden similarly calls attention to this dualism in the presentation of Yorick, saying that 'In an extremely subtle and ambiguous manner Yorick . . . represents at once the hope embodied in the sentimental ideal and the fear that it may prove inadequate'.[21] Such criticism contends that the *Journey* is neither one thing nor the other, neither sentimentalist nor satirical, but a delicate blend of both. Yorick may be fond of parading his feelings, but he often seems to have a degree of tongue-in-cheek awareness of how he is appearing to the reader. Such criticism points out that the question—like the traditional question of whether or not *Tristram Shandy* is obscene and immoral—is irrelevant.

This is criticism which is very aware of the traps set for those who have gone before, those who have committed themselves to either viewpoint. It is forced to admit that Sterne has designed his book to be two things at once. But this merely reasserts (although it does not acknowledge) that the text does pose the question. Stout and Brissenden are perhaps concentrating too hard on giving both answers to be able to see that the point of the original question was that it demanded an either/or response: that it played on the pre-established taste of the audience to good rhetorical effect.

Every accurate criticism of Sterne is a formalist criticism, in the sense that it is born of a consciousness of his work in relation to conventional novels. The more a commentator is aware of the various types of conventionality in the novel (even the 'anti-novel' is a convention), the more complete his criticism will tend to be. Similarly, every criticism which is incomplete or which misses the mark does so to the extent that it misapprehends or mistakes the nature of Sterne's complex relationship with the various species of prose fiction—and it will do this even when its appreciation of the kind of life which Sterne's works have about them is valuable. For instance when Work says, quite rightly, that 'The shadow of sexual impotence hovers like a dubious halo over the head of every Shandy male, including the bull',[22] the criticism is incomplete until one has also said that this condition is not merely one of the facets which make up the peculiar life of the Shandy household and the plot of *Tristram Shandy*. It is also partly satire of a received state of artistic affairs which was coming to control the form of the novel, whereby sexual potency (love, lust, etc.—see Northouck's 'base, abandoned, libertine lovers') is made a prerequisite of the plot. Take away the sex-urge and Richardson and Fielding fall to the ground. Not that Sterne says that the sex-urge is a ludicrous thing on which to found a genre of the novel: he merely moves the obsession with sex a few notches towards the more dubious end of the fastidiousness–grossness scale, and the complaints come rolling in. As with the point about the reader known as 'Madam', the joke is not to be fully appreciated inside the book. Inside the book it has one kind of meaning and one kind of life; outside, another. The moving of the obsession with sex along that scale is in itself a rhetorical engine, in that it virtually demands a stance from the audience.

Unlike the *Journey, Tristram Shandy* is not an example of a genre-novel: it 'fits uneasily into pigeonholes'.[23] Whenever a commentator decides that the book is part of a tradition, whether 'Tory satire',[24] 'learned wit',[25] an 'anatomy',[26] a 'rhetorical' work[27] or anything else, he always finds he has to admit that this is only true to a limited extent; that '*Tristram Shandy* is a novel and nothing else but a novel',[28] as Walter Allen puts it. It is always possible to go to the other extreme, and call the book the 'ultimate expression of *a*-literature in the eighteenth century',[29] but whichever way one turns, a certain width of definition is found to be necessary. One is led towards the paradox that *Tristram Shandy*, in setting itself in conscious opposition to conventional novels, becomes an entirely typical novel. The situation is analogous to that of the *Journey*: the book demands to be seen as one thing or the other. By showing that the novels which its audience takes to be conventional, representative works may well in fact be eccentric, it poses the question: Am I not myself, seeming eccentric, really a manifestation of true form? It is a playful, serious, rhetorical question which, in many different ways, lies at the heart of *Tristram Shandy*.

It seems to be an accepted fact that the function of Tristram's rhetorical conversation with the reader is basically to force choices upon him. The choices with which one is faced are multifarious, smaller and less specific than is the case with the *Journey*, where the choice is usually between two more or less opposite readings. Tristram is much more aware of the implications of his own position than Yorick is, and so more consciously concerned to present the reader with ambiguous material. R. S. Hafter says of *Tristram Shandy*,

> Perhaps the most insistent demand on the reader is that of choosing between alternative interpretations, which frequently lie at opposite ends of the emotional spectrum. Are we, for example, to regard Le Fever's death as pathetic or bathetic? . . . Sterne seems to design many passages to give free play to more than one response.[30]

He quotes the conversation between Tristram and Eugenius in Volume III, Chapter 31 as illustrating Sterne's conscious intention in this regard:

> Here are two senses, cried *Eugenius*, as we walk'd along, pointing with the fore finger of his right hand to the word

> *Crevice*, in the fifty-second page of the second volume of this book of books,—here are two senses,—quoth he.—And here are two roads, replied I, turning short upon him,—a dirty and a clean one,—which shall we take?—The clean,—by all means, replied *Eugenius*.[31]

From this, Hafter draws this lesson:

> His ambiguity, then, unlike that of the modern novelist, is not intended to charge his prose with multiple levels of meaning but to induce the reader's participation in that essential human activity of choicemaking.[32]

(Although to my mind the reader does not choose as *a man*, but as a reader.) Again, the creation of this ambiguity or ambivalence is in part duc simply to the choice of form. When Henri Fluchère is discussing the autobiographical convention and the tradition of the self-conscious narrator, he says this of the form:

> Elle a pour but d'établir des rapports personnels de pensée et d'émotion entre l'auteur et son lecteur, et se fonde sur une constante de raison, de sensibilité et de goût qui rend possible la compréhension mutuelle. C'est un aveu implicite que le livre n'existe pas en soi, dans l'impersonnalité indifférente de l'oeuvre d'art, mais qu'il recevra son sens et pourra remplir sa fonction d'après l'acceuil qui lui sera fait.[33]

Yet this is and is not true of *Tristram Shandy*, which adopts the traditional form of self-conscious narration only insofar as it is useful in adopting a position relative to other genres. Fluchère's second sentence applies perfectly to Sterne, the first hardly at all.

Ian Watt argues persuasively that Sterne's peculiar *syntax* is designed to be non-committal, designed to leave the reader to select his own personal attitude of response. In particular Sterne achieves this with his use of the dash—

> A special stylistic strategy was required to express the coexistence of humour and sentiment, and indeed of a very

> large diversity of attitudes, in a context that did not impose or imply a rationally-ordered hierarchy of values . . .
>
> His ostentatiously permissive syntax allows each category its own independent existence; the dash makes no assertion of relation, but allows the sense to flow forwards and backwards between the phrases which it conjoins, very much at the reader's pleasure; the emphasis is up to us, and if there is exclusion, it is we who make it.[34]

Watt points out that this gambit is by no means peculiar to the novel: 'This sort of intentional leaving of the final evaluative attitude up to the audience is a very common one in the stage comic'.[35] One thinks of Frankie Howerd's trademark—'Well, please yourselves'.

It is interesting that when Sterne himself comes to examine the fact that audiences of fiction *do* please themselves, he also emphasises how typical of fiction he believes his book to be. All these comments by Hafter and Fluchère and Watt in fact look very like glosses on one of Sterne's very few remarks about his own fiction outside of the novels themselves. This is the fascinating letter Sterne wrote in 1768 to Dr John Eustace, thanking him for a walking-stick Dr Eustace had sent him. The walking-stick had two handles.

> Your walking-stick is in no sense more *shandaic* than in that of its having *more handles than one*. The parallel breaks only in this, that in using the stick, everyone will take the handle which suits his convenience. In 'Tristram Shandy' the handle is taken which suits their passions, their ignorance or sensibility. There is so little true feeling in the *herd* of the *world*, that I wish I could have got an act of parliament, when the books first appear'd, 'that none but wise men should look into them'. It is too much to write books and find people to understand them . . . but it is not in the power of anyone to taste humour, however he may wish it—'tis the gift of God—and besides, a true feeler always brings half the entertainment along with him. His own ideas are only call'd forth by what he reads, and the vibrations within so entirely correspond with those excited, 'tis like reading *himself* and not the *book*.[36]

(It is worth noting that the central idea of the passage is itself an echo of uncle Toby's remark to Trim in Volume VIII, Chapter 19, that 'a man should ever bring one half of the entertainment along with him'[37] when he listens to a story: that his mood should predetermine him to sympathise with the tale.) Two different but related points can be made here, one by taking 'the herd of the world' to be referring more to the critics who attacked and belittled *Tristram Shandy*, and another by taking it as referring more to the audience in general. Either context might be suitable: the passage is deliberately unspecific. At the crucial point—'their passions, their ignorance'—the pronouns are left unsullied by any concrete reference to readers or critics. Practising what he preaches, Sterne leaves the reader to choose a handle to the passage itself.

If one assumes that it refers more to the critics, one could say that the passage swings round from being an apparently derogatory fling at amateur and prejudiced commentators on his book to a balanced statement about fiction in general ('a true feeler always brings . . .') which is intended to soften the impact of what he has just said: anodyne by generalisation. But the two elements of the passage, which are presented as being in harmony, in fact grate together. First Sterne says that something is happening and is a bad thing (when applied to his own book); then he says that the same thing happens and is good when applied to fiction in general. The two emotive phrases—'which suits their passions, their ignorance or sensibility' and 'a true feeler always brings half the entertainment along with him'—seem to work in opposite directions. In fact they are almost completely interchangeable as to their actual meaning. Sterne is playing with the relationship between the particular and the general, travelling between the two with great ease. He says that the laws that apply to fiction work visibly in connection with his own book. To this extent he applauds the representative nature of his own work. At the beginning of the passage he was applauding its eccentricity by providing an eccentric start to the argument—but only a conscious pose of eccentricity can give the demonstration (or the claim) of typicality its force.

If the passage is read as referring more to the ordinary readers, the more readily apparent movement from many to *one*—the 'true feeler' as an example of the herd of the world—is felt as more important than any sense of travelling from the particular to the general. As before, the apparent contrast between the two halves of the passage turns out to be spurious. The second part largely negates the impact of the first, by saying, in effect, that the reader's passions, ignorance and sensibility—that is, his personality—must be contributing to his response. Really only the *mood* of what is being said has changed. Sterne effectively makes a nonsense of his previous complaint, by acknowledging that what boils down to the same situation is right and just. It is all most disarming: but then, it is probably supposed to be.

The width of definition that was found to be necessary in relating Sterne to the traditions of writing which contribute to his novels is also needed when the question of Sterne's influence on other writers is considered. Almost any writer with an obsessive interest in the character of causality, or with a hyperaesthetic sense of 'riddles and mysteries' in the world around him, will bear some relation to Sterne. The traditional modernist writers, Joyce, Beckett, Woolf, Firbank, Nabokov, Durrell, Mann, are usually cited in this regard, but in fact the list could be extended indefinitely, to include many of the classical English novelists. For instance, *Tristram Shandy* is curiously like Joseph Conrad's novel, *Chance*, in some respects—in each case a sense of the strange intangibility of the causes of human action and motivation being conveyed by a work whose writer is confessedly uncertain or hesitant about approaching too closely or directly to the central 'story' of the book. Both men are novelists; Sterne should not be pushed into positions which imply that he is not quite a real novelist.

Victor Erlich provides an interesting criticism of that statement of Shklovsky's previously referred to, about *Tristram Shandy* being 'the most typical novel in world literature'. He says that this accolade is misapplied, and betrays 'the Formalist's "modern" bias in favour of non-objective art, his tendency to mistake the extreme for the representative, the "pure" for the "superior"'.[38] It is not a modern tendency to mistake Sterne's work for representative. To the ordinary eye, what Sterne does is doubtless extreme, but he has been taken to be representative of the order of the novel by those people who have made the best use of him, who have re-created his works by believing in their centrality, either in the interests of establishing a new literary form, or of evaluating their own position prior to establishing one.

It may help to substantiate this argument to provide a selective discussion of two such uses of Sterne—by Shklovsky himself, in the Russia of the early twentieth century, and by Goethe in the late eighteenth century.

II STERNE AND THE RUSSIAN NOVEL

Russian Formalism was a movement of criticism which flourished from around 1914 until 1930, when it was suppressed by the Russian establishment. Broadly speaking, it was the Russian manifestation of the Modernist movement which grew up rapidly in the world as a whole after 1910. It has affinities with the German Stilforschung and the American New Criticism.

The Formalists' situation bears some historical comparison with Sterne's own: the novel (and art in general, as the Formalists thought) was under threat from the outdated forms and prescriptions of the traditionalists. 'The Formalists as a group', says Victor Erlich, 'were as one . . . in postulating an acute crisis in Russian imaginative writing, especially in prose fiction, and in calling for a radical new departure.' 'The novel finds itself in an impasse; what is needed today is a sense of a new genre, i.e. a sense of decisive novelty,'[39] Yuri Tynianov complained in 1924. As they sensed this need, they set about discovering a new genre.

Some of the relevance to this situation of Victor Shklovsky's 1917 study of Sterne may be seen by looking at Richard Sheldon's introductory remarks to his own translation of Shklovsky's autobiographical history of the First World War. Shklovsky called this work *A Sentimental Journey*[40] in acknowledgement, if not in imitation, of Sterne. Sheldon says

> When *A Sentimental Journey* appeared, it was hailed by the Formalist critics Boris Eichenbaum and Yuri Tynianov as the start of a promising new trend in the Russian novel. The genre, they asserted, had been in a state of crisis since the deaths of Dostoevsky, Turgenev and Tolstoi. The subject-

> matter and technique of those masters no longer suited the postrevolutionary era; the genre required total renewal.
>
> *A Sentimental Journey* suggested a possible resolution of this crisis. It dispensed with traditional concerns of the nineteenth-century Russian novel; psychological analysis, the fictional hero, romantic intrigue, and lyrical nature descriptions. In Eichenbaum's opinion, this new novel relinquished the usual neat and artificial plot; instead, it simply presented a set of the author's observations and experience, with no particular effort to subordinate them to some overall scheme. It thus satisfied the craving of the Russian public for facts, seen in the new popularity of memoirs, letters, journals and biographies.[41]

It is, at first sight, hard to see how a study of Sterne could lead a writer to the position where he is able to control and adapt the genres of the novel in the interests of reconciling fiction and fact, novel and documentary. None the less, as the title of Shklovsky's book suggests, this control was in part learnt from a study of Sterne.

The particular aspect of Shklovsky's work on Sterne which seems to have contributed to his creative writing is an analysis of the relationship between the form and the content of *Tristram Shandy*. As 'form' and 'content' and the relation between them was one of the Formalists' favourite topics, it will be as well to describe the situation from within which Shklovsky produced his study.

Ignoring all historical considerations, it can be said that Shklovsky used the terms 'Motif' and 'Plot' as a pair of dynamic notions to replace the static concepts of content and form in literature. The Motif (also called Fable, Fabula and Material by earlier Formalists) corresponds to any pre-literary or pre-aesthetic aspects of the work. It is that material which would appear in a résumé of the plot; it is *what happens*, the sum total of events to be related, the material for narrative construction. Conversely, Plot (*Syuzhet*, Subject) is a term corresponding to *how* things are made to happen. It means the way in which the events are held together, the story as it is actually told. It is everything which stands outside a straight chronological résumé of the plot, everything subverting the résumé and holding it back. In order to become part of an aesthetic structure, the raw materials (the Motifs) have to be incorporated into the 'plot'. They only become eligible for participation in the literary work of art through the agency of the 'device', or more exactly a set of devices ('plot', again) peculiar to imaginative literature.

In this kind of analysis the particular 'tone' used in any literary work, the tone of voice that builds up from all the verbal details, becomes an integral part of the 'plot', the formal element. Shklovsky maintains that 'The methods and devices of *syuzhet* construction are similar to, and in principal are identical with, the devices, even with acoustic instrumentation'.[42] Sterne's devices of 'tone', his creation of an idiosyncratic tone of voice for Tristram, can thus be seen as being as important, in terms of his overall intention, as the larger devices of his plot. This looks very much like the distinction that Coleridge makes when he censures Sterne for combining true *humour* with questionable *wit* in his works.[43] The distinction is between the characters, who are formed from love and delicacy, and the tipping effect of Sterne's prose style. When style and tone of voice are taken to be formal elements, criticism of Sterne often comes to make this kind of distinction.

Shklovsky's contention is that the story-material, the content, is really only incidental to the overall work of art: 'the form creates content for itself . . . When we analyse a work of art, from the point of view of *syuzhet* potential, we have no need for the term "content"'.[44] His most general comments about *Tristram Shandy* reflect this attitude. He makes it plain that he respects the book insofar as he can show that it embodies all the laws of prose fiction which he considers important. As he says, it 'lays bare' all the devices it uses, comments on them—this being one of the conventions of book-as-object that Sterne uses:

> Sterne even lays bare the technique of combining separate story lines to make up the novel. In general, he accentuates the very structure of the novel. By violating the form, he forces us to attend to it; and for him the awareness of form through its violation constitutes the content of the novel.[45]

The awareness of form through its violation: as if Sterne had a general awareness of The Novel as a form, and was somehow writing a 'pure' (to use Erlich's word) novel.

Later in the same study Shklovsky tells us that 'The forms of art are explainable by the laws of art: they are not justified by their realism'.[46] Some other laws that Shklovsky describes, and which Sterne is said to embody, are the principles of Retardation and Impeded Form (which basically means the delaying of 'what happened next' by interposing digressive material), and of Alienation or 'making strange'—which looks rather like the Brechtian idea of the same name. Other writers have control over the devices of literature: Sterne exaggerates them so that they become perceptible. They stand in the way of the reader's complete imaginative identification with the characters and the story, and continually remind him of the conventionality of what he is reading (or so Shklovsky claims: but *Tristram Shandy* is in truth one of those works where imaginative identification can destroy the visibility of the devices—you can have your cake and eat it too).

A good many novelistic 'devices' seem to have been second nature to Sterne. It is interesting to see one aspect of Shklovsky's principle of 'Retardation' at work in Sterne's early composition, *A Political Romance* (1759), in its traditional novelistic form of retrospective digression. A situation is referred to (the wrangle over the commissaryship of Pickering and Pocklington, in the shape of the old-cast-pair-of-black-plush-breeches) and then Sterne goes back to another situation (to Topham's making out a patent for the Archbishop's Exchequer Court for himself and his son—the old watch-coat, in the allegory) to explain the 'true cause' of the one he has mentioned first. *A Political Romance* is an allegory rather than a novel, but Sterne, putting events in a sequence that will keep up the reader's interest, builds it *like* a novel. (What Shklovsky calls 'Retardation' might be simply called 'suspense' in other quarters.)

Because he concentrates on the narrative construction and the 'devices' employed in *Tristram Shandy*, Shklovsky fails to specify which of the motifs of the novel might be important. He picks out such things as 'knots' and 'Jenny': the fact that Dr Slop has to struggle with the dozen knots that Obadiah has used to truss up his obstetrical bag, and that the theme of 'knots' recurs from time to time later in the novel. The same thing is done with 'Jenny', the narrator's hypothetical sweetheart: she is treated simply as a recurrence. Shklovsky tries to pick out verbal leitmotifs which run through the novel and tie the whole edifice together. This is the general statement he makes about Sterne's attitude to his materials, his subject-matter:

> All of this diverse material, which is augmented by extensive excerpts from the works of various pedants, would undoubtedly tear the novel to bits were it not drawn together by crisscrossing motifs. A stated motif is never fully developed, never actually realised, but is only recalled from time to time; its fulfilment is continually put off to a more and more remote time. Yet its very presence in all the dimensions of the novel ties the episodes together.[47]

Shklovsky tied his own *Sentimental Journey* together with motifs in the same way. For instance, there is an evocative and powerful motif of the writer (who was an officer in the Russian army in the First World War) as a falling stone, with no control over what happens to him as the forces of war churn around him, but with a kind of blind power achieved by following his chosen course of action. Richard Sheldon describes this *Sentimental Journey* as employing narrative techniques similar to Sterne's, stressing the 'disjointed, polychromatic quality'[48] of the work and placing this quality in opposition to the leitmotifs. The inference is that without these leitmotifs the work would fall apart. Sheldon says:

> *A Sentimental Journey* does create a first impression of stylistic and compositional anarchy, but Shklovsky repudiated only the traditional methods of unifying a work of literature. In *A Sentimental Journey*, he offsets his disruptive devices with an intricate system of leitmotifs, recurrent images, and interlocking cross-references.[49]

These elements, and the author's habit of 'laying bare' his devices by making such remarks as 'This whole digression is based on the device which in my "poetics" is called retardation',[50] are presented as what Shklovsky learnt from Sterne. But this does neither Shklovsky nor Sterne much justice:

Tristram Shandy is not really organised in the way Shklovsky suggests, nor Shklovsky's in the way Sheldon would have it. A Sterne motif is not merely a recurrence: as Christopher Ricks points out,[51] the events caused or precipitated by some of those motifs—by those knots, for instance—have the same effect on the character within the novel as they do for the reader: they are a kind of epigrammatic metaphor for what the *form* of the novel is achieving. Slop struggles with his knots and cannot open his bag; Tristram struggles with the story of his life and cannot get it out; the reader struggles with the labyrinth of the book. Shklovsky never manages to demonstrate that the leitmotifs bring the subject-matter (in the traditional sense) of the novel to a point where it can be seen as a formal element.

Shklovsky's system of leitmotifs is not basically Sternean, but his attitude to what he writes and his particular awareness of genre is obliquely dependent on Sterne.

Once the critical energy that Shklovsky and the Formalists possessed had given them the desire to change a whole genre, their creative energy was free to develop separately. In fact, Shklovsky's *Sentimental Journey* does not make such difficult reading these days. It is an entirely absorbing narrative and can be read quickly and easily, because it uses a method that can now be recognised from the later examples that have consolidated the genre since Shklovsky wrote. Posterity has bestowed the ultimate accolade of conventionality on his *Journey*. Basically the form is what has become known as the 'non-fiction novel'; the subjective documentary. The effect is not dependent, as Sheldon would have it, on the irony in 'the tension between actual events and the author's detached view of them'.[52] It does work by a tension of this sort between content and form, but not primarily by irony. Shklovsky's material is too important for him to want to interfere with the impact that it can make by itself. The feeling is that of the pre-aesthetic material, or of material potentially art-fodder, being kept down, kept as pre-aesthetic (usually through the bareness of the brusque untrammelled tone of the work) for fear of distortion. Hence the irony of the title. Instead of being subjective, provided by the author, the 'sentiment' is to be left to the reader's discretion: though in truth it is hard not to be affected by the way the experiences are presented.

This is rather like something else that was said at the same time, under similar circumstances, though elsewhere:

> The subject of it is War, and the pity of War.
> The poetry is in the pity.[53]

Shklovsky's style is well tailored for his brusque effect: he knows for instance that 'a sentence is not emotional a paragraph is',[54] as Gertrude Stein has it, and so he favours the one-sentence paragraph quite a lot. But it is not dispassionate in the sense of being journalism. The formal quality is not absent, it is rigorously controlled. The necessity for this control of material, and hence of audience response, through the control of form seems to be what Shklovsky learnt from Sterne.

III STERNE AND THE GERMAN NOVEL

The Russian Formalists grew to be dissatisfied with the conventional novel as they inherited it from the nineteenth century. The Germans, in the mid-eighteenth century, were going one better than this. Not only the avant-garde of intellectuals but a whole reading public was dissatisfied with the state of contemporary German literature, and especially with the German novel. They had begun to idolise other literatures at the expense of their own. In the first half of the century this aesthetic xenophilia was mostly directed towards French literature, but in the 1750s the centre of interest began to swing towards England. The English novel in particular was held in high esteem. If an English book was successful in England, it could be virtually certain of a following in Germany. H. W. Hewett-Thayer says that

> The suggestion that a book, especially a novel, was translated from the English was an assurance of its receiving consideration, and many original German novels were published under the guise of English translations.[55]

Once again, the comparison with Sterne's own situation is suggestive. In each case the traditional forms begin to be seen as repressive and overinstitutionalised. The norms usually represented by vigorous conventional genres are felt to be lacking or false, with the result that eccentric or avant-garde works can propose themselves as norms; which, if they are taken up and become conventional, like Shklovsky's book, they indeed are.

As one might expect, this strong dissatisfaction with the conventional forms of German high art meant that this was an audience which was particularly susceptible to the impact of Sterne's novels. In general, though, the Germans' reception of Sterne was rather different from the Russian reception.

Most Germans seem to have gone through two phases of reaction to Sterne. The first was a period of uncritical adulation, in which the sentimental side of his writing was emphasised to the exclusion of his other gifts. *A Sentimental Journey* was thought by most Germans to be a more important work than *Tristram Shandy*, which by comparison was abstruse and incomprehensible. The *Journey* was accepted as the zenith of its genre. Imitation of English sentimentalism, which had begun with the response to Richardson, now intensified and became imitation of Sterne.

The second phase was to satirise Sterne, in the interests of satirising the sentimental genre. This process began as early as 1773, with Wezel's *Tobias Knaut*, although it did not intensify to become a strong countering force until the 1790s. It was not so much Sterne that they were satirising as their own particular conception of him, Sterne as pure sentimentalist. To watch this process happening is to realise to what extent Sterne's works could have been written specifically for the German audience—or rather, *against* the German audience. Sterne, in *A Sentimental Journey*, seems to be parodying the European response to the developments of the eighteenth-century novel before that response has taken place; so that when that response happens, it is already being burlesqued. *A Sentimental Journey* has this in common with Swift's *Tale of A Tub*, that it is what Ronald Paulson calls a 'parody-in-advance'.[56] Paulson does not apply his description of the *Tale* to Sterne's novels, which he describes as retrospective satires of existing genres of the novel: however it is the case that they are also calculated attempts to persuade the audience to take them as representative works in a situation where a desire for literary change has lent plausibility to this apparent paradox.

The Germans in their phase of enthusiastic reaction to Sterne tended to concentrate strongly on significant content at the expense of form. There was an almost universal belief in Sterne's 'formlessness'. He was simply an alternative, someone who had Made It New. For most of the German audience, the important things about Sterne were the characters and the basic incidents in which they found themselves. The specifically literary manifestations of the cult of sentiment in Germany are remarkable for their allegiance to Sterne, especially in copying his motifs. The most basic of these, the title of *Sentimental Journey*, was widely adopted, and could even be used for works which were modelled on *Tristram Shandy*. The most commonly repeated of the *Journey*'s motifs were: the priest begging with a snuff-box; the relation of man to the domestic animals; the poor girl with wandering mind seated by the roadside; the distressed aged soldier; 'filles de chambre' and waiting-maids.[57] Literary Germans took to adopting the names of characters in *Tristram Shandy* and *A Sentimental Journey* as correspondence names. Herder sometimes corresponded with his friends under play-names from *Tristram Shandy*. E. T. A. Hoffman and Hippel called each other Yorick and Eugenius. Also, the actions of characters in *A Sentimental Journey* began to be widely copied. Louise von Zeigler had a grave made in her garden for purposes of sentimental contemplation, and she led a lamb about which ate and drank with her. On the death of this animal, a 'faithful dog' took its place: all in imitation of Maria of Moulines. Following the first example of Johann Jacobi, cults of 'Lorenzodosen' sprang up, the members offering each other snuff from horn snuff-boxes, in imitation of the exchange of snuff-boxes between Yorick and Father Lorenzo in the *Journey*. The spirit of literary sentimentalism passed over into actual regulation of behaviour.

Concentrating on the periphera, the motifs, redoubles the unconscious irony. Here are the Germans acting in a sentimental manner which they consider specifically Sternean: but as often as not, Sterne has stolen his motif from some dubious source in the English background. The exchange of horn snuff-boxes smacks suspiciously of an incident in a book called *The Life and Memoirs of Mr. Ephraim Tristram Bates* (1756). An ancient Chelsea pensioner whom Bates talks to tells him a story about a 'brave fellow' who gets shot in battle and gives 'a brother Corporal' his trousers before he dies, as well as his horn tobacco-box: 'only Common Horn, but 'tis a Token'.[58] And as well as the name Tristram in the book's title, there is the interesting ejaculation of '*Alas! poor* Bates'[59] when the hero's death is recalled, paralleling Tristram's 'Alas, poor YORICK!'[60] at the end of Volume I, Chapter 12 of *Tristram Shandy*. As often as not, Sterne's novels are simply staging-posts for sentimental motifs as they pass on out towards acceptance in contemporary culture.

The one true exception to this naïve response is Goethe; and it is interesting that Goethe, quite as much as Sterne, knows the susceptible nature of his own audience and can consciously play upon those susceptibilities.

Goethe was extremely enthusiastic about Sterne:

> The influence Goldsmith and Sterne exercised upon me, just at the high point of my development, cannot be estimated. This high, benevolent irony, this just and comprehensive way of viewing things, this gentleness to all opposition, this equanimity under every change, and whatever else all the kindred virtues may be termed—such things were an admirable training for me, and surely these are the sentiments which in the end lead us back from the mistaken paths of life.[61]

But his appreciation is more discriminating than the credulous imitation and mimicry of Sterne that was taking place around him, and is based on an awareness of the particular quality of the English sentimentalism, as represented by Sterne and Goldsmith. He describes English sentimentalism as 'humorous and delicate',[62] while the French and German brands are respectively 'popular and lachrymous' and 'naive and realistic'. The English are thus credited with a greater degree of self-awareness than the other nations—and 'naive' is of course an excellent word for the contemporary German reaction to Sterne. He is certainly aware that the 'formlessness' his countrymen find so engaging in the English writers might be an illusion:

> The effect of Sterne and Goldsmith. Both have a high ironic humour, the one inclined to be formless, the other moving with ease in the strictest forms. After this, the Germans were made to believe that formlessness was humour,[63]

and at the end of the letter to Zelter previously quoted, Goethe says the same thing: 'the Germans have been persuaded that the characteristic of genuine humour is formlessness'.[64] He stresses the persuasion rather than the formlessness itself. His awareness of the 'ironic' quality of Sterne's humour is a good pointer to the degree of control of form and audience in his own creative work.

Goethe's own fictional effort in the sentimental direction, *The Sorrows of Young Werther* (1774), achieved much the same response from the audience in respect of the motifs as did Sterne's works. Werther's blue frock coat and yellow waistcoat were adopted by his readers, who on occasion even went so far as to copy the manner of his death when committing suicide. Goethe later commented on the extent of the reaction to Werther:

> The effect of this little book was great, nay immense, and chiefly because it exactly hit the temper of the times. For as it requires but a little match to blow up an immense mine, so the explosion which followed my publication was mighty, from the circumstance that the youthful world had already undermined itself; and the shock was great, because all extravagant demands, unsatisfied passions, and imaginary wrongs, were suddenly brought to an eruption. It cannot be expected of the public that it should receive an intellectual work intellectually. In fact, it was only the subject, the material part, that was considered, as I had already found to be the case among my own friends; while at the same time arose that old prejudice, associated with the dignity of a printed book,—that it ought to have a moral aim. But a true picture of life has none. It neither approves nor censures, but develops sentiments and actions in their consequences, and thereby enlightens and instructs.[65]

The statement looks strange, coming from Goethe. After all, there may be no seal of approval put on Werther's actions by the author's tone, but those actions are so obviously approved of in the novel, simply in the fact that they are written down, that they cry out for the audience's imaginative identification. Which they got. The principle of authorial objectivity which Goethe outlines in the last few sentences is spurious—or at least, a gambit. He may ostensibly be treating his subject in what he sees as an emotionally and morally neutral way, but the audience will already know what to do with it—after all, they have been primed for their explosion beforehand. Goethe's claim in the passage is that the process of enlightenment and instruction (as well as the 'explosion') comes from the actual story-material, 'the subject, the material part', rather than from the way the story is told or the author's 'moral aim'. As with Shklovsky in his *Sentimental Journey*, Goethe realises that he can leave the audience to provide most of the 'way of treatment' itself, and that it is not a question of their imaginative identification so much as a pre-existing tendency towards a particular state of mind being brought into contact with materials that will intensify that state. The audience, as Toby and Sterne say, must bring half the entertainment along with them: and this is also the process with which Sterne plays in his *Sentimental Journey* and in *Tristram Shandy*.

2 Plot and Character in *Tristram Shandy*

I PLOT AND CONSPIRACY

What the previous chapter has not done is to provide an unbiased argument about the 'typicality' of *Tristram Shandy*. Shklovsky and Goethe are both prejudiced to some extent by their historical situation, and Shklovsky's critical writing is polemical throughout. So this chapter will try to give other reasons as to why one might consider *Tristram Shandy* a 'pure' novel.

The assumption on which the argument is to rest is simple enough. It is that what characterises the eighteenth-century novel and makes it different from earlier kinds of prose fiction is the strength of its interest in the relationship between the idea of cause and effect, or plot, and the idea of character of personality. 'Plot' and 'character' are really the basic concerns of most fully-developed forms of narrative and dramatic literature. The novel begins to develop as a form at the end of the seventeenth-century partly because changes in society meant that writers of prose fiction began to be as well equipped as dramatists to express their interest in the relation between the two concepts.

It lies outside the scope of the present study to justify this assumption in any historical fullness. The only tentative attempt at discussing it is in Chapter 4, pp. 111–14. However the basic assumption is probably conventional enough in essence to stand by itself.

One of the fundamental concerns of *Tristram Shandy* is the exploration of many aspects of the relation between plot and character. It is a characteristic novel because it deals with the most characteristic problems of the novel. This chapter is by way of an enquiry into the nature of causality in the book.

There is a certain amount of ambiguity in the word 'plot', and it may be useful to bring this out at the beginning. Plot may be the actual weaving of the story, the linking of events—'sentiments and actions in their consequences'. This is plot in the traditional sense of the word, a device seemingly intrinsic to the fictional material itself, and usually taken by the reader to be an adequate and necessary framework for the characters and the events. It is the kind of plot in which *Tristram Shandy* is usually said to be lacking.

For some people, as we have seen, 'plot' is used to denote the formal quality of a work as revealed by style, tone of voice and so on. But there is another sense in which the word can be used. Plot may be a force which is presented as preliminary to the events of the novel: a power which broods over or behind the human action and affects its course—a power sensed either by characters or author, and sometimes by both. This is plot in the sense of conspiracy, and includes all the powers of causation which are external or preliminary to the story. It does not, of course, include the conspiracies or intrigues of the characters within the novel, which belong to the first kind of plot: it is a more general force.

This kind of plot is much favoured by some modern novelists who disapprove of the old formal patterns which the classical novelists are said to impose on their characters. Tony Tanner's book on modern American fiction, *City of Words*, brings this out well. Tanner's most general statement on the subject is probably this:

> One aspect of paranoia is the tendency to imagine plots around you; this is also the novelist's occupation and there is clearly a relationship between making fictions and imagining conspiracies. The difference is between consciousness in control of its own inventions, and consciousness succumbing to its inventions until they present themselves as perceptions. But the line between these two states of mind is a narrow one and a great deal of oscillation and overlap is possible.[1]

It would be possible to speculate at some length about this kind of plot, which in truth is as essential to the novel (and to the genre of tragedy in the drama) as any other. It is certainly not the prerogative of Pynchon and Kesey and Vonnegut, nor even of the nineteenth-century novelists (thinking of the feeling engendered by certain of Dickens's or Conrad's novels, that the plot as it appears in the novel is merely the surface construction, the 'surface shades', of some deeper or wider background power). In this sense, it could be said that the 'plot' of Richardson's *Clarissa* is the system of class-structure which leads Lovelace to see himself as an aristocratic Restoration rake, the Harlowes to see themselves as honest individualist burghers, and Clarissa to see herself as a Puritan virgin. It is this kind of plot which suffuses *Tristram Shandy*. To give two examples, one on a theoretical level and one on a naturalistic level: the form of the conventional novel is one of the plots of the book, a form against which the book reacts; and many of Walter's actions follow on from his awareness of strange, nebulous plots in the world and the whole cosmos.

Quite often, it is through Sterne's figurative language and leitmotifs—his playing with words, his wit—that one comes to an awareness of these plots. It is not unusual for a critic to see the wordplay and the patterns of motifs as substitutes for the *usual* kind of plot—for instance, A. D. McKillop says that

> Sterne . . . substitutes for the unilinear cause–effect sequence often called 'plot' a very elaborate set of patterns, themes and symbols, which invite comparison with devices used by later novelists.[2]

Although McKillop seems to be unaware of Shklovsky's writing, he shares his attitude to Sterne's 'techniques of verbal orchestration'—and possibly also shares Shklovsky's limitations. Both men bring together rather casually in the reader's mind two elements which should be separate, plot as cause-and-effect generally, and plot as the actual structuring of the work. The structural, 'storyline' kind of plot requires a conscious control only of the materials of the story. It has nothing to do with either style or tone of voice, whereas Sterne's uses of the various 'patterns, themes and symbols' have a great deal to do with these two things. McKillop and Shklovsky would have it that *Tristram Shandy* is held together by these leitmotifs, which themselves claim the reader's attention and distract him, whenever they appear, from the incidents and characters. But I do not think that this is so. McKillop says that the leitmotifs 'attempt to present or suggest firm order behind or alongside of the apparent chaos of the psychological flux'.[3] There is no such opposition. When a 'symbol' is used, it is not used by Sterne, it is used by Tristram the writer, and the use becomes a part of *his* character. (As with his rhetoric, Tristram tends to reserve the leitmotifs for his own conversation rather than distributing them in the conversation of Walter, Toby and the others.) No external devices are imposed, there is nothing like, for instance, the aeroplane flying over London in Virginia Woolf's *Mrs. Dalloway*, which is used to connect the scenes or characters of the book in the reader's mind. The figures also change to fit their context of use.

As usual, more might be gained from seeing Sterne as using techniques associated with the classical novelists than from seeing him as a premature modern. His use of these figures of speech might loosely be compared with the idea of a central controlling intelligence inside a Henry James novel. The device is made to perform something of the same overall function: to act as a 'reflector'. With James, the central character tends to act as reflector for the other characters, who are transmitted to the reader through him or her. In *Tristram Shandy* it is the ideas and the life of the writer as revealed by the power of his words which needs to be reflected from something in order to give them form and some kind of central point.

So it is not the mere presence of such 'techniques of verbal orchestration' which allies them to the concept of plot. Rather, it is the particular nature and action of some of Tristram's more persistent analogies and metaphors which achieve this. The Hobby-Horse is a good example of what happens: but first some general remarks about Tristram's mental habits as revealed by his literary practice are in order.

Tristram virtually never says anything which has only one meaning: his commonest mode of speech is simple pun and double entendre. But in moments of more complete virtuosity his figurative language lifts on to another plane, one on which each metaphor refers outwards not merely to one but to two levels of reference. Frank Brady puts it well: 'The reader, anxiously looking for unilateral analogy, finds himself like the resentful ass starving between two bales of hay.'[4] Brady is very good on Tristram's ability to conflate the worlds of thought, story and *sex* through this kind of treble entendre: he provides an infinitely suggestive analysis of one of Tristram's attempts at justifying his digressive technique, in Volume VI, Chapter 33. 'When a man is telling his story in the strange way I do mine, he is obliged continually to be going backwards and forwards to keep all tight together in the reader's fancy.'[5] I trust I may leave Brady's analysis to the reader's imagination.

Other treble meanings abound: thus in Volume III, Chapter 31, the word 'nose' can mean: a nose (Tristram insists this is what a nose means: a nose); wits, brains, presaging the *nasus/nasutus* pun in the Erasmus dialogue Walter gets hold of in Chapter 37 (Erasmus plays on *nasus* [nose] and *nasutus* [sharp-witted] in one of the dialogues in the *Colloquia Familiaria*[6])—Tristram's grandfather uses the word in this sense in chapter 33; and it can be an equivalent of the male sexual organ—as at the end of Chapter 33, and indeed at any point where Tristram insists it does *not* mean anything rude. The word 'bridge', in Volume III, Chapters 25–7, refers both to Toby's drawbridge and to the bridge Slop is making for Tristram's crushed nose.

In the case of certain important analogies, the doubleness is of a particular kind. One level of reference is established in the public and accepted thought of the 'real' world, while the other level brings out the connection between the original metaphorical object and the world of fiction, the aesthetics of the novel. What this does is to bring different aspects of plot, the external and preliminary and the intrinsic or structural, together in the same concept. The Hobby-Horse is a good example of this, and is doubly useful as it also has links with a related image, the Blow of Fate. This image is discussed in the third section of this chapter, to which this present section is a preliminary.

The word 'Hobby-Horse' in *Tristram Shandy* is a metaphor for one of the eighteenth century's conventional psychological concepts, the Ruling Passion, or more exactly for one facet of it. Seen in one light, the Ruling Passion is merely a person's dominant characteristic, around which the rest of his personality is organised, and without which it would lack direction and consistency—Pope uses the concept in this guise in the

Epistle to Cobham,[7] as a counter-weight to the sceptical argument about the instability and relativity of man's character which the first half of the poem puts forward. But Sterne's faintly derogatory metaphor stresses its other aspects. Michael Deporte develops the meaning of the image of the Hobby-Horse in terms of an equation often made in the eighteenth century between imagination and madness, and indicates the special importance which was attributed to the *idée fixe*, the Ruling Passion in its guise of irrational obsession. He talks about Walter and Toby Shandy's Hobby-Horses, their continual absorption in, respectively, occult systems of knowledge and military history:

> Though the benign insanity of the Shandys is most easily established by reference to Locke, it can be referred also to the medical theories of the period. The hobbyhorsism of Walter and Toby—it is at one point called a 'ruling passion'—has distant roots in the old doctrine of humours and more immediate ones in eighteenth-century theories of obsession. Doctors agreed that chronic preoccupation with a small number of ideas was an unmistakable symptom of mental disorder. Sir Richard Blackmore made prolonged obsession the criterion for distinguishing psychosis from neurosis, in which such preoccupation was only temporary. Insanity is characterised, he said, by a 'Continued Train of Thoughts, fixed on one sad object' ... Dr. Richard Mead asserted ... that madness could actually be induced by excessive concentration on a single subject, 'even though it be of the most pleasing kind'. Most important for *Tristram Shandy* was the common medical assumption that, in the words of Thomas Willis, men might be mad 'as to one particular thing, having their judgment concerning other matters for the most part right'.[8]

So that the Hobby-Horse, which is essentially a casual and frivolous thing in Tristram's eyes—

> no way a vicious beast ... 'Tis the sporting little filly-folly which carries you out for the present hour ... an *any thing*, which a man makes a shift to get a stride on, to canter it away from the cares and solicitudes of life.[9]

—becomes tangible evidence of insanity when referred to this background.

It should be stressed that this *is* a background and not a context: Mead and Blackmore are early eighteenth-century writers, Willis wrote in the late seventeenth century. Such ideas as Deporte refers to may well have had a period flavour by 1760, by which time madness was beginning to be seen as a subject worthy of an independent empirical science, rather than being treated in terms of more general and *a priori* notions such as the Ruling Passion. The Battie–Monro controversy which took place in London in 1758, and which is usually accepted as the first printed work on madness as such, rather than on more occult notions such as the Vapours or the Spleen, contains only one passing remark by Battie about '*unwearied attention to any one object*' being among 'the ninth class of remoter causes' of madness.[10] Battie looks for clinical symptoms where Mead and Blackmore were prone to call eccentric or neurotic behaviour mad. Deporte's background is itself a kind of plot. The plot lies in the application of very general notions from an occult background to individual characters. (The Ruling Passion is, as Deporte says, essentially only an evolution from Galenic theories of the dominant humour.) The effect of the presence of this occult background dressed up and accepted as science is to persuade the eighteenth-century reader to see Walter and Toby as lunatics.

Deporte implicates Tristram in this madness, pointing to his dedication to the Moon in Volume I, Chapter 9, his monomaniac energies and the correspondingly mad, mounted and digressive structure of his book. Writing is Tristram's Hobby-Horse: he is seen, at best, as a conscious zany, aiming at an antisocial but harmless eccentricity.

True as this may have been for eighteenth-century science, there is none the less a problem inherent in it. If Walter and Toby are mad, and yet we like them and sympathise with them, perhaps we are mad too. If Tristram's book is mad, then we must be mad to read it and enjoy it. (Reading itself is not unHobbyhorsical: Sterne plays a good deal with this fact of life, especially in *A Sentimental Journey*.) We are loath to make this connection, and we would be right not to make it. The Hobby-Horse is not an image which relates solely to the psychology of the individual. Deporte's reading of the image is very one-sided. Everything he says would be true if he were not dealing with a novel. Horseback riding is one of the archetypal images for fictional narrative, and indeed for literary art in general. This is due to the traditional image of life as a journey or pilgrimage. If novels are about life, then the narrative is seen as an analogous journey. Hence the picaresque novel, with its motifs of physical, social and spiritual voyaging.

The horseback journey is such a standard metaphor for the novelist's art that, on occasion, the writer will take the horse for granted. Thus Walter Scott, in the Introduction to *The Fortunes of Nigel*, can say

> When I light on such a character as Bailie Jarvey . . . my conception becomes clearer at every step which I take in his company, although it leads me many a weary mile out of the regular road and forces me to leap hedge and ditch to get back into the route again.[11]

One hardly notices that he is leaping hedges and ditches without having mentioned a horse: the figure has come automatically to the mind of both writer and reader. The best-known book-as-journey metaphor in the eighteenth century is probably Fielding's description of 'Divisions in Authors' in Book II, Chapter 1 of *Joseph Andrews*.

When Tristram stresses the Hobbyhorsicality of his writing, and uses the horseback metaphor in connection with it—'curvetting and frisking it away, two up and two down for four volumes together'[12]—he is using a professional formula. As well as emphasising his own individuality, he is taking refuge under a convention, a traditional reference. He stresses his kinship with the common forms and accepted energies of literature. Thus what the image of the Hobby-Horse does in *Tristram Shandy* is join the eighteenth century's ideas about madness and the unacceptable forces of the individual mind to a literary context in which the values are rather different, in order that comparisons between the literary and scientific contexts can be made. What the scientific background takes as mad, literature may take as agreeable and even normative. Tristram never uses the image without elements of both these aspects being present.

This kind of *convertibility* is often recognised to be central to *Tristram Shandy*: but commentators are not always very accurate in their descriptions of the character of Tristram's analogical and metaphorical world. Some describe the book as a literary reflection of a whole universe of correspondences: for instance Brady quotes McKillop to the effect that in *Tristram Shandy*, 'the universe is pictured as a great multiple system, in which sense and spirit, macrocosm and microcosm, are linked by analogies and correspondences',[13] a quotation which makes Tristram's wit appear to be the manifestation of a much safer and more secure world-picture than in fact is the case. It omits or disregards the highly idiosyncratic and eclectic nature of Tristram's wit, disregards the fact that analogy is not at all what it used to be.

Near the end of his book *The World and the Book*, Gabriel Josipovici makes some illuminating remarks about the differences between analogy in Dante and in modern writers:

> In modern literature analogy has become demonic—'le démon de l'analogie', Mallarmé called it. For to discover correspondences in the world around us does not lead to the sensation that we are inhabiting a meaningful universe; on the contrary, it leads to the feeling that what we had taken to be 'the world' is only the projection of our private compulsions: *analogy* becomes a sign of *dementia*. . . . In Dante the discovery of analogy serves to make us realize that the universe is meaningful, no longer isolated but a tune. The *trompe-l'oeil* effects of modern art, on the other hand, the playful inversions of the novel form and the parody of language and convention in modern fiction have the opposite effect, making us realize with a shock that we are dealing not with the world but with one more object in the world, one made by a human being . . .
>
> The effect of demonic analogy is to rob events of their solidity . . . We are in a world of infinite correspondences, but this time without any stable reality underpinning them all. The effect is to rob the content of the work of all its solidity and to turn the book into a field of play for form.[14]

This is beginning to get a good deal closer to the nature of *Tristram Shandy*. However I think it would be equally wrong to accept that *Tristram Shandy* is simply an example or embodiment of demonic analogy. When an argument of this kind is advanced about the book, the commentator tends to conclude that *Tristram Shandy* is no more than sceptical whimsy, utter relativity, and with no absolute standards whatsoever. Stephen Werner argues just such a case in a chapter devoted to Sterne in his book on Diderot. He uses the word 'Arabesque' to characterise Sterne's art, and describes analogy as the tool of this mode:

> *Tristram Shandy*, a work of scepticism and arabesque, is autotelic. There are no limits placed on the range of narrative invention. Analogy is a kind of infinite mode. Anything can be compared with anything else . . . Arabesque is a way of holding reality at bay, of denying ultimate meaning. The sceptic retreats from the chaos of everyday experience into a world of private mythology (what Sterne calls 'analogy'—'everything in the world has two handles').[15]

And he calls *Tristram Shandy* a 'profoundly dualistic' work, describing *chance* as 'the real principle' of its universe.

The mistake in this is, I think, easily found. *Tristram Shandy* is not 'autotelic' or self-enclosed: the correspondences point outwards to other worlds than the fictional. It is a work which is also about the process of analogy becoming demonic in the thought of the eighteenth and late seventeenth centuries. The 'plots' of the book, the awareness of conspiracies, attempt to persuade the reader that real plots exist in the real world, and that the text is conditioned by such preliminary and external plots.

To go so far as to believe the book and seek out such conspiracies is, of course, nothing short of quixotic. None the less, later chapters will show that it is the first of these truly demonic analogies, the misuse, by early-eighteenth-century medical and psychological theorists, of the principles of analogy when dealing with the religious and physical arguments from design, which stimulates to some extent the form, the purpose and the comedy of *Tristram Shandy*.

II THE CONFLICT BETWEEN CHARACTER AND SYSTEM IN VOLUME I OF *TRISTRAM SHANDY*

It is important to stress that neither Tristram nor most of his characters look with paranoid or cynical eyes on the systems of external causation which surround them. The plots predispose the book to comedy, and are mostly mischievous rather than truly malignant. Tristram and Sterne usually approach them in a spirit of playfulness rather than gloom.

There is, however, one place in *Tristram Shandy* where this appears to be untrue, where a good many of these external systems are taken very seriously. This is the beginning of the book, Volume I, which also apparently differs from the rest of the work in its attitude to conventional form, in the sense that it can be said to embody a fixed form rather than destroy or negate it. Fixed form is traditionally one of the locations of one kind of plot or external conspiracy (the structure or institution that the individual has to fight): it is interesting to see to what use Sterne puts the notion in the early chapters of his work.

The concession to fixed form is the organisation of the material into four sections of very nearly equal length. While the divisions between these sections are in no way absolute, it is clear that each section is designed to approach the idea of character from a specific and different viewpoint. In particular, they all raise the question of the relationship between character and some fixed, external system which mankind conventionally uses to codify and simplify the idea of character, and which Tristram here tries to present as having causal powers. He teaches the reader about plots: and the lessons he teaches in the first volume may also be applied to the reading of the book in general. This section of the chapter, however, is concerned primarily with what Tristram does in Volume I.

The first six chapters centre on the conflict between character and the idea of *Fate*, particularly Fate as Destiny.

In Chapters 7–12 the theme is that of character and *reputation*; character as it is publicly seen and appreciated.

Chapters 13–18 centre on the Shandy marriage-settlement: the external system is that of legal *documentation*.

The final section is mostly about *naming*, names and the power of words in relation to character, and about the actual characters of Walter and Toby Shandy. This is not an exhaustive catalogue of the systems Tristram presents, but these others will be considered in their place.

Chapters 1–6

Apart from the joke about winding up the clock, *Tristram Shandy* appears to get off to a rather depressing start. It is not characteristic of Tristram to gripe about his parents, as he does in Chapter 1; nor to be so completely mournful as to call earth 'this scurvy and disasterous world',[16] as he does in Chapter 5.

There may be a purely formal reason for this. It is not unusual for a writer to give a comic work a melancholy introduction, to point up the later humour and give it more bite. But there is also a more specific reason for Tristram's gloomy tone of voice. In the third chapter, Tristram ascribes the anecdote he is recounting—the joke about the clock—to his father Walter. Walter had the events in the anecdote happen to him and told them to Toby, who passed the story on to Tristram. Tristram is borrowing Walter's tone of voice while he tells the story, and this tone of voice is carried over into the rest of these early chapters. It is Walter's gloom, for Walter weeps at the memory of misfortune when he thinks of the mistimed conception of his son and of the spanner his wife threw into the workings of his system of astrologically-motivated conception.

In fact Tristram is borrowing not just Walter's tone of voice, but his entire outlook on life. This may become clearer when the first dramatised example of Walter's outlook is examined.

In Chapter 3, Walter is complaining to Toby about the disastrous effect of the events surrounding his son's conception: '*But alas! . . . My Tristram's misfortunes began nine months before ever he came into the world*.'[17] But what catastrophe has brought the memory of this original misfortune into his mind? Nothing more than his observing Tristram's 'unaccountable obliquity, (as he called it) in . . . setting up my top, and justifying the principles upon which I had done it'[18]—and this is not a catastrophe at all. Tristram's character is a disaster only for Walter; and it has to be a disaster because his system proves that it ought to be so. Others might have inferred from

Tristram's originality that he would be different from his peers, but Walter must infer that he is inferior. By reading the present situation in terms of his own system and drawing his sufficient conclusions from an insuficient premise, he lays himself open to the reader's amusement.

Going back to the opening chapter with the benefit of this hindsight, we can see that Tristram's complaint is in fact an echo or a parody of Walter's. Tristram claims to draw the same conclusions as his father from the same premises. He ascribes his unhappy life to the unhappy nature of his conception, and the unhappiness of his conception to the principle of the association of ideas, as manifested in his mother's response to the clock being wound up. He complains that if his parents had 'duly considered' the cast of the 'humours and dispositions which were then uppermost', he would have made 'a quite different figure in the world, from that, in which the reader is likely to see me'.[19] His parents were not scientific enough in their choice of the moment of conception; but this is precisely Walter's complaint.

In Chapters 4 and 5 the reasons for Tristram's adopting Walter's attitude begin to emerge. Tristram is in effect creating a polarisation inside the text, setting up claims in the rhetoric, the 'telling' part of the prose, which he will then immediately negate by what he *shows* the reader. He is entering wholeheartédly into Walter's attitude at the beginning in order to be able to comment obliquely on it later.

This polarisation begins in Chapter 4, where at last we find the anecdote which renders intelligible Mrs Shandy's interruption of her husband in Chapter 1. It is the story of her association of the winding-up of the clock with 'some other things'. Tristram lays the blame for this state of affairs heavily on the principle of the association of ideas, rather than on anything in his mother's own individual character. By quoting Locke's belief in this principle, he can make it appear that it is the association of ideas which is in charge of Mrs Shandy, and is thus directing the whole situation. The phrasing is delicate: 'from an unhappy association of ideas . . . it so fell out at length',[20] but Tristram reinforces it a little to make it appear as a mechanical principle of cause and effect: '—which strange combination of ideas, the sagacious *Locke* . . . affirms to have produced more wry actions than all other sources of prejudice whatsoever'.[21] Thus, like Walter, he makes the claim that the sources of action and of character are external to the individual. Walter perceives that man's character is determined by the conspiracy he feels as Destiny or Fate—perceives that character is written in the stars. Tristram leads the reader towards perceiving that actions are governed by an equally general principle, association.

But what Tristram tells the reader and what he shows him are two very different things. The anecdote as Tristram renders it is much more about Walter's being a slave to ordered time than it is about his demonstration of the association of ideas—which is what Walter was trying to use the anecdote as. Also, Mrs Shandy's enquiry about the clock is only carrying Walter's habitual association of *activities*—clock-winding and sexual intercourse—half a stage further. As Ian Watt notices, the 'strange combination of ideas' is in fact produced by a strong element of conditioning circumstance in the physical and sensory world:

> In the opening passage, we have a classical example of Mrs. Shandy's association of ideas between the dual monthly routine of Mr. Shandy in his timekeeping and his connubial roles. But there is nothing very unconscious about this in the modern sense; Pavlov's dog, had it the gift of tongues, would, under similar circumstances, have echoed Mrs. Shandy's words.[22]

So the shown cause of the circumstances of Tristram's conception is the conjunction of the states of mind, and the characters, of his mother and father. It is very typical of Walter to be that precise and well-regulated. It is typical of his wife to be ruled by her husband's careful organisation of life, and to be vaguely worried when it lapses—or when she *thinks* it lapses: Tristram, beginning early his technique of presenting opinions about actions and not the actions themselves, omits to say anything on the subject of whether the clock really had been wound up that night.

That these things are typical of the Shandys becomes clearer when the reader has gained some knowledge of the Shandy character and of Tristram's methods. As R. F. Brissenden points out, Tristram will only describe an individual action when it is in some way typical of the person in question:

> Sterne usually accompanies his account of some habitual action with a precise and vivid memory of a particular occurrence... usually the habitual cross-fades so gently into the particular instance that it is difficult to say where one begins and the other leaves off.[23]

So while Tristram tells the reader that Destiny is Character, that external laws determine both personality and actions, he is simultaneously showing him that Character is Destiny:[24] that the individual, having the character he has, is the immediate cause of his own actions. But for the moment the telling is in control, and Tristram's professed attitude continues to be conditioned by his father's outlook.

This is of some interest in Chapter 5, where Tristram's apparent acceptance of destiny's control over man's life leads him into what is, in *Tristram Shandy*, a most peculiar statement. His belief in this system of control, which he here personifies as 'the ungrateful Duchess', Fortune, tempts him into describing his own life, and the book he will make from it, in terms of a fixed *literary* system or genre.

Chapter 5 is a typical first chapter of a picaresque novel. The comparison with the picaresque cannot be upheld by detailed reference to any one example—perhaps it would be better to substitute something more non-committal such as the ethos of the picaresque. The parallels lie mainly in the writer's being able to make promises of misadventure. It is like Roderick's mother's dream at the beginning of Smollett's *Roderick Random*: she dreams that she is delivered of a tennis-ball instead of a baby, and that the devil then picks up this ball and hits it clean around the world with a racquet.[25] Tristram makes promises of the picaresque 'low life', with such phrases as 'this vile, dirty planet of ours'.[26] He also creates a strong sense of life as a battle between the picaroon and Fortune or circumstances, with the picaroon having to contend with the malevolent energy of the great world which buffets him to and fro. It is, in short, the sense of Tristram as Fortune's Plaything.[27] Both aspects of Fortune are involved: the Duchess represents the singleminded Fortune of Destiny;

the 'cross accidents' she pelts Tristram with remind the reader of the Fortune of Chance and Caprice. The presence of the two elements together emphasises what Stephen Werner, talking about Jacques' belief in the cosmic 'grand rouleau' in *Jacques le Fataliste*, calls the 'mystifying connection between necessity and accident which we call fatalism, that combinatoire of chance and fate which signifies the rule of the great scroll'.[28] It all produces a satisfyingly gloomy determinism.

Tristram uses the same material to support his attitude in Chapter 5 as he used in the first chapter, where he was going along with his father's attitude. In Chapter 1 he referred to the Galenic/Hippocratic system of humours as lying behind the more local theories of well-timed conception which Walter tries to practise. In the phrase 'humours and dispositions' he also links this to the older system of astrology on which the theory of humours is based: 'dispositions' means the arrangement of the stars and constellations. Each of the four humours, blood, phlegm, choler (or yellow bile), melancholy (or black bile), is associated with a combination of two of the four elements—'The four elements of Empedocles—Earth, Fire, Air and Water, "the four-fold root of all things" '[29]—each of which is in turn placed under the control of one quarter of the zodiac, thus:

Earth:	Taurus, Virgo, Capricorn:	Phlegm (and melancholy)
Fire:	Aries, Leo, Sagittarius:	Choler (and blood)
Water:	Cancer, Scorpio, Pisces:	Melancholy (and choler)
Air:	Gemini, Libra, Aquarius:	Blood (and phlegm)

In Chapter 5 Tristram gives the date of his birth, and then deliberately reminds the reader of the system of astrology: 'this scurvy and disasterous world',[30] he says, disastrous meaning ill-starred. He was born, he reminds us, on earth, but he wishes he had been born 'in the Moon, or in any of the planets'.[31] By going back to this general system of external causation he raises the suspicion that he might be describing a system of literature (the picaresque) which he wants to associate with his father's awareness of conspiracies.

Yet in truth he is teasing as much in Chapter 5 as he was in Chapter 1. He makes comments that will remind the reader of astrology, but he does not place enough credence in it to want to give us his own horoscope, nor indeed to discuss his own character in these formalised terms at all. Similarly, in Chapter 1 he was most unspecific about just which 'humours and dispositions' were in fact uppermost at the time of his conception.

The general claim in Chapter 5, the promise of misadventure, is also most untypical of Tristram, who usually goes out of his way to stress that he can make *no* promises as to what will happen. His attitude stands in absolute contrast to remarks he makes elsewhere about the nature of his book. Consider for instance the last words of Volume I: 'if I thought you was able to form the least judgment or probable conjecture to yourself, of what was to come in the next page,—I would tear it out of my book'.[32] This is a very different thing from promises of misadventure. Nowhere but in Chapter 5 does he try to engage the reader's trust in this way. He may say (in Volume IV, Chapter 32) that he is going to write about uncle Toby's amours—which he eventually does—but he also promises (in Volume I, Chapter 18) that he is going to explain the relationship between himself and his 'dear, dear Jenny'. This he never does. He is almost ostentatiously proud of the independence of his effects from any mechanical system of causes. Nothing in his book happens because something else has previously happened to dictate events; everything happens because his characters are the way they are.

But this does not mean that Chapter 5 is an anomaly or a piece of misdirected rhetoric. In the context of the book as a whole, this chapter is not statement: it is part of the polemic between 'telling' and 'showing'. It describes a kind of literature which seems to share Walter's attitude to plot: and while telling us Walter's version of reality with great conviction and aplomb, Tristram has none the less managed to dissociate himself from it. The first chapters of *Tristram Shandy* ask the reader to believe, with Walter, that life runs on mechanical principles. At the same time they begin to let the alert reader see that Tristram does not believe that life—or literature—does in fact run on such principles.

Chapters 7–12

Here the central theme is the relation between character and its public reception, i.e. reputation; and especially the relation between character and its treatment in fiction. Writing or telling about a person is taken to be the same thing as making a person's character public property through gossip or other forms of social broadcasting.

The section begins with the story of the midwife and the parson, who, later in the story (at the start of Chapter 11) is to be named as Yorick. He pays the fees that enable the midwife to obtain her licence and to practise.

There is then what appears to be a digression, about Hobby-Horses, in the course of which Tristram writes a bit of slanderous gossip about a highly esteemed and respected London physician, Dr Richard Mead, who had died in 1754. It seems to have been an open secret that Mead ('Dr Kunastrokius') had this eccentricity—that he took pleasure in 'combing of asses tails, and plucking the dead hairs out with his teeth'[33]—but no-one had yet had such bad taste as to refer to this in print. Tristram merely describes this habit as Kunastrokius's Hobby-Horse, and says 'De gustibus non est disputandum'—every man to his own taste—which in the context of Tristram's very dubious anecdote is a little ironical.

After a sub-digression for the Dedication, and after then referring to the universality of Hobby-Horses, Tristram returns to the story of Yorick and the midwife in Chapters 10–12. It now becomes clear that the apparent digression was not a digression at all, but matter introductory to this story. Yorick's habit of making slanderous jokes about his neighbours arouses their hatred: they pay him back in kind by noising it abroad that his motives for paying the midwife's fees were suspect, that he keeps a percentage of her profits. Yorick, discouraged, dies. Alas poor Yorick.

So Yorick's character as reported by Tristram is, in one respect, very close to Tristram's own character as it appears in this first volume. When Tristram describes Yorick's satirical jests against his contemporaries and neighbours, he is also describing the process which he himself has been providing and will continue to provide—a process of anecdote and caricature directed against worthy citizens. Tristram offers his gossip about Kunastrokius with just the same insouciance as Yorick offers his jests:

> —he never gave himself a moment's time to reflect who was the Hero of the piece, —what his station, —or how far he had power to hurt him hereafter; —but if it was a dirty action, —without more ado, —The man was a dirty fellow, —and so on: —And as his comments had usually the ill fate to be terminated in a *bon mot*, or to be enliven'd throughout with some drollery or humour of expression, it gave wings to Yorick's indiscretion.[34]

So Tristram presents Yorick as practising his own arts of character disfigurement. But in order to appreciate just how this reflects back on to Tristram, and on to his methods of writing, two other parallels between Tristram and Yorick need to be examined: they both ride horses, and they both have blows fall on them.

In the digression or introduction in Chapters 7–9, Hobby-Horses are almost indistinguishable from real horses. It is the real quadruped, Kunastrokius's ass, which first suggests to Tristram the notion of the Hobby-*Horse*: at least, the one follows the other. From the original physical detail the image has shifted to a concept; by the end of the same chapter it has moved on, or back, into metaphoric physical detail: 'so long as a man rides his HOBBY-HORSE peaceably and quietly along the King's highway . . .'.[35] And in this form it passes over into the next chapter, Chapter 8, where Tristram refers to his practising of the arts as his own Hobby-Horse:

> for happening, at certain intervals and changes of the Moon, to be both fiddler and painter, according as the fly stings:--- Be it known to you, that I keep a couple of pads myself, upon which, in their turns, (nor do I care who knows it) I frequently ride out and take the air.[36]

Fiddling and painting are not the only arts he practises. Another of his Hobby-Horses is his writing, and particularly his description of other people's Hobby-Horses: the quotation just given comes only some hundred words after the description of Dr Kunastrokius.

Then in Chapter 10 Tristram lingers so long over a detailed description of Yorick's horse that it becomes far too drawn-out for the demands of the episode. Its real purpose might be to raise the question of whether Yorick's horse is a Hobby-Horse: the reader is unsure of the status of this beast, and of the connection between it and Yorick's reputation, because what 'horse' and 'character' mean to the reader's imagination has been coloured by Tristram's introductory activity in Chapters 7 and 8. It is this lead-in that gives the story of Yorick the atmosphere of a parable. It seems to hint at some kind of moral, to have the power to talk about more than it claims to be talking about.

The last of the hints towards a moral lies in the other parallel between Tristram and Yorick. In Chapter 5, Tristram has said that his life is a continual history of being 'pelted' by Fortune. Yorick is also 'pelted', but this time the blows are more specific: he describes the actions of his irate neighbours, who answer his unconsidered slanders with more deliberate denigrations, as 'blows . . . in the dark'.[37]

This may in turn remind the reader of a larger pattern of retributive violence in *Tristram Shandy*. Fortune pelts Tristram: the world buffets the man. Tristram's reaction to this is to write a book in which the theme of retaliation by the writer appears to be strong. He pokes fun at the world: the kick the physical Tristram receives, the mental Tristram gives.

It is Tristram's habit to express this second blow—the writer's retribution—in terms of the image he has already established as representative of his art, in terms of blows from the hooves of the Hobby-Horse he rides. (He is helped in this by the coincidence of the journey, and especially the horseback journey, being a standard metaphor for the progress of a man through life, and also for the progress of a work of fiction.) Tristram's is a particular kind of journey: as he himself says, he 'writes galloping'. The book is always in violent motion, and when Tristram uses the metaphor of a brisk horseback journey in connection with his book, he tends to stress the damage that can be caused by such a trip:

> I'll tread upon no-one, —quoth I to myself when I mounted——I'll take a rattling good gallop; but I'll not hurt

> the poorest jack-ass upon the road . . . Now ride at this rate with what good intention and resolution you may, —'tis a million to one you'll do some one a mischief, if not yourself.[38]

This damage is caused to characters: Tristram is travelling too fast to have time to describe anything but the dominant characteristic, the ruling passion or Hobby-Horse. Because writing is a Hobbyhorsical pursuit, and because of the element of retaliation in it, any kind of systematic description must be reductive to some extent. It reduces characters from the roundness of their real-life selfhood to the flatness of literary presentation: and the more the writing tends towards caricature, the more violent this process will be.

The plot against Yorick disfigures his reputation and his character in the same way that Yorick disfigured his antagonists': it flattens and reduces them. Yorick expresses this as a physical distortion; his head is 'bruised and mis-shapen'.[39] He loses his character and dies. As Yorick has been practising Tristram's arts, it seems possible that what happens to him is what would happen to Tristram (or perhaps to Sterne-as-writer) were the subjects of his satire to take offence. Yorick is a sacrificial victim of a literary technique, a scapegoat for Tristram.

The *ostensible* moral behind the story of Yorick and the midwife is that to lose one's good character or good name is tantamount to losing one's life: the metaphorical blows Yorick receives cause his physical death. But this is only the bare bones of the action. The status of Yorick's death is as equivocal as that of his horse.

The moral is a literary as well as a naturalistic one—Yorick loses his character *twice*. It is suggestive that the only character of whom Tristram ever gives a full and systematic description is Yorick—in Chapter 11. He loses his character to Tristram as completely as he loses it to his neighbours, and having been described, he dies. There is possibly something of the same joke in the case of the midwife, who also has her character (and her good reputation) established in the classical and conventional fashion (in Chapter 7), only to be permanently written out of the book after Chapter 13, where Tristram sarcastically reminds the reader of her existence and promises to introduce her to him 'for good and all'. It is the same kind of death as Yorick's, if less theatrical.

So it might be more accurate to say that the external system in this section is not just character-as-reputation, but also the literary description and reduction of character. Tristram again does his best to tell us that this is a causal system, in that character description (whether of the fictional kind or real-life slander) appears to cause real events— even death. But this is not consistent with Tristram's usual literary practice: the telling opposes the showing. Tristram does not usually describe people systematically, and does not kill them off. What this section does is to indicate that Tristram knows that some of the conventional methods of fiction might be a trap—a conspiracy against the fictional character—and that he is consciously trying to avoid this in the rest of his own book. (The only other important character that Tristram will approach as directly as Yorick is Dr Slop, in Volume II, and the caricaturing of Slop stands in pointed contrast to the methods used on the other characters at Shandy Hall.) What Chapter 5 did with a genre of the novel, this section does with its traditional tools. Sterne demonstrates, through the character of Tristram, a similar awareness of the limitations of conventionality.

Chapters 13–18

J. M. Stedmond says this about the many documents, or shards of documents, which turn up in *Tristram Shandy*:

> But Sterne has taken pains to weave these bits and pieces into the fabric of his narrative, either by having them act as catalysts which cause revealing reactions in his characters, or making them serve as indicators of Tristram's mind, as much by the fact that he considers them worth passing on as through the things he has to say about them.[40]

He goes on to refer to an article by B. H. Lehman, which he paraphrases like this:

> . . . reality its own hypothesis. The constant expansion of a hypothesis to fit the facts can only end in a view of nature as

> perceived by a given mind . . . he was interested in theory only as it manifested itself in experience.[41]

Neither of these two quotations seem to me to have got the relation between document and character, system and experience in *Tristram Shandy* quite right. Stedmond says that the documents act as catalysts to the characters. In fact they also represent the external and publicly-visible *effects* which result from private emotional experiences happening 'inside' the characters. They form a systematised debris of personality. The Shandys' marriage-settlement, with Toby's added clause, sets out in due form and process the Shandys' knowledge of each other's wishes, and also demonstrates their knowledge of each other's characters.

So perhaps it is right to add to the second quotation the proviso that Sterne is also interested in the evolution of theory out of experience. Tristram would certainly like us to believe that system and theory dictate experience and that that is the end of it, but if we *do* come to believe this we have yielded to his playful rhetoric and adopted terms of reference which belong to Walter—not to Tristram. Tristram has a much greater awareness of the 'inventions' of his own mind and his father's than at first appears to be the case.

To further the reader's belief in system dictating experience, Tristram takes up the theme of cause and effect once more, at the end of Chapter 15, after he has explained the workings of his parents' marriage-settlement. 'But I was begot and born to misfortunes . . . I was doom'd, by marriage articles, to have my nose squeez'd as flat to my face, as if the destinies had actually spun me without one'.[42] He represents the document to the reader as a new system of external causation, and repeats the theme of 'begot and born to misfortune' to remind us of the more general systems which have previously been set up.

The truth of the matter is that Tristram is not doomed by marriage articles at all, and that this becomes quite plain as early as Chapter 17 of this volume. He is 'doomed' to be born in Yorkshire, where Slop can get his hands on him, by the article which his father has had put in to VOID the settlement should it be misused—if his wife should get a trip to London on the strength of a false pregnancy. This is precisely what does happen, so (and this is really the joke) it is as though the settlement had never existed, for all practical purposes.

As in the previous sections of the volume, the turn of events is actually determined by the characters of Walter Shandy and his good lady—and here also by Toby's character, for, interestingly, it is Toby's insight into Mrs Shandy's nature which prompts Walter to insert his clause.

What the reader remembers from this section is not the long, slow joke of the marriage-settlement, with its tortuousness of phrase; it is Walter's character, his 'peremptory insistence' upon his rights once his wife has cried wolf, and the fact that his vexation stems principally from his missing the correct time for the pulling of his greengages back home. Yet Tristram goes on claiming that the document is important for its own sake, that it is a Cause. Given the clarity with which he has shown that the settlement is the cause of nothing, it is interesting that he has the temerity to make the claim, and to repeat it at the end of Volume II—inviting the reader to 'raise a system to account for the loss of my nose by marriage articles'.[43] The reader's belief in these systems seems to be as important to Tristram as Walter's belief in systems is to Walter. The reader is again invited to be his own Shandean character, invited to force his mind to be aware of the conspiracy.

In Chapter 17 Tristram provides a momentary break from this procedure, which forms enough of a contrast to point up his usual method. He tells the reader the same thing as he shows him. Instead of setting up an inscrutable or capricious system of external causality—Fortune, astrology, the association of ideas, the forms and methods of fiction, legal document and so on—and deducing effects from it while at the same time negating or opposing the whole process, he makes the chain of causality appear to originate with the characters, and says no more about it.

The effect of this is to create, for the first time, a sense of the characters existing in lived time, an evolving present moment. He makes a paragraph which contains one single sustained sentence and tone of voice. There are two clear points of time for the reader to latch on to: the ride home from London to York, and the post-conceptive chat between Walter and his wife. There is an established time-scheme to link these, and to enable the material in the previous chapters to be briefly summed up. For a little while everything is comparatively naturalistic.

It is also the first point where there is no stress on either Walter's or Tristram's yearning for an order, coherence, plan or system. Like Walter, Tristram wants to create an ordered system, but unlike Walter he makes a system which involves a personal step into the past, as well as the systematic retrieval of material to shore up a present moment. It only begins to be felt as a whole and satisfying imaginative order when Tristram leaves off persuading us into other orders.

Chapters 19–25

The first part of this section is about Naming, and through this, about the power of words and rhetoric. But the last chapters of the volume are also used to recapitulate and reinforce some of the other systems of external causation Tristram has thought of so far.

Chapter 19 is ostensibly about Walter's ideas on the significance of different Christian names:

> His opinion, in this matter, was, that there was a strange kind of magick bias, which good or bad names, as he called them, irresistibly impress'd upon our characters and conduct.[44]

The name for which he has the greatest contempt is TRISTRAM; he would rather bequeath any other name to his son. His plan is patently going to fail, what with Tristram being Tristram's name.

Tristram does not trouble to answer this new sytem on its own terms, and does not directly oppose it or show its falsity. Instead he provides a subtle ironic counterpoint to it in the rest of the chapter, which consists of a description of Walter's natural powers of eloquence. Walter defends his theory of good and bad names while he is at Jesus College, Cambridge for the day, entering Tristram's name(!) for a place at the college. He trains all his rhetorical guns on the dons. The dons, despite their scholastic reservations, are very impressed:

> —it was a matter of just wonder with my worthy tutor, and

> two or three fellows of that learned society, --- that a man who knew not so much as the names of his tools, should be able to work after that fashion with 'em.[45]

Walter's eloquence is not part of any conscious pattern or system, but is simply part of his character. He is 'the natural orator, who knows and uses all the devices of rhetorical artifice'.[46] The irony begins with the fact that he does not know the names of the arguments he uses to defend his theory of names so successfully. It is completed by Tristram's being in total possession of those names Walter lacks. He has read the rhetorical handbooks—he casually mentions an impressive list of the books Walter never read:

> he had never read *Cicero* nor *Quintilian de Oratore*, nor *Isocrates*, nor *Aristotle*, nor *Longinus* . . . nor *Vossius*, nor *Skioppius*, nor *Ramus*, nor *Farnaby* . . . *Crackenthorp* or *Burgersdicius*, or any *Dutch* logician or commentator,[47]

and displays his familiarity with formal rhetorical terms which Walter uses without knowing their names: 'he would sometimes break off in a sudden and spirited EPIPHONEMA, or rather EROTESIS, raised a third, and sometimes a full fifth above the key of the discourse'.[48] As John Traugott comprehensively shows, the techniques of rhetoric are in constant use in *Tristram Shandy*. The book is one long, conscious pattern of rhetorical figures from the 'Optatio' of the very first words—'I wish'.[49] Tristram's natural eloquence or garrulousness finds an outlet through these forms, and he writes his book. He has inherited his eloquence from his father, who has bequeathed to him without knowing it his most important characteristic. Tristram needs no help from magic names.

Chapter 20—the Sorbonne doctors' consultation on the ticklish baptismal point—looks at first like a pure digression, but it also shows the reader that what Tristram finds of interest is not the *act* of naming or any intrinsic significance it might have, but the grotesque verbal structures which men are prone to erect around such events. And the theme does remain the same: the significance (this time a religious one) of the Name.

This unconscious bequeathing of names, i.e. words, to his

son colours the reader's attitude to Walter. The pity that Tristram suggests as the appropriate response begins to be tempered by an awareness of Walter's powers, and a memory of the fact that Tristram is writing the book at least partly in imitation of him. Having Walter impress the fellows is a shrewd move. He would not ever impress us by what he said, because we see behind his eloquence into his curious habits of mind. But we are impressed that others are impressed, that Walter's eloquence works, has an effect in the real world.

In Chapter 21, Walter uses the family story of great-aunt Dinah's marriage to a coachman to bolster his theory of the 'magick bias' of Christian names. (His point is that as Diana was the goddess of hunting and horseriding, Dinah was obviously destined to marry a coachman.) This leads into the theme of character as reputation: Toby does not like Walter telling the story about Dinah, as it offends his personal modesty and his family pride.

> [Toby] – – how can you have so little feeling and compassion for the character of our family? . . .
>
> [Walter] What is the character of a family to an hypothesis? . . . Nay, if you come to that – What is the life of a family?
>
> [Toby]——The life of a family![50]

The equation between character and life is the same as in the story of Yorick. Just previous to this point in the chapter Tristram has made the same equation in a different way, by restating the connection between formal description of character and a sort of death. He has given the reader a glimpse of Toby smoking his pipe, 'in mute contemplation of a new pair of black-plush-breeches which he had got on',[51] skilfully immersing the reader in Toby's character, building up the suspense in three lines—and then interrupting Toby after two words with a promise of, and a beginning of, a systematic description of his character, in the course of which all he says is that Toby is modest, and that he is a Shandean sort of a character. As he leads the discussion away from Toby, Tristram uses one phrase with particular sarcasm: 'you must be made to enter first a little into his character'.[52] Once again a promise of formal description leads to a state of imaginative death for the character in question, in the sense that he disappears for a time from the book.

In Chapter 23, Tristram gives a list of the various 'mechanical helps' he might have used in his delineation of Toby's character. He could have drawn him 'with wind instruments', or by way of his 'evacuations',[53] or with a Pentagraph, a mechanical copying device. At the end of this list, he insists that he will avoid the errors inherent in all these methods by drawing Toby's character from his Hobby-Horse. In the next chapter he claims that the relationship between Toby and his Hobby-Horse (and between men and their Hobby-Horses in general) is a close and organic one. But he chooses the metaphoric physical mode for his description, Toby mounted and riding and absorbing Hobbyhorsical matter via the parts of his body which come into contact with the beast. In this mode the Hobby-Horse is not seen as an integral part of the character, but as an external source of energy and direction. It makes a man's impulse to action appear to originate from outside himself. In this it is analogous to Walter's systems. It does not avoid all the errors of the other 'methods' of drawing character, not when the metaphor is used as a system in its own right. Tristram uses a slightly suspect phrase about his desire to describe characters: 'if we would come to the specifick characters of them'.[54] Before the discussion of the Hobby-Horse gets under way Tristram refers to Momus, the Roman god of ridicule and satire. This colours the following discussion, by reminding the reader that Tristram's aim in coming at 'specifick characters' has, in Volume I, often been Momus's own—the aim being caricature, or the reduction of a person to his dominant characteristic or Hobby-Horse. To describe Toby from his Hobby-Horse would smack of satire; and Tristram is too fond of him to poke fun at him. Toby's Hobby-Horse is eventually described, in Volume II, but nothing is learnt about the rest of his character from this description.

As has been said, Tristram writes his book partly in imitation of his father Walter. Walter's fascinated interest in a variety of systems of knowledge is matched in intensity by Tristram's fascinated interest in his father, a fascination which leads him to adopt or assume some of Walter's own attitudes as he writes. In the first volume of *Tristram Shandy*, the systems themselves are mostly kept within bounds by Tristram's subtle policy of divide-and-rule: he presents each system more or less separately, and gently distances it by some of the dramatic—as opposed to the rhetorical—elements in his writing. But in the book as a whole such systems are felt as presences both more general and less directly confronted. Tristram is not in control of them to the same extent. They have more of a life of their own. The following chapter, and the remaining section of this chapter, take the form of an enquiry into the nature of these larger systems in *Tristram Shandy*, and into the background which lies behind Sterne's imagery and behind his selection and treatment of material in the book. Later chapters will illustrate in detail the presence of this background in the text.

III GRAVITY AS PLOT AND HOBBY-HORSE

The relevance of tracing the sources of *Tristram Shandy* at least partly through the history of ideas lies in the fact that it is through ideas that Sterne makes the readers aware of the typicality of his characters. In eighteenth-century literature, says E. R. Wasserman, the only people who are truly representative of the mental life of the period, 'those who were moulded wholly by the indigenous and cultural forces—are to be found among the members of the Shandy household'.[55]

This, of course, is very unusual in a novelist. The Great Tradition of English novel-writing chooses to do things differently. The writer shows the reader characters who have specific places in a recognisable social or family structure, and the reader identifies with the characters' ambitions or dilemmas inside that structure. But the reader must not assume that because the social levels of existence are secondary in *Tristram Shandy*, Sterne is indulging himself by describing eccentrics. It is not hard to show how close a parody of public thought and discourse *Tristram Shandy* is. There are many opinions to quote. Even respectable historians pass remarks about the mentality of the eighteenth century which can be seized on as evidence of 'Shandyism' on the loose in society at large. For instance, when Gustave Lanson attempts an overview of the data his period has provided him with, it is easy to say that the serious philosophers he is talking about are made to appear close cousins to Walter Shandy:

> On a surtout reproché à la philosophie du XVIIIe siècle son abus de l'a priori. Tous les faiseurs de systèmes posent des principes, donnent des définitions, et ils tirent des conséquences sans avoir songé à établir leurs principes ni a justifier leurs définitions . . . Ils ne songent pas à se demander si la réalité autorise leurs· principes ou leurs définitions: ils trouvent la réalité au terme de leur analyse; et s'ils ne la trouvent pas, ils la condamnent . . . La réalité est citée par eux pour être jugée par leurs systèmes.[56]

As with Walter, reality exists merely as an obstacle to finer perception. But it is not quite enough simply to point to some philosophy and say that it is *used in*, or *appears in, Tristram Shandy*. Flippant reference to serious thought is a part of the tradition of the self-conscious narrator, who is often anxious to display his own familiarity with popular or abstruse philosophy.

It is not the naked 'use' of philosophy that characterises Sterne's book.[57] The image of the Hobby-Horse has already given a good example of the method. A particular metaphor will have material arranged around it in such a way as to suggest that there is a correspondence or figurative relationship between the real, public world (what might be called the world of published knowledge) and the world of fiction: and the metaphor will draw attention to both worlds at once.

The crucial metaphor (or cliché) in *Tristram Shandy* seems to be one from which the discussion was diverted in a previous section of this chapter: the Blow of Fate. It is crucial in that it forms a point of intersection for several interrelated metaphors and discussions. So it may be wise to preface the examination of the general cultural background to *Tristram Shandy* with a discussion of the context of this metaphor inside the book.

Tristram tends to use the final chapter or chapters of the volumes of his book to stress the *systematic* elements either of a character, or of the book, or of the world in general. At the end of Volume V (Chapter 43) there is Walter's most sustained exposition of his system of auxiliary verbs, the 'white bear' passage: the penultimate chapter (Chapter 34) of Volume VIII contains his dietary system, which he is communicating to uncle Toby in a letter. The last chapters of Volumes II, III and IV all bring the reader back to the idea of systematic thought, either by referring to the book as an entity (at the end of Volume II there is the invitation to the reader to form his own system of plot: the same kind of general recapitulation at the end of Volume IV expresses Tristram's opinion that 'such a building do I foresee it will turn out, as never was planned, and as never was executed since *Adam*'[58]), or by referring to some other system: Volume III, Chapter 42 mentions Slawkenbergius's tales as 'all of them turning round somehow or other upon the main hinges of his subject'.[59] A common feature of these examples is the tone of gentle mockery or self-mockery which usually occurs whenever Tristram talks about things having to do with the concept of design, or designed systems.

But the two most interesting examples of this process come near the ends of Volumes I and VI. Here the systems are huge and various. Tristram parcels up together the visible movement or laws of movement of the universe and the movement of the characters' minds, and then tries to tie up the parcel with a remark about the visible movement of his own book. All three spheres of reference revolve together, after the manner of others of Tristram's virtuose and hydra-headed metaphors. This happens in Chapters 21 and 22 of Volume I —he begins with the universe and Walter's mind:

> My father, as I told you, was a philosopher in grain, —speculative, —systematical; —and my Aunt Dinah's affair was a matter of as much consequence to him, as the retrogradation of the planets to *Copernicus*: —The backslidings of *Venus* in her orbit fortified the *Copernican* system, call'd so after his name; and the backslidings of my aunt *Dinah* in her orbit, did the same service in establishing my father's system, which, I trust, will for ever hereafter be call'd the *Shandean System*, after his.[60]

Then in the next chapter Tristram explains how, although his digression on aunt Dinah has 'led us a vagary some millions of miles into the very heart of the planetary system',[61] this digression in fact helped the main plot, i.e. the drawing of Toby's character, and that

> By this contrivance the machinery of my work is of a species by itself; two contrary motions are introduced into it, and reconciled, which were thought to be at variance with each other. In a word, my work is digressive, and it is progressive too,—and at the same time.
>
> This, Sir, is a very different story from that of the earth's moving round her axis, in her diurnal rotation, with her progress in her elliptick orbit which brings about the year, and constitutes that variety and vicissitude of seasons we enjoy;—though I own it suggested the thought . . . I have constructed the main work and the adventitious parts of it with such intersections, and have so complicated and involved the digressive and progressive movements, one wheel within another, that the whole machine, in general, has been kept a-going.[62]

The conflation is a little obfusc, and perhaps deliberately so. The first quotation, from Chapter 21, is seen (if the reader grasps just how clever and exact the comparison is) as a piece of sheer mental virtuosity on Tristram's part; but then he extends this conflation in the second quotation, book/earth, and this is not quite so well expressed. Why does he approach it by calling it 'a very different story' if he wants to make a comparison? It makes the metaphor just a little bit more mystifying and occult.

The example at the end of Volume VI is even more confusing, because the metaphor is produced so much more quickly. Chapter 40, the chapter which contains the drawings of the various lines of narrative, ends thus:

> Pray can you tell me,—that is, without anger, before I write my chapter upon straight lines—by what mistake—who told them so—or how it has come to pass, that your men of wit and genius have all along confounded this line, with the line of GRAVITATION.[63]

This is a strange joke. The metaphor works between two spheres of reference, as follows.

Firstly, 'Who told the critics that the best, most serious (grave) way to write a book was straight forwards? My book is very serious indeed, and is written (as the lines of narrative show) parabolically, digressively, hyperbolically . . .'

Secondly, the sphere on which the first really depends, because it refers to the more usual sense of the word GRAVITATION. 'Why did men believe that the track of a projectile through gravitational space was a straight line and not a parabola, or a hyperbola?' This refers the system of the book to the universal law of gravity, which is manifested in the book through Toby's Hobbyhorsical studies of the science of ballistics in Volume II.

But there are anomalies in all this. If one follows up the second reference, one finds that Tristram was previously (Volume II, Chapter 3) taking pains to show that 'men of wit and genius' haven't confounded the straight line with the 'line of gravitation' since before Niccolo Tartaglia, *circa* 1536. Tristram is trying to make a joke out of a comparison between the erroneous dogma of science and the erroneous dogma of criticism, but he doesn't quite succeed. Since he is usually a very good and precise writer, it may be that his intention is larger than this, that his methods here are part of a wider argument in the book.

In making these conflations, Tristram is using his own variant of a conventional figure. The eighteenth-century writer, wishing to refer to his construction of a heterocosm, an alternative imaginative world in his book, will refer to it as a *machine*, and will invoke the pattern of the larger world, the laws of 'Nature', to justify the pattern of his book. Ian Donaldson, in an article called 'The Clockwork Novel: Three Notes on an Eighteenth-Century Analogy', points out the use of this figure in the Introduction to Hobbes's *Leviathan*, in *Tom Jones*, in Locke's *Essay Concerning Human Understanding*, and in Richardson and Samuel Johnson. In all the examples he gives, the idea of a machine or mechanism is used as a metaphor for the idea of pattern or system, to link together 'human motive and action . . . artistic design, and . . . the design of the world at large'.[64] This kind of use tends to leave the reader with a sense of something more rigid and inflexible than does Tristram's use of the figure, which emphasises the mental energy needed to make the analogy work properly, rather than making a comparison with clockwork. None the less, the cosmic clockwork is what is in Tristram's mind at the end of Volumes I and VI.

Another difference is that in *Tristram Shandy* it is not just an externally-applied metaphor, but an integral part of the book. The gravitational laws of the cosmic machine are embodied not only in Toby's study of projectiles, but also in the blow of the cannonball which strikes Toby in the groin in Volume I, Chapter 25, and determines, or appears to determine, his Hobby-Horse through the book. A body obeying the universal laws of motion becomes the stimulus to human action and motivation. Indeed, there is a noticeable tendency for the plot of *Tristram Shandy* to evolve and develop by way of the blows which are delivered on the characters, and which they deliver on each other. In Volume I there are the blows that fall on Tristram from the arm of 'the ungrateful Duchess', Fortune, the blows of the 'cross accidents' with which he promises his book will deal: and there are the blows which fall on Yorick and send him to his fate; as well as Toby's more specific blow. In the rest of the book there is the window which falls on Tristram and neatly circumcises him while he is ******* out of it; there is the gentle but devastating blow of the hot chestnut upon Phutatorius's tenderest part; and there is the crushing blow of Slop's forceps on the infant Tristram's nose. Also, characters themselves undergo slapstick falls, Slop from his horse, and Trim and Bridget through the drawbridge and into the fosse.

Nor is this the end of such things. As the story of Yorick's death made clear, Tristram's Hobby-Horse of writing delivers blows of its own on the characters, the flattening, bruising and mis-shaping of caricature. Thus the metaphor of the blow is made to carry associations of violence directed by one individual (the writer) against others (the characters). The metaphor comes to be as supple and various as that of the Hobby-Horse: not only is the reader unsure as to whether the blows that fall on people are merely real or are metaphorical physical detail, he may also feel that he is being invited to relate the blow to either, or even both of, two contexts: the personal, literary context and the cosmic plot. Even when a blow can be explained as the result of a character's own action or personality, Tristram will prefer to see it as a blow of

Fortune, one of the cross-accidents and coincidences that fall on to suffering humanity from an ingenious and faintly conspiratorial cosmos. This sense of the causal power of the mischievous universe is usually expressed in terms of falling bodies, bodies conforming to the constant laws of that universe, the ultimate external system of *gravity*. Whenever Tristram can blame something on gravity, he does so: if *Tristram Shandy* were a whodunit, gravity would be the butler.

This, of course, is a virtually timeless method of ironically referring events which are felt to be ruled by chance and circumstance when contemplated on the purely human level, to the macrocosm, in order that they may be felt to be ruled by Fate and Destiny. Thus Bob Dylan:

> It was gravity that brought us down
> And destiny that kept us apart.[65]

Tristram's use goes beyond irony, in that the characters—especially Walter—do genuinely feel that they have a lot of trouble from such systems; and as the book's motto says, it is not things but opinions concerning things which disturb men. But all this does nothing to explain what Tristram is doing with the system of the world at the ends of Volumes I and VI.

His deepest intention may be to issue an invitation to the reader to respond in a particular way. It is one of his many traps for the unwary. As there is an excellent example of a critic falling into this trap all unawares, the general point can perhaps be best introduced by way of this specific response.

In an article called 'Tristram Shandy's Law of Gravity', Sigurd Burkhardt evolves a theory that Sterne saw his words as having *weight*, and as following parabolic curves downwards like projectiles, in that when they are directed towards the reader's reason (his head) they invariably 'curve downwards and hit the reader's concupiscence instead',[66] meaning that they so often contain sexual innuendo. He tries to find a parallel for this phenomenon in the characters' continual 'misplaced faith in the efficacy of mechanical devices',[67] citing among other things Dr Slop's faith in his forceps, and several of the formal documents—the Shandys' marriage-settlement, for example. If engines and devices fail to work, this might be due to the action of a similar 'law of gravity' which works to frustrate the characters' intentions, just as Tristram is continually finding that his verbal and artistic intentions are frustrated—his Life will not progress. This theory is supported by Burkhardt's noticing Tristram's preoccupation with gravity at various points in the book—he deals with the example at the end of Volume VI:

> The question, therefore, why men of wit and genius have all along confounded the straight line with the line of gravitation is asked by Sterne in honest bewilderment; nothing seems so obvious—and nothing should *be* so obvious—as that, if you want to project something (meaning words) over a gap, your line can never be straight, but must be indirect, parabolic, hyperbolic, cycloid.[68]

From these and other instances he feels able to make a surprising claim, that *Tristram Shandy* is governed by 'a causality as binding and as precise as that of classical mechanics'[69]—meaning Newtonian mechanics. He continues like this:

> I feel on shaky ground here: what sustains me in my speculations is the conviction that in these figures the secret of the book is hidden and revealed, and that careful reading and supple and rigorous thinking may ultimately come up with a satisfactory formulation of the law of this most curious machine.[70]

Shaky ground is right; it's Tristram's trap. Burkhardt makes a claim which Sterne takes great care not to let Tristram make at this point—that the book is a machine. Burkhardt does not notice that when one is dealing with a novel, an intellectual concept applied from a system outside the book—a Law of Gravity—*is* a mechanical device, in that the law cannot, of itself, be an organic part of the book. He falls, in short, into much the same error as the characters he has just described, putting a misplaced faith in the efficacy of an engine, a device—and it is the misplaced faith of the characters, not the nature of the engines themselves, which causes the mishaps in the book. To show a man searching for order, patterns and the universal laws which might control those patterns (as

Tristram shows Walter) is a different thing from making patterns and formulating laws.

I think Burkhardt is right to be interested in this curious aspect of the book, and to associate Newtonian mechanics with the causality of *Tristram Shandy*: but what he gives is really a response rather than an answer. It is tempting to respond to Tristram's invitation to indulge in mental speculation, an invitation which is held out particularly strongly in the questions about gravity. His enthusiasm is contagious, the reader finds himself making the same kind of enthusiastic hypotheses as the characters; he sympathises. Even the intellectual reactions to the book are worked by sympathy, by the reader's being caught in the peculiar vibration of Tristram's mind. Ultimately, it is the sense of himself as a friend and confidant to the reader which Tristram can engender that is responsible for the critical indulgence in theme-theory and hypothesis.[71] This reflects back on to the nature of that emotion. A word like 'sympathy' is usually used as if it applied primarily to the characters in *Tristram Shandy*, as if it helped only to explain Sterne's notions about the psychology of the individual mind. In fact it applies much more widely (the same is true of 'association'). Sympathy, far from being the 'final doctrine'[72] of the book, embodied in the emotional rapport between the Shandy brothers, is an intellectual premise from which the book develops.

What Tristram is doing is to exploit the latent Hobbyhorsical tendencies which exist in every reader's mind. It is strange and ironic that he is able to do this by way of a subject as apparently cut-and-dried as the laws of gravity. Newton's formulation of these laws in the *Principia Mathematica*, which was published some twenty-five years before the action of *Tristram Shandy* takes place (the first edition of the *Principia* dates from 1687), is after all a model of the results of the pure scientific method, the final expression of the mechanical world-picture which developed in England towards the end of the seventeenth century. Once demonstrated, these laws must be allowed to be correct and absolute. Yet Tristram insists that the study of gravity is somehow a Hobbyhorsical activity, that there is something about the subject that leads to Hobbyhorsicality.

The obvious illustration of this is uncle Toby, whose study

of the motions of projectiles is made an essential part of his Hobby-Horse. But there are two minor characters in *Tristram Shandy* whom it is worth investigating on a documentary level, to show that Sterne is also interested in the connections between gravity and Hobbyhorsicality in the 'real world'. In the first example (Simon Stevin) the comments really have only the curiosity value of occult resemblances or coincidences; the second (Thomas Aquinas) has more to do with the text, for he shows that two themes associated in *Tristram Shandy*, gravity and sexuality or generation (associated in that the blows that fall on the characters tend to fall on their genitals) are associated elsewhere.

Simon Stevin is the extremely versatile sixteenth-century Dutch mathematician and engineer who gets into *Tristram Shandy* in Volume II: his famous sailing chariot turns up in a discussion between Walter and Toby, and Yorick's sermon falls out of Stevinus's book on military fortification, which is in Toby's library. Stevin was, among many other things, a gravitational scientist: it was he who performed the experiment involving the dropping of balls of different weight from a tower, which legend attributes to Galileo.[73]

Stevin's sailing chariot, a sort of oversized Renaissance land-yacht, which he designed and built for his patron, Maurice of Nassau, is instantly recognisable as a Hobby-Horse. Not only is it a vehicle capable of extremely swift motion, it also induces extreme enthusiasm in the minds of those who regard it, whether this be 'the learned *Peireskius* . . . who walked a matter of five hundred miles . . . in order to see it',[74] or Toby, who is so enthusiastic about it, or Walter and Slop, who are both impelled by the chariot to launch into a favourite dissertation ('on trade').

Stevin himself seems to have been quite well-known for his Hobbyhorsical character, and is thus fully compatible with the effects of his invention: W. W. Rouse Ball says that he was

> somewhat dogmatical in his assertions, and allowed no-one to differ from his conclusions; 'and those' says he in one place, 'who cannot see this, may the Author of nature have pity upon their unfortunate eyes, for the fault is not in the thing, but in the sight which we are unable to give them'.[75]

Isn't life beautiful when you know you're right: an essential ingredient of the Shandean happiness. Stevin isn't *visibly* a Shandean character in the book, but the reasons for his inclusion are.

Thomas Aquinas gets into the book in Volume I, Chapter 20, in the Sorbonne doctors' consultation on the question of the baptismal squirt: can an infant still in its mother's womb be baptised? Thomas says no, but the doctors say yes, with reservations and a little squirt. Is this discussion pedantic, or merely Hobbyhorsical? There is a connection between the squirt and another Hobbyhorsical engine or device, Dr Slop's marvellous new obstetrical invention, the forceps; in Volume III, Chapter 15, Slop's squirt falls out of his bag when he pulls out the forceps, and Toby makes his inadvertent joke about it: '*are children brought into the world with a squirt*?'[76]

—But what on earth could be the real-world connection between the administering of the sacraments and the study of gravity?—

To answer this question, it is necessary to extend Toby's studies a little, and briefly to digress as far back as Aristotle, with whom the recorded search for the true cause of the motion of falling bodies originates.

Artistotle's theory that a projectile, once separated from its projector or thrower, acts on its surrounding material—the air—in such a way as to transfer its projector's power into the layers of air immediately adjacent to the projectile, was overtaken in the Middle Ages. A certain Johannes Philoponus formulated the concept of an immaterial intrinsic motive power in order to improve the theory of projectiles. In medieval Scholasticism this power was discussed under the name of *vis impressa*, or *impetus*, and by the thirteenth century it was generally assumed that it was this force, imparted by the projector to the projectile, that formed the true power of the body. This theory of gravity, says E. J. Dijksterhuis,

> was treated as a familiar matter in the thirteenth century. Thomas Aquinas rejected it in his commentaries on the *Physics* and on *De Caelo* . . . but elsewhere he cites it three times to illustrate a metaphysical problem, without any evidence of a critical attitude . . . on two of the three occasions it arose in connection with the problem frequently

> discussed in the Middle Ages, of how the human embryo is endowed with a soul; is this effected directly by a creative act of God, who adds the *anima sensibilis* to the purely physical foetus evolved through natural causes, or does this *anima* originate from that of the father through the semen? In the latter case, a force would have to be operative in that semen as instrument, and this would be impossible, according to peripatetic conceptions, as soon as it was divorced from the paternal soul, which is its *movens*. Here the *projectum separatum* is cited for the purposes of comparison: just as this has received from the *projeciens* an intrinsic *virtus movens*, the *virtus in semine patris* may also be a permanent intrinsic power.[77]

The real weapon in the arsenal of the artillery of love.

Thomas discusses one sort of little squirt in the context of gravitational studies: but squirts in their baptismal function also figure in this serious discussion. Dijksterhuis continues:

> The first to subscribe fully to this theory (of impetus) was the Italian Scotist, Franciscus of Marchia. He refers to the concept of *impetus* (by the name of *vis derelicta*) in a discussion of the mode of operation of the sacraments: does an intrinsic derivative force reside in them, which effects grace, or does God interfere directly through the local motion of the means of grace? In order to elucidate the former view, Franciscus gives a detailed exposition about falling bodies and projectiles in the sense of the impetus-theory; the question of whether it can be accepted will depend on whether an instrinsic *virtus* may be assumed in a *projectum separatum*.[78]

It is interesting to find that material in *Tristram Shandy* which appears to be of very local interest only—i.e. the Sorbonne doctors' deliberations, which appear to relate only to the theme of names and naming—in fact has unexpected connections with some of the leading general ideas that are used in the construction of the book. But I think that this present chapter of the study has now lain itself open to several criticisms, to wit:

Surely these obsolete philosophical notions, fascinating as

they may be in their Hobbyhorsicality, have very little to do with the universal law of gravity as it appears in Newton's *Principia*? Surely they have only curio value as ideas—isn't this what John Ferriar was talking about when he said that Sterne 'laughs at many exploded opinions, and forsaken fooleries'?[79] Is not Sterne simply interested in drawing parallels between the wayward minds of all the characters, the Sorbonne doctors, Toby, Stevinus, and so on, who are caught up in some lunatic fringe of the subject? Is it not totally unwarranted to connect these carefully-selected examples of Shandyism with the strictly scientific exposition of Newtonian mechanics—and what could Newtonian or even post-Newtonian science have to do with the literary methods of *Tristram Shandy*?

To answer these criticisms, it is necessary briefly to consider the particular character of Newtonian gravity in relation to the science of the time, and the uses made of Newton's ideas by the succeeding generation of thinkers.

3 Sterne and the Scientific Study of Man

Sir Isaac Newton was not a particularly Hobbyhorsical character. He even expressed the opinion that his system of philosophy was not Hobbyhorsical—as for instance in Rule One, from 'The System of the World', Book III of the *Principia*: 'We are to admit no more causes of natural things than such as are both true and sufficient to explain their appearances'.[1]

Unfortunately his impact on the scientific and cultural audiences belies this opinion. His thought can induce violent and extreme Hobbyhorsical motion in the hearer. There are particular reasons for this, as follows.

When the *Principia Mathematica* first appeared in 1687, the scientific community was not altogether happy about Newton's ideas on gravity. His formulation of the law of universal gravitation (that every particle of matter attracts every other particle with a force which varies directly as the product of their masses and inversely as the square of the distance between them) was generally felt to be retrogressive, reactionary and essentially unscientific, in that it was not an evolution from the post-Cartesian mechanistic philosophy then in vogue. All of Newton's most important terms—gravity, attraction, sympathy and so on—revert back to the medieval terminology of occult resemblances. 'Gravity, interpreted as an innate attraction between every pair of particles of matter, was an occult quality in the same sense as the scholastics' "tendency to fall" had been.'[2] Scientists who had spent their lives conscientiously weaning themselves from the old animistic explanatory principles operating with semi-magical ideas of sympathy and antipathy and had built corpuscular theories of motion, were now asked to return to the idea of *actio in distans*: and of this, they were naturally somewhat mistrustful. Christiaan Huygens, in *La Cause de la Pesanteur*, says that

Newton's concept of the mutual attraction of two particles of matter is unacceptable to him

> par ce que je crois voir clairement, que la cause d'une telle attraction n'est point explicable par aucun principe de Méchanique, ni des règles du mouvement comme je ne suis pas persuadée non plus de la nécessité de l'attraction mutuelle des corps entiers.[3]

Similarly Leibniz, in a letter to Huygens on 20 March 1693, discussing the problem of the explanation of *cohesion*, disapproves of introducing a new and inexplicable concept for it:

> laquelle estant accordée, on passeroit bientost à d'autres suppositions semblables, comme à la pesanteur d'Aristote, à l'attraction de Mons. Newton, à des sympathies ou antipathies et à mille autres attributs semblables.[4]

What these men find difficult to accept is that Newton's gravity appears to belong more to the realm of supernature, to some ancient covert system of cosmic analogy, than to the visible, natural world. In its own supramechanical way, the mutual attraction of particles was as much a metaphysical concept as was the harmony of the spheres; indeed, it almost amounts to a scientific expression of this belief of cosmic order. Yet it exists in an age which thinks mechanically and scientifically. The rest of Newton's works conform largely to this other ethos; his *Opticks* for instance describes light in terms of material corpuscles.

The post-Newtonian universe may be a machine, and clockwork may be the analogy which is felt to apply most appropriately to it, but this is not specifically Newton's doing. Newton does not kill off the universe, he animates it. He populates the cosmos with qualities almost of *mind*, as if it were some sentient, self-regulating organisation, rather than a grand, impersonal machine: yet with this approach he is equipped to describe the absolute laws of the purely physical universe.

In particular, this aspect of Newton seems to sanction the principle of argument by analogy between the natural and the human orders. He anthropomorphises the cosmos, and thus makes argument in the other direction legitimate—man must be like the natural universe. In terms of the eighteenth-century reception of his ideas, this is the most important quality of his thought.

Medical, psychological and aesthetic philosophers in the first part of the eighteenth century have a great fondness for making analogies between their own systems and the universal laws of Newtonian gravity. They take these laws and concepts as a model for their own intellectual activity. As early as 1710, George Berkeley alludes to the fashionable nature of Newton's physics, and especially of the concept of gravitational attraction. He calls Attraction 'the great mechanical principle now in vogue',[5] and takes it to be a paradigm of the entire scientific method, whose function he says is to discover 'analogies, harmonies and agreements'[6] in the natural world.

The thinkers who make the most comprehensive use of the analogy with Newton are the *associationist* psychologists of the mid-eighteenth century, who operate under the belief that the universal laws of external nature can be used to demonstrate the universal laws of *human* nature. (It is one of the most complete of the *a priori* systems of thought to which Lanson was referring.) By making use of a specific aspect of the analogy with Newton—the conflation between the macrocosm and the 'Little world of man'—these writers justify their development of a psychology in which the individual is largely reduced to a passive agent, controlled by external forces, responsive to them. Man becomes a model of the cosmic clockwork.

Association is not usually mentioned in connection with *Tristram Shandy* without the name of John Locke being quite close at hand. Recently, however, there has been something of a reaction—and quite properly—against the practice of referring Sterne's fictional treatment of association to Locke's chapter 'On Association' in the *Essay Concerning Human Understanding*[7] and indeed a reaction against the previously widespread practice of saying that *Tristram Shandy* is not much more than a fictional rewriting of the *Essay*. R. S. Hafter, when he wants to diverge from this opinion, can muster a list of some twenty or so critics who subscribe to it.

This has led to something of a vacuum of ideas about association in *Tristram Shandy*. Hafter, with some plausibility, says that a better reference for Sterne's attitude to association is David Hume—saying that Sterne keeps to, and illustrates, Hume's three categories of association: Hume says that association is induced where the mind habitually perceives relations between things and ideas involving cause and effect, contiguity in time and place, or resemblance and contrast.[8]

There may well be something of Hume's spirit in *Tristram Shandy*: the connections between Sterne and Hume—and indeed Sterne and Locke—will be touched on later. But it seems to me to be more important to point out that Sterne's endowing his narrator and his characters (most notably Toby and Mrs Shandy) with habits of association which, to say the least, draw attention to themselves, has a strong connection with the *plot* of the book—plot in the sense already mentioned, of a sense of conspiracies which are felt to condition the characters' actions. Toby is *at the mercy of* his associative habits, his Hobby-Horse: or so Tristram says.

In this chapter I shall try to show that Sterne's interest in the association of ideas may well be a single aspect of his much more pervasive interest in analogy and correspondence. The concentration on false or casual association in the Shandys is Sterne's way of approaching the general notion of analogy through the vitality and divine spark of *wit*. It makes the characters appear to be more Lockean than in fact may be the case: demonic association or analogy is not the prerogative of Locke. Most of the chapter, however, is not concerned with Sterne's fictional practice, but with trying to see what it is in the background that could lead Sterne to see it as a 'real' plot.

To go back for a moment to David Hume: the ostensible connection between psychological association and Newtonianism is at its clearest in a fully-fledged system of associationism such as Hume's *Treatise of Human Nature* (1739–40). He makes the analogy enthusiastically and forcefully near the beginning of the *Treatise*; association, he says,

> is a kind of *attraction*, which in the mental world will be found to have as extraordinary effects as in the natural, and to show itself in as many and as various forms. Its effects are everywhere conspicuous; but as to its causes, they are mostly unknown, and must be resolved into *original* qualities of human nature, which I pretend not to explain. Nothing is

> more requisite for a true philosopher, than to restrain the intemperate desire of searching into causes.[9]

Even the caveat about not searching into causes is Newtonian, paralleling Rule One of 'The System of the World'. Hume makes the comparison between the two species of Attraction a second time in Book II of the *Treatise*: 'nature has bestowed a kind of attraction on certain ideas and impressions, by which one of them, upon its appearance, naturally introduces its correlative'.[10] Such a procedure is not really logically sound, unless the writer is prepared to offer concepts equivalent to distance, force and mass which can be measured in the mind. John Passmore points out the unsuitability of Newtonian attraction as an adequate pattern or model for Hume's brand of association:

> Attraction operates universally: therefore we cannot sensibly ask why it operates in a particular case. In contrast, association is 'a gentle force which commonly prevails'; we are not to conclude that 'without it the mind cannot join two ideas', since 'nothing is more free than that faculty'. Thus there is a genuine problem, and one which Hume does nothing whatsoever to solve, why association sometimes operates and sometimes fails to operate. Hume . . . leaves us with a 'science of man' which is quite incapable of explaining why the mind works in one way rather than another. This is certainly not Newtonianism . . .[11]

But then, Hume does not show the slightest interest in such problems—and other associationists are never worried about technicalia such as those mentioned above. They do not think them worth bothering about. This is perhaps an indication that what interests them is not so much Newton himself as the process of mind by which they find themselves able to claim the authority of Newtonian science, the process of analogy. Analogy is after all a sort of association itself, one which operates between different levels of reference: at one point in his *Observations on Man* (the eighteenth century's most thorough-going associationist work) David Hartley even uses the phrase 'Association, i.e. Analogy'.[12] It is only reasonable to justify one's theories simply by using a manifestation of the principles on which one's theories run.

At this point, informed criticism would make a remark to the effect that in making this analogy with Newton, these writers are simply attempting to shelter under the wing of a straightforward theological argument which has a strong tradition of use in the eighteenth century. This is the argument from design; the inference, from the evidence of a cosmic plan, of a cosmic planner, as discussed in the Introduction to this study.

Nothing demonstrates the cosmic plan so convincingly as Newtonian physics: so if a writer can demonstrate an alliance between his own work and the Newtonian cosmic machine, he will feel that he can claim a religious and moral justification for his work, as well as scientific justification. It might be concluded that there is nothing more than this in the analogy with Newton.

However in historical and methodological terms, eighteenth-century associationism is based neither on the divine analogy, nor on Newtonian laws. It is based on a quite specific evolution of *medical* principles from the design-argument, principles which in themselves are not associationist in character but which are based directly on the analogy with Newton. They occur in a tradition of popular science written in the vernacular. Without the establishment of this intermediate layer of thought between 1690 and about 1740, the associationist writers' adoption of the design-argument would not carry very much weight.

It will be as well to give a reasonably thorough rehearsal of the evolution of this set of ideas. There are of course connections between the later associationists and Sterne, but as well as this, a number of Sterne's practices in *Tristram Shandy* will be found to take on voice and point when considered in the light of these earlier developments.

Just as the theological argument from design exists in a Christian and Platonic tradition going back many centuries, so medical arguments involving analogies with design are found well before the start of the eighteenth century. It is, after all, a highly traditional approach to man's physical ills—that 'everything that is within can be known from what is without'.[13] In the Galenic–Hippocratic theory of humours, for instance, illness is the result of an imbalance in the body of the four universal humours or elements, which results in an exaggeration of one or more functions or attitudes.

One of the most interesting developments of this tendency in the generation before Newton is Sir Kenelm Digby's *Discourse in a Solemn Assembly at Montpellier*, entitled *Of the Sympathetic Powder; A Discourse of the Cure of Wounds, by the Powder of Sympathy* (1658). This extremely engaging work is distinguished by a belief that apparently magical correspondences between the natural and human worlds are in fact manifestations of natural laws. The 'Powder of Sympathy' is a preparation which, according to Digby, 'doth, naturally and without any Magick, cure wounds without touching them, yea, without seeing of the Patient'.[14]

This medical equivalent of the philosopher's stone seems to have been one of the seventeenth century's favourite legends. Digby's account was one of several attempts to persuade a public of the powder's reality: Ephraim Chambers described the powder, in 1713, as 'a mere piece of charlatanry, whatever Sir Kenelm Digby, and others before him, and after, plead in its favour'.[15] The cure is effected by sprinkling the powder on a piece of clothing belonging to the person wounded; the powder was then supposed to return to the wound by following the particular vibrations given out into the air by that person, and to close up the wound: a kind of psychometric healing bloodhound. Digby's *Discourse* tries hard to make this old wives' tale scientifically respectable. (Chambers's explanation of the powder, by the way, is that it is merely a chemical which has mild coagulative powers when placed on the wound.) Near the end of the work, Digby is quite clear about the particular objection he has had to overcome. 'I am perswaded my Discourse hath convincingly shewed you, that in this Sympathetical cure, there is no need to admit of an action distant from the Patient.'[16] He copes with the problem of *actio in distans* by positing a universal medium (akin to the Newtonian *ether*), in which the force of sympathy or attraction may work mechanically. He uses a beautiful and striking analogy of the diffusion of scents—he tells of being on a sailing-ship six miles off the Spanish coast and yet being able to smell the rosemary in the fields.

In the main body of the *Discourse*, Digby relates the powder's action to an amazing variety of occult phenomena, all of which, he claims, operate by this process of *sympathy*. The shape of birthmarks is of course determined by events which happen to the pregnant mother: vibrations travel in the blood between the mother's imagination and the baby's body. Naturally, one can cure horses by hanging toads round their necks—the toads give off therapeutic vibrations: and

> 'Tis an ordinary remedy, though a nasty one, that they who have ill breaths, hold their mouths open at the mouth of a Privy, as long as they can; and by the reiteration of this remedy, they find themselves cured at last; the greater stink of the Privy drawing to it, and carrying away, the lesse, which is that of the mouth.[17]

Unless, of course, you have very bad breath and a clean privy. It's an interesting example in two ways—firstly because Doctor L——n, in Smollett's *Humphry Clinker*, still appears or affects to believe in a variant of this remedy in 1771.[18] Secondly because Digby is arguing that the cure works in a way exactly analogous to the terms of gravitational attraction: the greater body/stink causing the lesser to be drawn towards it. But what is of most interest is his desire to include all his examples in one system which works by natural laws, and the fact that sympathy is the quality through which he believes he can do this. His system of medicine is based on the assumption that there is a pattern of correspondences, a harmony between the natural and the human world. Any evidence of harmonic or vibrational correspondence, whether scientific or artistic, is grist to his mill—for instance, he regards a cure involving music as of great support to his thesis. He saves until last the example of the bite of the tarantula spider. Victims of this beast, he says, sink into a swoon and die; but if they have music played to them they are seized with a desire to get up and boogie, thereby dispelling the effects of the poison. (The more usual variant of this story is that the bite of the tarantula itself causes tarantism, or dancing mania; the dancing is thus supposed to be a symptom as well as a cure. But this would interfere with Digby's hypothesis.) Digby leaves the example to speak for itself: in as plain a case of vibrational and harmonic correspondence as this, no argument is felt to be needed. So long as there is a pattern to be argued from, whether the laws of gravity or the harmonies of music, Digby feels safe. This is still the world of the late Renaissance, full of enthusiasm and holy simplicity where metaphysical correspondences are concerned. The atmosphere in the 'Solemne Assembly' cannot have been wholly solemn: the *Discourse* is three hundred pages long, and the audience must have had some natural predisposition to sympathise with Digby's ideas.

Dr Richard Mead (Sterne's 'Kunastrokius') is also impressed by the tarantula and the apochryphal cure for its bite. In his *Mechanical Account of Poisons* (1702) he gives a list of references for the dancing cure which includes Galen, Apollonius and Democritus. His own contention is that music, besides being able to stimulate the nerves as directly and effectively as can the will, can also prevent the coagulation of the blood, which, he supposes, causes the lassitude of the victims. The blood responds to the vibrations in the air.

At this point he expresses succinctly the dependence of his biological and chemical ideas on the laws of physics. The action of music on the blood is explained by reference to a theory of Lorenzo Bellini's, that the response of fluids to stimuli depends on the degree of *cohesion* inherent in the fluid. Cohesion is the effect of gravitational attraction operating at very small distances; music can affect the blood by means of its vibrations interfering with the natural vibrations of gravity to which the blood is always subject. This quality of cohesion Mead calls fermentation:

> And hence it follows, that whatsoever *Power* is sufficient to make a change in the Attraction, or Cohesion of the Parts, makes an Alteration in the Nature of the Fluid; that is, as the Chymists express it, puts it into a *Fermentation.*[19]

The mechanical nature of an apparently occult phenomenon has been demonstrated, thanks to the close analogy with gravity. In the Preface Mead explains the basis of his thought:

> My Design . . . was, to Try how far I could carry Mechanical Considerations in Accounting for those surprising Changes, which Poisons make in an Animal Body; Concluding (as I think, fairly) that if such abstruse *Phaenomena* as These did come under the known Laws of Motion, It might

> very well be taken for granted, that the more obvious Appearances in the same Fabrick are owing to such causes as are within the *Reach* of Geometrical Reasoning.[20]

And behind the physical analogy lurks the divine analogy, which is thus beginning to be implicated in a tradition of justification of medical science—or rather, of sympathetic magic masquerading as medical science:

> Nor ought any One indeed to doubt of this, who considers that the *Animal Compages* is not an irregular Mass, and disorderly Jumble of Atoms, but the Contrivance of Infinite Wisdom, and Master-piece of that Creating Power, who has been pleased to do all Things by Established Laws and Rules, and that Harmony and Proportion should be the Beauty of all his Works.[21]

It is not yet the fashion, in 1702, to refer to Newton in person, but a generation later the position is different. In 1725 Thomas Morgan published his *Philosophical Principles of Medicine*. The long introductory poem by Samuel Bowden expresses the unconscious tension in the work between the scientific principles from which Morgan feels free to argue and the occult nature of his own theories. The importance that he claims for Morgan's idea is really astonishing:

> Mature in Thought, you NEWTON'S Laws reduce
> To nobler Ends and more important Use.
> You show how heav'nly Orbs affect our Frame,
> And raise, or sink by turns the Vital Flame:
> How *Moons alternate*, in their changing Sphere,
> Impress their Force, and agitate the Air;
> How as without successive Tides advance
> While the pale Moon pursues her silent Dance,
> So does the *refluent Blood* her Influence know,
> And tides within *roll high*, or creep on low.[22]

In Morgan's book the equation between gravitational attraction and the cohesion of the blood is absolute and all-pervasive; and as Morgan defines animal life simply and wholly in terms of the circulation of the blood, he feels able to argue that all diseases have their original cause in the organism's response to changes in this attraction. Almost all his book is devoted to demonstrating that the condition of the human organism necessarily depends on the state of external nature then prevailing.

Morgan attempts at one point to include the emotions in this discussion, by means of a virtuoso piece of physiological deduction involving the arrangement of the nervous system.[23] The details of this argument are perhaps not as important as its implications. The analogy with Newton is now beginning to be used, *via a medical argument*, to deal with problems involving behaviour and motivation as well as purely physical questions. The external system of gravity begins to be scientifically accepted as one of the first causes of human action. This, of course, is what Walter Shandy would say, were he to contemplate gravity for long enough. But this is not the only sense in which Morgan is Shandean. He is using Shandean materials and dealing with Tristram Shandy's problems: using gravity and the process of licensed analogy to explore the relation between the individual and the sources of his behaviour.

Morgan's book *Physico-Theology*, published sixteen years later in 1741, takes this idea much further. In section one of Chapter 3 ('Of Human Nature, and the general laws of Sensation and Intelligence') Morgan discusses the 'internal Sensations, or Modifications of Pleasure and Pain, which we call the Appetites, Instincts and Passions of Animals',[24] and states plainly that

> the Creature, with respect to these Appetites and Instincts, is purely passive, and performs no Action nor exerts any active Power at all, no more than Bodies in the necessary passive Motions to which they are subject.[25]

Then in the next chapter ('Of Active Power, and Liberty, or Free Agency') Morgan provides a crucial and exquisite extension of the argument, into the area of morals. He equates, or associates, pain with *evil* and pleasure with *good*, and says that it is a law of the sensitive soul that it should always move away from pain/evil towards pleasure/good, to gratify its appetites. Evil, he argues, is as necessary as good, for without it there could be no movement of this kind. This demonstrates that an animal body is under the same dynamic laws as an inanimate body:

> Here, then, we have the true and only principle of Motion or Action in the Brutes; when a Beast, for Instance, feels the Pain and Stimulus of Hunger, and is thereby moved or impelled to his Food, this Action, though Spontaneous, and in that sense free, as not being externally forced, is yet as necessary, as the Motion of a Body, when impelled by an extrinsic, moving Force acting upon it.[26]

Finally Morgan copes with the objection that all pain is an evil, and that there is more evil than good in nature, by reverting to a different part of the argument of design.

> To admit the Objection, as grounded upon any Thing of Truth or Reason, would be to condemn God and Providence, and to subvert or destroy the fundamental Principle of all Morality and Religion: For if any Thing be evil, irregular, unnecessary and ill-ordered, upon the Whole, the Reflection and Blame must rest upon the Author, Contriver, Preserver and Director of the Whole.[27]

As the natural and unceasing movement of the sensitive soul is away from evil and towards good, evil is not an autonomous principle but a necessary aspect of the divine plan. However, this argument is based on what is really a separate analogy, that between the physical macrocosm of nature and the microcosm of the animal body.

All evil is to be described in terms of the universal good. Morgan has reached the attitude which Pope expresses in the *Essay on Man* (1733–4):

> All Nature is but Art, unknown to thee;
> All Chance, Direction which thou canst not see;
> All Discord, Harmony not understood;
> All partial Evil, universal Good.[28]

and he has reached it by a series of scientific deductions which are intended to give it the status of scientific law. Morgan uses virtually the same idea as Pope, but he uses it for an entirely different purpose. Pope gives what seems to him—and at first to the reader also—to be a modern version of the traditional Christian belief in the power of God and the goodness and worth of His universe. He is unaware that the new scientific tradition (of which Morgan is a later representative) is taking up these ancient expressions of correspondence between the human order and the larger orders of nature, and that the context and meaning of those concepts is changing. In the seventeenth century, such correspondences are nothing short of fact: they are simply *there*. 'The *Scripture* witnesses, that the World was made in *Number*, *Weight* and *Measure*; which are all qualities of a good *Poem*. This order and proportion of things is the true Musick of the world,'[29] says Cowley in 1668. In the eighteenth century, they are not just there: they are there to be argued from. The scientific tradition, in its attempts to impose the pattern and laws of external nature on man, begins to interfere with the traditional vocabulary and way of thought of ethical and literary discourse.

Pope is by no means the only representative of literary and philosophical culture who does not see that the feet of the enemy are breaking up the ground in his own camp. The eighteenth century's second most popular philosopher, the Third Earl of Shaftesbury (most popular in terms of numbers of editions—only John Locke's *Essay* was reprinted more times in the eighteenth century than Shaftesbury's *Characteristicks*: see Chapter 7, p. 194, for details) is extremely fond of claiming that his own thought, with its foundations in the Platonistic analogies of the Latitudinarians and Cambridge Platonists, stands in absolute opposition to the modern 'mechanical' philosophies of Hobbes and Descartes. He does not notice that his own position, that of the elegant, civilised, sincere upholder of a tolerant and feeling brand of Christianity, has been undermined by the scientific tradition. Shaftesbury is not of any particular relevance to *Tristram Shandy*, but is recognised to be an important element in the background to *A Sentimental Journey*, and will be discussed in Chapter 7.

The particular form of the argument about design which is used by Morgan and by Pope is one which is very widely employed in the period between 1720 and 1750. Medical writers use the analogy with *gravity* in this way, as an explanation of how disease can occur in a God-governed world. George Cheyne ingeniously does this by putting the analogy into the conditional tense, thus:

> As in *Bodies* there is a *Principle* of *Gravity* or *Attraction*, whereby, *in Vacuo*, they tend to one another, and would *unite*, according to certain *Laws* and *Limitations* established by the *Author* of *Nature*: so there is an *Analogous Principle* in *Spirits*, whereby they would as certainly, in their proper *Vacuity*, be *attracted* by, *tend* to, and *unite* with one another, and their first *Author, Centre*, and the *Rock out of which they were hewn* . . . as the *Planets* would to one another, and to the *Sun*. And this is nothing else but what in Scripture is called CHARITY.[30]

The proposition tries to show how wonderfully suitable the fallen and imperfect nature of man is to the universe he lives in. Just as the celestial bodies only aspire to join together, and are held in their orbits by a mysterious counter-force, so man can only (but must) aspire towards God, not reaching him in this world, only in the next.

The same form of the argument is also used at a crucial point in the development of eighteenth-century associationist writing, to transform the hints given by Locke and by medical theorists into an autonomous science. It is not mere figurative language: the *shape* of the idea, the necessary aspiration towards perfection, is central.

In 1739 the English translation of William King's *De Origine Mali, An Essay on the Origin of Evil*, was published, with John Gay's short work, 'Concerning the Fundamental Principle of Virtue or Morality' as a preliminary dissertation.[31] Gay's work is seminal to eighteenth-century associationism: David Hartley refers to it at the beginning of the *Observations on Man*, and the shape of Hartley's ideas bears a strong resemblance to Gay's.

The argument in Gay's short work is dependent on the attitude to design which is developed in the first half of King's *Essay*, an attitude which I hope is by now familiar. A reductive paraphrase of the first two hundred pages of the *Essay* might run as follows: 'God is distinguished from his created works by being *perfect*. Nothing can be created to be perfect, otherwise it would also be God. Absolute perfection is absolute goodness.

As man is created and is not God, he is therefore imperfect. Hence the origin of evil, that is, imperfection. Evil is thus a concept relative to goodness: it is less-than-perfection.'

In a later chapter,[32] King offers the opinion that were it not for man's mental imperfections, he would always judge rightly of his possible choices and would always choose good, i.e. choose that which would give him most pleasure. His imperfections lead him into Error, Negligence, Levity, Obstinacy, and hence away from good/pleasure.

For Gay however, the association of ideas is the faculty whereby man can overcome these imperfections. Gay produces his argument by making a most peculiar conflation of Habit and Pleasure. He claims that pleasure is derived solely from habit, and cites the pleasure derived from money as an example. A man gets a specific sense of pleasure from receiving a specific sum of money; when this specific sum is given again and again, the sense of pleasure becomes automatic. Thus, says Gay, the man comes to make a direct connection or *association* between happiness and money in general. Gay presents this as being typical of mental events, and goes on to speculate more generally:

> The same might be observ'd concerning the Thirst after Knowledge, Fame, etc., the delight in Reading, Building, Planting, and most of the various Exercises and Entertainments of Life. These were at first entered on with a view to some further End, but at length become habitual Amusements; the Idea of Pleasure is associated with them, and leads us on still in the same eager Pursuit of them, when the first Reason is quite vanish'd, or at least out of our Minds . . . The Association remains even after that which at first gave them the Connection is quite forgot, or perhaps does not exist, but the Contrary.[33]

He describes association as a series of 'RESTING PLACES' which is given to the human mind in order that it be able to cope with 'the narrowness of our understandings'; after a course of experience and habit, man comes to substitute these automatic responses for the principles, the individual judgments, on which he ought to act. This contradicts King, who says that Habit ('Obstinacy') leads to Error. Gay has taken King's general argument about perfection and put his later chapter about choice and imperfection strictly into line with it. Habit and association, for Gay, are elements in the divine plan: they are only positive—

> our Approbation of Morality, and all Affections whatsoever, are finally resolvable into *Reason* pointing out *private Happiness*, and are conversant only about things apprehended to be means tending to this end; and . . . whenever this end is not perceiv'd they are to be accounted for from the *Association of Ideas*, and may properly be call'd *Habits*.[34]

He finds himself in a position to ignore completely the demonic and irrational aspects of the association of ideas which Locke had pointed out in the *Essay Concerning Human Understanding*. Association, for Locke, is an entirely casual phenomenon. It can just as well be false as true, for there is in the mind a 'Connexion of *Ideas* wholly owing to Chance or Custom: *Ideas*, that in themselves are not at all of kin, come to be so united in some Men's Minds, that 'tis very hard to separate them'.[35] That Gay can ignore this is due to the nature of the attitude to design in King's *Essay* and in medical science. He manages to assimilate all the casual, chance qualities of association at which Locke hints, into a system of cosmic mental and moral *direction*.

It is interesting to speculate as to whether he would have managed to sustain the argument, had he been forced to select negative rather than positive data. There can be no such thing as a *bad habit* in his system—but what if he had had to use the example of a man having his face knocked against a wall every day, instead of one continually receiving money? His system in fact hinges on this arbitrary selection of positive material.

Commentators usually assume that the difficulties with communication that the Shandys' associative processes impose on them are a kind of 'Lockean madness'. Michael Deporte, for instance, was previously noted as describing their 'benign insanity . . . with reference to Locke', and thinking that the Shandys embody Locke's ideas about *false* association. This may be so: it is certainly true of the inaugural associationist joke in *Tristram Shandy*, Mrs Shandy's confusion of clock and 'some other things' in the early chapters of Volume I. But it is interesting to see that in terms of the eighteenth-century associationists, Toby and Walter are perfectly normal. Their habits of association always tend to make them happy. The paradise which they attain through these habits is rather more bizarre than the one Gay and Hartley have in mind, being much more private, but it is quite secure.

At one point in *Tristram Shandy* this situation is hinted at in the text. Walter has a natural (I mean natural-because-habitual) defence mechanism in his mind which takes the force from all the misfortunes that befall him: when misfortune occurs, he invariably tries to become eloquent. He enjoys making speeches, and even when it is inappropriate as a response he will always use it. He associates misfortune and eloquence, eloquence and pleasure. This happens even when his son Bobby dies—or rather, when news of Bobby's death reaches him. His funeral oration is a great comfort to him, so much so that he manages to forget Bobby completely and take refuge in his own generalisations. 'He succeeds where Cicero had failed',[36] says Richard Lanham. But this is a strange time to achieve a thorough consolation. Tristram comments:

> A blessing which tied up my father's tongue, and a misfortune which set it loose with a good grace, were pretty equal: sometimes, indeed, the misfortune was the better of the two; for instance, where the pleasure of the harangue was as *ten*, and the pain of the misfortune but as *five*—my father gained half in half, and consequently was as well again off, as if it had never befallen him.[37]

Walter's response is highly incongruous; as always, he is somewhat removed from the usual springs of emotion. But this incongruous response is perfectly normal in terms of Gay's statement that association is the agent of pleasure. It might even be designed to show or to imply the limitations and the comic potential of this attitude to association.

There may even be specific connections: Tristram appears to be stealing *phrasing* from one or both of King or Hartley. In Chapter 5 of his *Essay*, King discusses the misfortunes that befall us:

> We can choose to bear these Things, and please ourselves in that Choice . . . if one feel two Degrees of Pain from a Distemper, and receive six Degrees of Pleasure from an Election to bear it with Patience and Dignity; subtracting two Degrees of Pain from these six of Pleasure, he has four of solid Pleasure remaining; he will be as happy therefore as one that has four Degrees pure and free from all Pain.[38]

David Hartley, in the second part of the *Observations on Man*, puts King's general attitude and Gay's associationist theory together, to correct King on this point:

> when any small Pain is introductory to a great Pleasure, it is very common for us, without any express Reflection on the Power of Association, to consider this Pain as coalescing with the subsequent Pleasure, into a pure Pleasure, equal to the Difference between them; and in some Cases, the small Pain itself puts on the Nature of a Pleasure, of which we see many Instances in the daily Occurrences of Life, where Labour, Wants, Pains, become actually pleasant to us, by a Lustre borrowed from the Pleasures to be obtained by them.[39]

The use of association as what modern psychologists term a 'tension reduction model' is widespread in the eighteenth century. As P. McReynolds points out in an introduction to the associationist writer James Long, it may derive from Locke's concept of 'uneasiness' as the stimulus to action:

> Long adopted Locke's concept of 'uneasiness', and posits that the removal of uneasiness—i.e., the gratification of the desire which led to the uneasiness—is pleasurable. It is in this sense that his system is a kind of tension reduction model.[40]

In several other places, Tristram gets comic mileage from this notion of consolation outweighing the original misfortune. In Volume VII, Chapter 29, for instance, his chaise breaks in pieces. Unworried, he rhapsodises on the benefits of travelling 'by water', and, reminding himself of his usual method of dealing with calamity—'making a penny of every one of 'em'[41]—goes on to illustrate his theme by telling (or hinting at) his failure to**** Jenny. He is, or was at the time, embarrassed, but

> —Every thing is good for something, quoth I.
> —I'll go into Wales for six weeks, and drink goat's-whey——and I'll gain seven years longer life for the accident. For which reason I think myself inexcusable, for blaming Fortune so often as I have done, for pelting me all my life long, like an ungracious duchess, as I call'd her, with so many small evils: surely if I have any cause to be angry with her, 'tis that she has not sent me great ones—a score of good cursed, bouncing losses, would have been as good as a pension to me.[42]

In Volume V, Chapters 27 and 28, Walter's discoveries of classical precedents for circumcision lead him to accept the only one of his son's early misfortunes which Tristram himself feels as a misfortune ('Fifty thousand pannier loads of devils . . . could not have made so diabolical a scream of it'[43]) as quite natural and even desirable: '—But is the child, cried my uncle *Toby*, the worse?—The *Troglodytes* say not, replied my father.'[44] Here it is Walter's consolation outweighing Tristram's misfortune; which brings out well Walter's typical enwrapment in his own ideas. Elevating a specific truth (that misfortune can bring its own compensations) into a generalisation about life makes that truth seem ludicrous. Of course on a purely novelistic level what Tristram says is true. He writes about his 'misfortunes'; the writing is a consolation to him (and it earns him money: hence the reference to a 'pension'); so the more misfortunes he has, the more he has to write about, the greater consolation he gets. But it is still a comic principle. This is also what it is in King and in Hartley, except that they present it in all seriousness, as a paradigm of their vision of the world.

Hartley's moral cosmos in the *Observations on Man* is shaped much like King's: a static divine pattern of perfection, and a necessary but constantly frustrated attempt on man's part to learn and live up to this pattern. This shape is once again strengthened by the pattern of the Newtonian universe, for Hartley's doctrine of Vibrations, from which his associationist system derives, is based on 'the Hints concerning the Performance of Sensation and Motion, which Sir *Isaac Newton* has given at the end of his *Principia*'.[45] The setting-up of these patterns enables Hartley to ignore, even more completely than Gay does, the perversity and casualness of association. In the ninth of the 'Corollaries' to Part I, in the course of a mathematical demonstration that by regulating one's associations one may increase control over the degree of pleasure one feels, comes the statement that 'Association, under the Supposition of this Corollary, has a tendency to reduce the State of those who have eaten of the Tree of the Knowledge of Good and Evil, back to a paradisiacal one'.[46] He takes it for granted that association can be controlled and regulated. At one point in these 'Corollaries' the possibility of control by conditioning is hinted at, as Hartley forgets for a moment that it is God who is supposed to be in ultimate control of man's associative patterns.

> If Beings of the same Nature, but whose Affections and Passions are, at Present, in different Proportions to one another, be exposed for an indefinite Time to the same Impressions and Associations, all their particular Differences will, at last, be over-ruled, and they will become perfectly similar, or even equal. They may also be made perfectly similar, in a finite Time, by a proper Adjustment of the Impressions and Associations.[47]

He half-consciously recognises that a system of necessary response could be understood and manipulated by man himself. This is exactly what does eventually happen to this tradition of thought—what is being explored here is actually the early history of the modern psychological science of behaviourism. The Renaissance world of meaningful analogy and correspondence between mundane and divine worlds is being exploited and turned into a science which will eventually produce Pavlov. (This connection is explored a little more fully in Chapter 5 of this study.)

Hartley's associationism, unlike Locke's, is highly deterministic. Coleridge's examination of Hartley's thought in the *Biographia Literaria* brings out Coleridge's irritation at the idea that man's patterns of thought are controlled from outside himself, and also makes much the same point as Josipovici made on the nature of modern analogy. He begins by restating the general principle under which all the associationists work:

> ... the law of association being that to mind, which gravitation is to matter ... according to this hypothesis, the disquisition, to which I am at present soliciting the reader's attention, may be as truly said to be written by Saint Paul's church, as by me: for it is the mere motion of my muscles and nerves; and these again are set in motion from external causes equally passive, which external causes stand themselves in interdependent connexion with every thing that exists or has existed. Thus the whole universe co-operates to produce the minutest stroke of every letter, save only that I myself, and I alone, have nothing to do with it, but merely the causeless and effectless beholding of it when it is done ...
>
> ... To make myself intelligible as far as my present subject requires, it will be sufficient briefly to observe:
>
> 1. That all association demands and pre-supposes the existence of the thoughts and images to be associated.
> 2. That the hypothesis of an external world exactly correspondent to these images or modifications of our own being, which alone, (according to this system,) we actually behold, is as thorough idealism as Berkley's, inasmuch as it equally (perhaps, in a more perfect degree,) removes all reality and immediateness of perception, and places us in a dream-world of phantoms and spectres, the inexplicable swarm and equivocal generation of motions in our own brain.[48]

Received opinion on the subject of the breakdown of the divine analogy and arguments about design seems to be that they simply passed peacefully away, being replaced by more 'dynamic' theories which said that the relation between man and his world was established through emotive acts rather than through outward perceptions. Earl Wasserman for instance says that

> In the eighteenth century ... there is to be found the last

> significant vestige of the myth of an analogically ordered universe, but significantly weakened by the rhetorical tradition, associationism and science, all of which had become of far greater importance than the heritage of correspondences. The divine analogy... had become enervate as it waited to be replaced by other world-schemes for relating matter and spirit.[49]

This greatly underestimates the degree to which the divine analogy was undermined from within, by being adopted and extensively used in associationism and other sciences which sought to use the 'heritage of correspondences' for their own ends. The energy with which the analogy was used in incongruous contexts was, in part, the reason for its discarding and discrediting.

If any general conclusion can be drawn from this, it is that when writers ignore the demonic nature of association, they also ignore or do not see the demonic element which develops in their own systems of associationist theories. At the same time as they sanctify the principle of association, they betray an unquestioning and almost irrational attachment to analogical argument, which they license by reference to the Newtonian and the spiritual analogies with design, via an equally occult medical argument. In particular, they tend to discredit the ancient ideas about sympathy, correspondence, right proportion and harmony which they inherit, by applying them in contexts for which they are not suited.

This chapter has tried to show that Sterne's interest in association might be an aspect of his interest in analogy and correspondence. In turn, his interest in correspondences seems to be an aspect of his fascination with the concept of pattern and design.

The rupture of order, symmetry and pattern is one of the most consistent processes in *Tristram Shandy*. It is a very positive destruction, paradoxical as that may sound. It is not just a question of there being no patterns in the book. A pattern has to be established before it can be questioned. This was one of the things that the examination of Volume I was designed to show—Tristram setting up Walter's patterns in order to be able to comment on them.

As I hope the following chapter will make clear, Sterne does not break up order and symmetry gratuitously or at random. Almost always, he is trying to take patterns other people have made during the previous decades of the eighteenth century, and to show that what, there, appears to be an harmonious and viable set of ideas and beliefs is in truth based on a conjunction or arrangement of ideas which is perverse or which has comic or quixotic overtones. In a sense he does not break anything that was not already broken; all he does is show the reader the cracks. In a sense the Shandean relations between ideas—the wild Shandean analogies—are the true relations.

4 Breaking Patterns: Analogy and Proportion

I ANALOGY AS MODELLING

This chapter is intended as a general and miscellaneous illustration of some of Sterne's uses of the idea of design in *Tristram Shandy*, seen in the light of the background suggested in the previous chapter.

The best way of describing the Shandean flavour of early eighteenth-century science is to say that it often takes the form of an obsessive modelling, of taking all-pervasive universal patterns and trying to re-create them in the smaller world of man. Toby and Walter Shandy both enjoy a kind of modelling, making miniature replicas of things. Toby works with physical things, constructing his scale models of the towns besieged in the French wars of 1689–97 and 1702–13. Walter works with ideas, constructing mental systems. In Toby's case, the reader is never shown the big, 'real-world' analogue of Toby's modelling, the world of real battles, sieges, fighting, blood, guts, and so on, which is utterly foreign to Toby's nature and which is not conveyed to us except in formalised or idealised ways. Apart from the blow of the cannonball, it has not impinged on him and is not conveyed to us. Everything happens in miniature, in the few square yards of the bowling-green and the few cubic inches of Toby's head. The same is almost true of Walter. We are never directly shown any one overriding system from which all of his devolve. This is probably because the brothers never ask each other to justify their activities, their Hobby-Horses.

On two occasions, however, this larger system does come into view in an oblique way in *Tristram Shandy*, in connection with Walter's efforts at modelling. In one instance it appears in the shape of the universal system of gravitational attraction and weight. In the second, the pattern of divine or spiritual harmony which is felt to lie behind all physical harmony appears in the same sidelong way. These, of course, are the patterns which the associationists invoke to justify their own modelling: the links between the Shandys and their background are not always built with such occult material as falling bodies and false association.

The first of these cases comes in the last chapter of Volume II, in the course of Tristram's description of Walter's theories about the relationship between body and mind. Walter's ideas are of interest on their own account and will be discussed later in this chapter. Briefly, he believes that there is a sympathetic correspondence between body and mind which means that events that happen to the body must necessarily affect the condition of the mind. However what is of most interest here is the shape of the argument Walter uses to justify his system.

Before Tristram tells us about Walter's ideas, he describes Walter's views on the true philosophical method. Walter would like us to believe that he is only interested in minute details of knowledge, questions which are only important for their own sakes and which do not refer to any larger systems of thought. He issues what appears to be a disclaimer:

> 'Tis the same, he would say, throughout the whole circle of the sciences;—the great, the established points of them, are not to be broke in upon. —The laws of nature will defend themselves;—but error—(he would add, looking earnestly at my mother)—error, Sir, creeps in thro' the minute-holes and small crevices, which human nature leaves unguarded.[1]

He does his cunning best to make himself appear to be an empiricist, basing his beliefs not on any 'popular tenets' existing beforehand, but on 'the minutiae of philosophy, which should always turn the balance'.[2] He tries to make the traditional pastoral concept of relative size work for him, stressing the virtues of not aiming too high, not dealing directly with grand, universal ideas. But the arguments he puts forward are much more in the nature of a defence than an explanation. By expressing the question of *a priori* versus *a posteriori* argument in simple physical terms, he betrays a highly sophistical attitude to argument-by-proportion. Properly speaking, the 'big end' of Walter's argument or analogy is as important to his overall outlook as the 'little end' to which he claims to be restricting himself. The connection between the two ends is felt even as he is trying to refute it:

> Knowledge, like matter, he would affirm, was divisible *in infinitum*;—that the grains and scruples were as much a part of it, as the gravitation of the whole world. —In a word, he would say, error was error,—no matter where it fell,—whether in a fraction,—or a pound,—'twas alike fatal to truth, and she was kept down at the bottom of her well as inevitably by a mistake in the dust of a butterfly's wing,—as in the disk of the sun, the moon, and all the stars of heaven put together.[3]

All the small things that Walter is interested in are in fact important to him only insofar as they are small fragments of a larger pattern, or as they aspire to the clarity and perfection of that pattern. Here the pattern is nothing less than the system of the world, the laws of nature. Walter is not just using a figure of speech when he refers to the *weight* of knowledge; he is invoking the design of the post-Newtonian cosmos.

Tristram provides the reader with another important clue to the true status of Walter's argument, by referring it to the 'sorites' of Zeno and Chrysippus. A 'sorites' is a particular kind of syllogism, one which uses proportional argument in a devious way. It is a

> form of sophism leading by gradual steps from truth to absurdity, and based on the absence of precise, especially numerical, limits to terms (e.g. a man with only one hair is bald, therefore a man with two, three, four . . . ten thousand, hairs is bald).[4]

It is a wool-pulling method: Tristram lets the reader know that this is Walter's method too.

The second example comes near the end of Volume III. Tristram has been conducting a lengthy and varied examination of various aspects of proportion and harmony in this volume. The most recent tendency has been for him to apply such ideas to the construction of the book, taking several opportunities of showing the reader that his work is based on a conscious awareness of literary design. Thus in Chapter 24 he has remarked on the felicity of having Trim's affair with Bridget as a sub-plot to Toby's amour with the Widow Wadman—'an amour thus nobly doubled'—and has even suggested that subsequent dramatists 'have ever since been working upon *Trim's* and my uncle *Toby's* pattern'.[5] In Chapter 39 he has reminded the reader of the skill with which the Shandy family has been put together, and modestly (if rather backhandedly) ascribed this skill not to himself but to God: 'the hand of the supreme Maker and first Designer of all things, never made or put a family together ... where the characters of it were cast or contrasted with so dramatic a felicity as ours was'.[6]

Then, in Chapter 41, as a kind of coda to this discussion, God's skill in right proportion is referred to in a more suggestive context. Walter is doing his best to impress on Toby the quite extraordinary scientific significance of the various systems of *long noses* written by Prignitz and Scroderus, Ambrose Paraeus, Ponocrates, Grangousier and Erasmus—'the various accounts which learned men of different kinds of knowledge have given the world, of the causes of short and long noses'.[7] Toby is not at all impressed:

> There is no cause but one ... why one man's nose is longer than another's, but because that God pleases to have it so ... 'Tis he ... who makes us all, and frames and puts us together in such forms and proportions, and for such ends, as is agreeable to his infinite wisdom.[8]

Although this appears to be only a sentimental piousness in Toby, it is also a very successful answer to Walter. Toby has in effect stolen Walter's ultimate argument and denatured it. Walter, one imagines, would dearly love to argue from cosmic and divine pattern to his own lesser systems. But Toby's pre-emptive piousness, his Christian peevishness, has been offered in *opposition* to his brother's theories, and has perhaps hinted that he would prefer him not to make a false analogy between the divine harmony of man's proportions and the harmony of a set of scientific laws.

It is interesting that Toby does this again when Walter is

trying to make a speech to him (in Volume IV, Chapter 7) on the subject of affliction and consolation, a subject which, as we have seen, has some connection with the associationist sciences. Walter is telling him

> by what hidden resources the mind is enabled to stand it out, and bear itself up, as it does against the impositions laid upon our nature. —'Tis by the assistance of Almighty God, cried my uncle *Toby*, looking up, and pressing the palms of his hands close together—'tis not from our own strength, brother Shandy . . . we are upheld by the grace and the assistance of the best of Beings.
>
> —That is cutting the knot, said my father, instead of untying it.[9]

Most of Walter's attempts to 'undo the knot', his extravagantly displayed systems of knowledge, are doomed from the start, because they fit so poorly into the fabric of the real world. His *Tristrapaedia* for instance, his system of education for his son, proves of little practical use because Tristram manages to grow at a much greater pace than his father's book, which thus inadvertently becomes a fine example of the modern commercial principle of built-in obsolescence. Where his systems are not answered by events, they are answered by other people: in the case of his systems of *noses* and *consolation*, by Toby, and in several other cases by Tristram. Tristram's answers are usually oblique, probably because Sterne does not want to imply that Walter is wrong in his beliefs. Walter is not really a figure of fun despite his comic frustrations, and it would be a bad idea to destroy his credibility as a character by sneering. Also, Tristram cannot answer Walter on Walter's own terms, because he has to answer in character. He has terms of his own, those of a writer and novelist. When Walter presents him with a 'scientific' system, he will reply from the point of view of someone interested in plot and character.

The most interesting of Tristram's answers is given to Walter's ideas about the relation between body and mind in Volume II, Chapter 19. However to see what Tristram is answering, and why, we must first look at the system itself.

Tristram begins by insisting that Walter's theories show that he is a complete individualist:

> -- Mr. *Shandy*, my father, Sir, would see nothing in the light in which others placed it;—he placed things in his own light;—he would weigh nothing in common scales;—no, he was too refined a researcher to lay open to so gross an imposition.[10]

Walter goes along with this, insisting that it all comes out of his own head. Yet Tristram documents enough sources for Walter's system of physiology to convince the reader that it derives its framework from philosophical writers, real or otherwise: Descartes on the pineal gland, Borri on the cerebrospinal fluid, 'Dutch anatomists', the apochryphal Adrianus Smelvgot, and generally 'all kinds of books'. Tristram goes back on his word a little, and stresses that the foundations of Walter's beliefs are quite in harmony with respectable medical ideas of a good many eras, including Walter's own, the first decades of the eighteenth century. 'So far there was nothing singular in my father's opinion,—he had the best of philosophers, of all ages and climates, to go along with him.'[11] These premises or foundations, which Walter shares with all the above writers, are simply that the rational soul has a physical existence, and must lie in some specific part of the body. Walter favours the Medulla Oblongata. He expresses reservations about these gentlemen's theories, but his reservations actually come from an extension of their way of thinking rather than a rejection of it. Having taken up their assumptions about the physical existence of the soul, he argues from this (via Smelvgot) to his idea of the necessity for delivering children by Caesarean section. His reasoning, which is his own, is impeccable: his premises, which are those of other people, are dogmatic. Locke makes a comment which is perhaps relevant to this situation: 'mad Men put wrong Ideas together, and so make wrong Propositions, but argue and reason right from them'.[12] This puts the philosophers in an interesting position.

Although Tristram goes back to his original attitude and represents the conclusions Walter draws as Shandean and eccentric, this is not really the case. The final step of the argument, the necessity for Caesarean section, may seem pure Shandyism, but it is based on an intermediate step which is in fact close to the beliefs of the 1730s and 1740s (the *succeeding* generation of medical theorists)—that there is a necessary sympathetic correspondence between the body and the mind or *sensitive soul*. What happens to the body must have an influence on the mind, and vice versa. So (according to Walter) the pressure on the baby's head during the normal process of childbirth must surely have a detrimental effect on the infant soul, located as it is in the back of the neck and head.

Although this succeeding generation tended to uphold the idea of an immaterial soul, the belief in a necessary connection between it and the body remained strong. A typical metaphor expresses this connection in terms of the relationship between a stringed instrument and its player, with the reservation that a blow or stroke on the strings (i.e. an impression on the sense-organs conveyed along the nerves to the brain) would affect the 'musician'; rather like a player-piano, or in this case a player-violin. For instance George Cheyne, in the Introduction to his *English Malady* (1731), sums up his philosophical outlook for the benefit of those readers who wish to skip the theoretical sections of this work:

> These need only suppose, that the Human Body is a Machine of an infinite Number and Variety of different Channels and Pipes, fill'd with various and different Liquors and Fluids . . . That the Intelligent Principle, or *Soul*, resides in the Brain, where all the Nerves, or Instruments of Sensation, terminate, like a *Musician* in a finely-fram'd and well-tun'd Organ-Case; that these Nerves are like Keys, which, being struck on or touch'd, convey the Sound and Harmony to this sentient Principle, or *Musician*.[13]

Cheyne uses the same figure in Chapter 6, 'Of the Passions', of his *Essay of Health and Long Life* (1724). It is another instance of science making use of a concept from another level of discourse to justify the shape of its own ideas. Musical harmony, and through this the ancient harmony of man and macrocosm, are here used to sanction an early form of the theory of *vibrations* which Hartley and other associationists will find of so much use. In this instance the sympathetic relation between body and mind is a development from the analogy between man and the natural world which was discussed in

Chapter 3. The natural world presents the body, the sense-organs, with stimuli; the body responds; the mind in turn responds. Neither body nor mind is credited with power to cause, or even to interpret. Everything is at the mercy of the elements, the stimuli.

Tristram does not actively disagree with Walter when, a few chapters later (Volume III, Chapter 4), he sets out his own idea of the relation between body and mind, but he does take care to qualify what Walter has said. At first he seems to be going along with his father's attitude—in fact he virtually reproduces it, in metaphor: 'A Man's body and his mind, with the utmost reverence to both I speak it, are exactly like a jerkin, and a jerkin's lining;—rumple the one—you rumple the other.'[14] But then through the rest of the chapter he claims to make an exception of himself and a long list of Stoic writers, all of whom claim (he says) that they have a 'jerkin made of a gum-taffeta, and the body-lining to it, of a sarcenet or thin persian',[15] a combination apparently guaranteed to preserve the lining from creasing ('persian' is chintz, which certainly does not crease easily). In his own case the claim is demonstrably true, at least on his own terms. The critics have torn his 'jerkin', his body, to shreds (meaning the body of his book, the first published unit of Volumes I and II), but they have not been able to tear his lining, his mind: obviously not, since he is still writing his Opinions in the same spirit as he did before. At the end of the chapter Tristram refers to, and uses, uncle Toby's brand of passive or unresponsive sentiment, dismissing the critics with as good a wish as that with which Toby dismissed the fly in Volume II, Chapter 12. In doing this, Tristram shows how the sympathetic circle of reflex action between body and mind which Walter's beliefs imply can, in this case, be broken to advantage. And because he has done it obliquely rather than directly and angrily he has done it without 'vibrating the note back again', without making his answer seem to be part of a circle of revenge.

—But has Tristram not qualified Walter's system just because it pleases him to do so? In order to assert the independence of his own mind and to score a point off the critics?—

I think not. I think that Tristram examines this belief in Walter as a corollary to his own belief in certain ways of depicting character in fiction. It might be a pointer to another reason why Sterne does not want to write a conventional or naturalistic fiction.

Walter's belief in an exact correspondence between body and mind begins to take on some point when he tries to put it into practice. He does this in an episode early in the sixth volume, and trespasses on to Tristram's territory as he does so. His mental search for the perfect governor for his son leads into the story of Le Fever: in fact Tristram uses Walter's search as an artificial introduction to get to that story. In Chapter 5 the basic correspondence between body and mind is translated into an interest in the relationship between body and *character*, or into character as revealed by body. It reveals itself in Walter's belief in the significance of the visible external bodily characteristic:

> There are a thousand unnoticed openings . . . which let a penetrating eye at once into a man's soul; and I maintain it, added he, that a man of sense does not lay down his hat in coming into a room,—or take it up in going out of it, but something escapes, which discovers him.[16]

A man's character, says Walter, can infallibly be known from his actions: so his son's governor shall be a man who 'shall neither lisp, or squint, or wink, or talk loud, or look fierce, or foolish;——or bite his lips, or grind his teeth',[17] and so on. From these physical details Walter switches straight into details of character, as if there were no difference: 'I will have him . . . cheerful, faceté, jovial; at the same time, prudent, attentive to business, vigilant, acute, argute, inventive.'[18] Only Toby's interjection—'Now this is all nonsense again'—comes between them. As usual someone (usually Toby, if it is not implied by Tristram or Sterne) knows what is sense and what not.

As Richard Lanham points out, these notions of Walter's are in a sense the foundations for a certain kind of fiction, one which Lanham himself calls 'realistic':

> The premises of realistic fiction are not only scientific but Platonic. A reality exists beyond words which words can point to . . . [on the other hand] The rhetorical orchestration of man views him as an incorrigible roleplayer. He is *essentially* a speaker of lines. No Platonic self exists.[19]

Yet curiously it is Walter, who is a rhetorician by nature, who posits an inner self separate from words, a *man within*, a Platonic 'real' exhibited in outward signs. It is a sensible enough thing to believe in; Tristram himself is a brilliant exponent of the system Walter suggests, drawing character from minute particulars of gesture and behaviour. But as soon as you believe in it as a system you start to abuse it, as Walter does here. Walter translates all those details as having inherent worth or value, whereas for Tristram they are simply interesting in themselves. They are characteristics, but they are not characteristic *of* anything in particular, except the person described.

Walter is here descanting on one of Tristram's own favourite subjects, for insofar as someone has a Hobby-Horse, or ruling passion, he has a visible characteristic and is thus open to analysis of the Walterian kind. Tristram said something on this subject as early as the chapter about 'Momus's glass in the human breast', Volume I, Chapter 23: 'our minds shine not through the body, but are warpt up here in a dark covering of uncrystallized flesh and blood'.[20] Tristram often refers to his own interest in Hobby-Horses and usually has a lot to say in their favour, but he absolutely refuses to use it as a method of drawing his main characters. Toby for instance has a Hobby-Horse, but it is described separately, at the start of Volume II. Paradoxically, his 'characteristic' is not at all characteristic of him. In naturalistic terms, he is not 'like' a soldier; and in dramatic terms, his function in the book is usually to be unHobbyhorsical in relation to his brother—to be 'fatalistic' in a way that brings Hobbyhorsical speculation to an abrupt halt. ('Fate', in the Toby-sections of the book, is usually a jocular term for chance or accident or it-just-was-so: it is (for instance) in this guise that she prepares Toby's bowling-green for his models of besieged towns, in Volume VI, Chapter 21:

> When FATE was looking forwards one afternoon, into the great transactions of future times,—and recollected for what purposes, this little plot, by a decree fast bound down in iron, had been destined,—she gave a nod to NATURE—'twas enough—Nature threw half a spade full of her kindliest compost upon it . . .[21]

Whereas in the Walter-sections, 'Fate' is something to be learned from, argued from and controlled.)

Tristram also expresses his dislike of the characteristic as a system when he talks about his intentions in writing. His book, as he takes care to say in Volume IV, Chapter 22, is not 'wrote against any thing'; just as Toby is not representative of 'militating spirits', nor Trim to be taken as being *like* or representative of the Duke of Ormond, so the events in the book are not representative of any other events: the book is not 'wrote against predestination, or free-will, or taxes'.[22]

Probably the strongest characteristics of the fiction Lanham calls 'realistic' are firstly that the characters *are* representative, of either particular social or personal attitudes, and secondly that the events in the book are meant to be 'like' the events which happen in real life: to be interesting, they must be typical of something visible. This, it seems, is denied to Tristram. Of course it may be denied for purely artistic reasons, because Sterne does not find that it is a true and satisfying way of writing about characters and events and life. But in Walter's character and his theories about body and mind, with their foundations so firmly in the successful and accepted sciences of the eighteenth century, there seems to be a suggestion that Tristram's extremely defensive attitude towards character—'riddles and mysteries'[23]—and his caginess about the legitimate methods of fiction, are conditioned by Sterne's awareness that he is writing in an unusual and specific historical and intellectual context.

One thing should be said about the story of Le Fever in the light of this introduction that Tristram provides for it. When Toby recommends Le Fever's son to Walter as an ideal tutor for Tristram, he is recommending someone whom Walter does not appear to have seen, and thus someone who has no checkable 'character'. (The story of Le Fever senior takes place rather pointedly in the middle of the fourteen years—*circa* 1700–14)—during which Toby and Trim are living out at Shandy Hall by themselves, while Walter is still away carrying on his business '*in town*'.) Perhaps this is why Toby's suggestions meet with such a deafening silence from Walter at the end of chapter 13—'We'll talk of them, said my father, another time'.[24] There are good naturalistic reasons, though. If one pays pedantic attention to the chronology of this story, one finds that Le Fever junior is about twenty-three years of age by the time he leaves school (he was 'about 11 or 12 years of age' in 1707/8, at the death of Le Fever senior)—that he quits it 'without leave', implying that his eleven years there have not completed his education—that he tries his fortune in the French army, fails ('a series of unmerited mischances'[25]) and returns to Toby six years later, when Tristram is five (1723: see Volume V, Chapter 17). Is this supposed to speak for Le Fever junior's character, in the face of Toby's enthusiasm? Or is it shaky chronology from Sterne?

I think that the story of Le Fever, with all its possibly dubious details of content and style, is to be read as a genuine sentimental episode. In fact the story, I take it, is there largely to illustrate Toby's character, his transparency, the genuine and visible correspondence between his actions and himself:

> There was a frankness in my uncle *Toby* . . . which let you at once into his soul, and shewed you the goodness of his nature; to this, there was something in his looks, and voice, and manner, superadded, which eternally beckoned to the unfortunate to come and take shelter under him.[26]

Sometimes it does apply, then. The same notion as is exposed to satire when Walter believes in it as a pattern of knowledge is used—has to be used—to describe Toby's character, because Toby's soul really does shine through the body. First an idea is true (for Walter): then it is shown to be false (by Toby's awareness of its nonsensicality, or by Tristram's presentation of it and his distrust of it): then it *can be* true when it is a question of applying to a specific character. As usual, Tristram works in threes. He will approach an idea in the same way as he approaches an object which he wishes to work up into a double-headed metaphor, establishing not one but two perspectives on it: thesis, antithesis and synthesis: or pattern, breaking of pattern, and qualification of pattern.

His success at doing this has a great deal to do with the rhetorical nature of the text. Both Tristram and Walter are fond of taking up dogmatic positions to defend which turn out to be untenable. But the opposite or contradictory position is equally false, being logically dependent on the first—'merely an obverse vocabulary'[27]—the problem known to Gilbert Ryle as 'the dogma of the Ghost in the Machine', albeit in another context.

The implied truth must lie somewhere in between the two rhetorical extremes. Not that Tristram is interested in the truth. He is much more interested in the process of rhetoric, or in the dualisms of the process of analogy. This interest has led critics to call *Tristram Shandy* a 'profoundly dualistic' work,[28] one that is *based on* the principles of licensed analogy and 'free' association. Yet those principles have such a strong perspective established on them in the book that it seems truer to say—to reiterate—that it is *about* them rather than embodying them.

It might be profitable to consider the motto of the book in this light. The motto comes to Sterne from Epictetus, via Montaigne. 'Men (says an ancient Greek Sentence) are tormented with the Opinions they have of things and not by the things themselves.'[29] Nothing is, but thinking makes it so: it is one of the laws of the book. Or is it? It is also, in 1760, becoming one of the *topoi* of modern aesthetics. It might have come to Sterne from Burke, who in 1758 wrote: 'Certain it is, that the influence of most things on our passions is not so much from the things themselves, as from our opinions concerning them';[30] or from works such as Diderot's *Paradoxe sur le comédien*. It is in fact the *antithesis*: it is a rhetorical contradiction of the original neo-classical position of the early eighteenth century, that there are absolute standards to be observed: that there are absolute standards of value just as there are absolute physical laws. The *law* that everything is relative is in fact merely the obverse of another law. The most basic law of *Tristram Shandy* is that there are no laws; but if there are no laws, the law that everything is relative must be to some extent untrue.

II TRISTRAM'S RELATED ARTS

One of Tristram's favourite occupations when he is talking as narrator, as custodian or curator of his own story, is the making of analogies between his own art—writing prose—and various other arts, painting, music, drama and so on. In fact it is quite common practice in Sterne criticism to assume that because Tristram tells the reader, in Volume I, Chapter 8, that he happens, 'at certain intervals and changes of the Moon, to be both fiddler and painter, according as the fly stings',[31] and because it is known that Sterne himself was an enthusiastic amateur of both these arts, *Tristram Shandy* is either a 'pictorial novel' or a 'musical novel'. For instance, W. V. Holtz's book, *Image and Immortality: A Study of 'Tristram Shandy'*, comes to the conclusion that Sterne is an exponent of 'literary pictorialism';[32] that he tries to draw scenes in such a way as to make the reader aware of their visual content. Tristram's overt analogies with the art of painting are represented as supporting this practice. On the other hand, William Freedman, in an article called '*Tristram Shandy*: The Art of Literary Counterpoint', insists that the book's art is that of the musical composer: that the

> analogies with music . . . state figuratively what he states more literally elsewhere (I, 22; IX, 12): that it is the balance, the equipoise, the harmony that counts, and that his book, if it seems to conform to no *a priori* rules of literary production, is at least consistent and harmonious with itself. In short, in *Tristram Shandy*, as in music, the criterion of truth and value is not so much external correspondence as internal coherence and consistency.[33]

But Tristram never makes an analogy with a related art for the sake of making an analogy, or in order to make the reader think of the other art. Instead, the analogies contribute to the quality of the book itself. They are not inconsistent with the rest of Tristram's 'techniques of verbal orchestration', in that they help to diversify and extend the sense of plots, of conspiracies, inside the novel.

As the previous chapter has shown, many people in the eighteenth century use analogies with aesthetic and artistic theory. Medical, social and aesthetic writers all exploit the same metaphors. The custom of expressing the correspondence between the physical and human orders in terms of music, the human body and mind vibrating to the natural tune or key of the macrocosm, has already been discussed. In the later associationist writers the pattern of sympathy between men, between their ideas and emotions, is likened to harmony and right proportion as it is used in music, painting and literature. All these analogies are based on the concept of an absolute higher power, a trustworthy macrocosm; or, to speak more plainly, they assume that a pattern exists which can be argued from.

Tristram is also fond of making this assumption, or pretending to make it. He hardly ever refers to pictorial or musical art—or indeed to poetry or drama—without the ideas of design, harmony and proportion which those arts make use of being present. The difference is that all his analogies parody the idea of a trustworthy pattern, and show up those who believe in it. Tristram establishes and uses analogy—analogy between arts, between things which exist on the same level—to examine and satirise the use of analogy between different levels, between absolute standards and the relative standards which prevail in the human world.

Tristram's analogies with painting begin as early as Volume I, Chapter 9, and immediately the concept of harmony, of putting pieces together to make a well-balanced whole, is involved as well. Tristram lauds his own Dedication in terms of a painting—'measure my piece in the painter's scale'[34]—and is particularly proud of the *design* of his offering: 'and the design, —if I may be allowed, my Lord, to understand my own *design*, and supposing absolute perfection in designing, to be as 20,—I think it cannot well fall short of 19'.[35] But along with this expressed sense of design, there is an attendant attitude of self-ribbing, self-directed sarcasm, conveyed in this case by the fact that Tristram is advertising the Dedication for fifty guineas. The same sarcasm appears in connection with the design of Corporal Trim's posture, in Volume II, Chapter 17, when Trim is to orate the sermon. Tristram puts him in a still frame: 'to take the picture of him in at one view'.[36] His posture is perfect to a mathematical nicety, and he harmonises prettily with the cosmic laws of nature, the force of gravity and the laws of mechanics. He is in harmony with the universe. Tristram draws in the lines and angles for us. But this harmony cannot help him when his sympathetic *human* nature has to respond so feelingly to the emotive parts of the sermon. The method, or theme, is really a particularly elaborate form of an ancient comic device, the pratfall; the enthusiasm or presumption of man in attempting to acquire or emulate an ideal of order. The attempter, the aspirer to order, always gets into trouble. He has to make the attempt because it is in his nature to do so, but his imperfections always lead to an elliptic kind of response.

So from the art of painting as it appears in the book, the reader quickly gets a sense of conspiracy and plot, of an external force demanding a response from the character. The plot exists in the absolute perfection implied by the system of rules: the fact that there exists somewhere an ideal painting which gets 20 out of 20 on all counts. This plot exists externally in the sense that it is supposed to have an independent, absolute nature, but it also exists as an observed and envied model in the mind of the individual who is compelled to try to live up to it. The idea of the related arts is being used to bring the concept of plot and the concept of character closer together.

Where Tristram tries to use the existence of this sytem of rules without reference to any fully realised character, the process does not work quite so effectively, and sticks at the level of satire. There is an example of this in Volume III, Chapter 12. Here the 'Excellent critic!' (as his partner in the conversation calls him) tries to take David Garrick down a peg for not speaking his lines with the requisite regularity, then denigrates a book and a poem for being 'out of all plumb' and deplores a painting which exhibits a regrettable lack of adherence to the 'principle of the *pyramid*'.[37] This critic is then much abused by Tristram in his turn.

Tristram does three things in this passage, none of them very well. He satirises the critic: but the opinions the critic puts forward are extreme and rather obsolete. He is also justifying the irregularity of the construction of *Tristram Shandy* (if the works of the other artists are out of plumb, then his book can be so too): but this is also a bit simple. On another level, he is building up an impression of the diversity of systems-builders; but it is not in character for Tristram to pour scorn on someone simply for being a systems-builder. As the critic is a figure rather than a character, Tristram cannot do anything very positive with the idea here. (Tristram might in fact intend this criticism of the 'Excellent critic' to be limited in its effects and success—or rather Sterne might; this possibility will be examined in the third section of the present chapter.)

Another example of Tristram using the analogy with painting to introduce a joke about symmetry and proportion comes in Volume IV, Chapter 25. This is the chapter after the missing chapter, which contained (so Tristram says) a description of Toby, Trim and Obadiah riding on horseback to visit Aunt Dinah, riding on horseback rather than use the coach with the bend-sinister incorporated into its coat-of-arms:

> But the painting of this journey, upon reviewing it, appears to be so much above the stile and manner of any thing else I have been able to paint in this book, that it could not have remained in it, without depreciating every other scene; and destroying at the same time that necessary equipoise and balance, (whether of good or bad) betwixt chapter and chapter, from whence the just proportions and harmony of the work results.[38]

His argument is that the book is 'the more perfect and complete' for not having the chapter. Here the notion of proportion is wholly ironic, because Tristram directs it against himself. The argument is based on the proposition that *Tristram Shandy* embodies not just self-consistency, but self-consistency *and therefore* order and design. Yet anyone may see that the book is not at all regular or designed in this visual sense. Visually it is a mess, and this mess is exacerbated by the chasm made by the missing chapter. Tristram is complimenting himself on avoiding the pratfall: had he presented his ideal chapter, his failure in the rest of the book would have become obvious. Yet in talking of his pratfall he has made it. In talking of his absent perfect chapter he draws attention to the confusion of the text. It is in fact satire of the idea of self-consistency, of being 'in tune with yourself', as an adequate aesthetic.

One might notice (though it has nothing to do with painting) how this chapter is complemented by Volume VII, Chapter 28, the chapter in which the two stories about Auxerre and the 'real' moment of writing all come together in 'the most puzzled skein of all'. Having worked up this fine confusion, Tristram explains that 'There is but a certain degree of perfection in every thing; and by pushing at something beyond that, I have brought myself into such a situation, as no traveller ever stood before me.'[39] Aiming at an ideal order: except that he has not been. He has been aiming at an ideal confusion, which he has attained. This is Tristram at his most perfect.

There are indications in the pictorial art of the mid-eighteenth century that the same analogy used the other way round—describing painting in terms of literature—produces just the same entanglement of plot and character. The particular example is William Hogarth, with whom Sterne has a special relationship.

Hogarth did not think of himself as the purveyor of artistic designs with simply spatial relationships. His two major works, *A Harlot's Progress* and *A Rake's Progress*, are both concerned with cause and effect. (The full title of Hogarth's longest series is *The Effects of Industry and Idleness Illustrated*.) In the Advertisements to *A Harlot's Progress*, Hogarth describes himself as 'The Author' of the series, and insists that he is a 'dramatic writer' rather than a mere artist.[40] By doing this he draws attention to two related facets of his work. He means that he is a describer rather than a transcriber of events; that his art must pass through the highly individual filter of his own character in order to portray clearly a more general, external, social subject. He also means that he is interested in plot and character—in particular in the situation of a certain defined ruling characteristic of an individual being able to start off the plot of a work of art. The process of cause and effect must originate at least partly from within the character of his protagonist. Thus in the first plate of *A Harlot's Progress*, Mary Hackabout's gullibility is signalled to the reader—spectator, rather—by the dead *goose* in her basket. Because she has a goose in her basket she is a silly goose; because she is a goose she makes a bad assessment of character, and because she makes a bad assessment of one particular character she ends up as a harlot. The detail of the goose in the basket lets the reader-spectator (who is the third character or personality needed to complete the picture) make his own inference between the external signal and the overall situation. It is at least two steps from the goose to the plot, and the reader has to get there by the efforts of his own mind. In this way the idea of an audience is as integral to Hogarth's art as it is to Sterne's.

In some of Hogarth's panorama-scenes all the indicators

exist at the same time. In the picture of the progress of the king's army near Twickenham,[41] there are about a dozen figures in the centre and centre right who are all involved in a simultaneous train of cause-and-effect; a milk-selling maid who is too full of the milk of human kindness to refuse a kiss to a trooper, and thus loses her milk to a thief, and so on. The interest of this to a reader-spectator is that when he picks up a figure and notices one or more of its relations, he will then be unsure as to whether he is looking at the beginning, middle or end of a sequence. Solving the picture, coping with the plot, constitutes the pleasure of reading it.

Hogarth is not valuable or interesting just for his plots. There is also the particular realism, the social-documentary aspect of his work. But perhaps this ability to create representative characters who are also individuals without being caricatures, and to put them into a world whose detailed physical interest gives it the flavour of being the real world intensified rather than formalised, also depends on Hogarth's sense of plot. This would be plot in a larger sense; the aspect of his art which decrees that the Harlot and Rake cannot stop themselves sliding down the slippery slope to destruction, because they are caught in a society which somehow has come to represent a trap, a malevolent external force operating on their characters. Perhaps the right way to put it is this: that an awareness of the individual personality as being important in its own right can only develop when people begin to have a sense of society, the whole world, as a conspiracy against its individual human components.

It has of course been argued (by Ian Watt) that the social and economic 'individualism' of the seventeenth and eighteenth centuries was a factor which contributed directly to the development of the novel as an art-form. The climate of political, religious and social thought provided a world-view which emphasised the importance of the individual and his relations with society: the novel is characterised by an interest in the perceptions and choices of the autonomous individual. But individualism has many facets. The same background of thought as freed men from old fetters also laid the foundations for the bureaucratic vastness of the corporate nation state, and also for a century of ferocious exploitation of man by man in the name of utility, the greatest happiness of the greatest number. John Locke, for instance, may have been a pioneer of the notions of the liberty of the individual and the equality of men, but this doesn't stop his thought being at the same time a *denial* of individuality. C. B. MacPherson even argues that 'the result of Locke's work was to provide a moral basis for a class state from postulates of equal individual natural rights'.[42] Social and economic individualism stresses the individual *in* the world: literary individualism tends also to examine the world acting *against* the individual.

It is of course true, as a generalisation, that people in stories tend to be defined against their opposite—St George would not be St George without the Dragon; Robin Hood needs the Sheriff. But I also think it is true that between the seventeenth and eighteenth centuries there is a change in the way the world outside is seen and presented in literature. The change occurs quite suddenly and dramatically with Defoe. In the seventeenth century personality or character is almost taken for granted—characters tend to take the sources of their own action for granted. Even Hamlet does not ask how his actions are being determined—what has made Denmark a prison, how his mother and father came to have the characters they had. His nature is almost subdued to what it lives in. But with Defoe you have characters who reflect on the nature of the world outside, the way it conditions and determines action, and who thus slowly come to understand more about the limits of their own freedom, and about themselves. The 'world outside' does not have to be society—Crusoe has to be on his island before the strangeness of his situation leads him to reflect at all seriously.

Although this change may be dependent on social and economic changes, it is primarily intellectual and emotional. A sense of conspiracy in a particular or 'real' situation must depend to some extent on a deeper or more pervasive sense or 'idea' of conspiracy.

Sterne does achieve, in his writing, the vivid and detailed texture of immediate reality, but it is very much an incidental realism. His main interests are plots, characters, and the varied entanglement of each with the other. However this is also an underlying interest of some of the practitioners of social documentary, as the previous few pages have perhaps shown. Thus the reader of *Tristram Shandy* can find himself in a position to bake, in his own imagination, the cake of the real Shandy world from the grains of physical and gestural detail that Tristram lets fall. Sterne does not involve himself in the manifestations of the documentary mode, but he achieves its realism through an awareness of its ethos.

The aspirant towards *musical* harmony in *Tristram Shandy* comes up against exactly the same problems as Trim and Tristram meet with. His human limitations let him down in the face of an ideal of order; or, to be more precise, two ideals of order. Diego, in the 'Slawkenbergii Fabella', wants to compose the only original song in *Tristram Shandy*, a song to his mistress Julia.

ODE

Harsh and untuneful are the notes of love,
Unless my Julia strikes the key,
Her hand alone can touch the part,
Whose dulcet move-
ment charms the heart,
And governs all the man with sympathetic sway.

[2d.]

O Julia![43]

Diego has a terrible time of it here, although he comes out of it quite well. He tries hard to give voice to one ideal of order, the old sympathy between the harmony of music and the harmony of the microcosm of man. But words conspire against him to wreck his pretensions. His mistake of course is the unconscious ambiguity of the word 'part'. But 'part' is a good rhyme for 'heart'; Diego succumbs to the conventional *literary* order of the poem, towards which his love is impelling him to strive. He ends up with what is actually rather a charming comparison of the effects of genital manipulation on the male body with the effects of musical harmony. His search for order unconsciously frustrated, he is left with a much more stimulating second-best.

This of course is of the essence of *joke*, and one would hardly be tempted to make these remarks about it, were it not being delivered in *Tristram Shandy*. These things count for more here, in the context of Tristram's rhetorical awareness of a cosmic plot against mankind which affects the destinies and course of his book and himself. Here even Diego's tiny attempt at the decorous modelling of a well-turned phrase must lapse into a slide on the universal bananaskin. It is Tristram's ability to convince the reader of the ambiguity of that bananaskin which extends its influence so far. Is it a real or imagined one? Does it lie mainly in the mind, in the quality of words, or in the real world?

Tristram sometimes expresses the sympathetic nature of his characters in directly musical terms. When he does so, he makes their emotion appear almost entirely passive. What kind of sympathy is this?—'... he wants a shoe, poor creature! said *Obadiah*. —Poor creature! said my uncle *Toby*, vibrating the note back again, like a string in unison'.[44] It is hard to say. It is, however, the same kind of sympathy as David Hume uses in his *Treatise of Human Nature*, to back up his theories on association with an extension of the vibrational metaphor:

> As in strings equally wound up, the motion of one communicates itself to the rest, so all the affections readily pass from one person to another, and beget correspondent movements in every human creature.[45]

When Tristram notices himself responding to music, notices the benevolence it engenders in him, he does not leave the description of himself without a little equivocation as to the value of this benevolence:

> Ptr . .r . .r . .ing— twing— twang— prut— trut— 'tis a cursed bad fiddle. —Do you know whether my fiddle's in tune or no? ...Your worships and your reverences love musick —and God has made you all with good ears—and some of you play delightfully yourselves—trut-prut, —prut-trut.
>
> O! there is—whom I could sit and hear whole days, —whose talents lie in making what he fiddles to be felt, —who inspires me with his joys and hopes, and puts the most hidden springs of my heart into motion. —If you would borrow five guineas of me, Sir, —which is generally ten guineas more than I have to spare—or you, Messrs. Apothecary and Taylor, want your bills paying, —that's your time.[46]

Is this sentiment or sympathy, or both? If sympathy is only reflex action, is sentiment so too? Does it matter, do other people think it matters? I think that as sympathy and sentiment are so central to Sterne's work, these are important enough questions to require a separate examination, in Chapter 6.

This section of the chapter concludes with a note on Sterne's use of the related art of poetry. Tristram does not actively analogise between his own writing and poetry, but at two points in the book he adapts Pope's *Essay on Man* to his own ends. These ends turn out to be the reworking and distorting of analogies, of correspondences between different worlds in the poem.

In the first case Tristram picks lines which express a sense of universal order and harmony through reference to gravity, and treats the idea contained in them in such a way as to stress his own idiosyncrasy rather than a sense of pattern. By the mid-eighteenth century, the concept of gravitational attraction (as has already been noted) exists as a very general and conventional point of reference for writers who wish to express the goodness of God and His strength as a designer of physical and social patterns. Thus Pope:

> On their own axis as the planets run,
> Yet make at once their circle round the Sun:
> So two consistent motions act the Soul,
> And one regards itself, and one the Whole.
> Thus God and Nature linked the gen'ral Frame,
> And bade Self-love and Social be the Same.[47]

It is the same figure as Tristram uses in Volume I, Chapter 22 of *Tristram Shandy* (see Chapter 2, note 62 and ref.), in relation to his book rather than to social philosophy. But Tristram uses it to confuse and perplex, or at least to stimulate, the reader, not to express harmony. The relation of great world to little becomes more complicated, and more interesting.

The second adaptation of Pope comes in Volume IX, in the Dedication. In this case the correspondence is between earth and heaven: once again Tristram turns what was quite a straightforward passage into something rather more equivocal. Volume IX is about love—about Toby's amour with the Widow Wadman—at least, some of it is. In the Dedication Tristram, arguing that 'Nothing is so perfectly *amusement* as a total change of ideas; no ideas are so totally different as those of Ministers, and Innocent Lovers',[48] dedicates the love-story to Lord *******, i.e. to William Pitt, Earl of Chatham. Extending his argument-by-opposites, he promises to dedicate some future volume (which will be concerned with matters of State) to 'some gentle Shepherd'—the traditional Pastoral lover—whose 'passionate and love-sick Contemplations' will thus receive some healthy '*Diversion*': some gentle Shepherd,

> Whose Thoughts proud Science never taught to stray,
> Far as the Statesman's walk or Patriot-way;
> Yet *simple Nature* to his hopes had given
> Out of a cloud-capp'd head a humbler heaven;
> Some untam'd World in depth of woods embraced—
> Some happier Island in the watry-waste—
> And where admitted to that equal sky,
> His *faithful Dogs* should bear him company.[49]

This is a free adaptation of lines 99–112 of Epistle I of the *Essay on Man*. In Pope, the passage is about a 'Poor Indian' rather than a 'gentle Shepherd', and the thought is a fine thought. But Tristram has chosen to write himself into something of a corner, by exchanging the Indian for the Shepherd without adapting the passage sufficiently to cope with this new context. The traditional objective of a 'passionate and love-sick' Shepherd is a 'heaven' only in a metaphorical sense. It may be the 'heaven' of his beloved's favour, or of something more physical. Pope's ambiguous language ('in depth of woods embraced' and 'admitted to') becomes ambiguous meaning in Tristram's new context. Pope becomes Diego, his intended heaven exchanged for another. The Shepherd is to be admitted to an 'equal sky' by his beloved: all men are equal there. This does not speak well for the lady's character: it also reinforces the Shepherd's comicality ('cloud-capp'd head'). From being a touching concluding thought, the last line now takes on hints of comic grotesquerie.

III THE HEART OF THE WORK: A TREATMENT OF PROPORTION IN VOLUME III

Tristram may not be entirely joking when he draws the lines of narrative of the first six volumes, in Volume VI, Chapter 40, and draws a distinction between the first four volumes and the next two, Volumes V and VI.

He has been, he says, resisting the temptation to digress as freely from the story as he did in the earlier part of the book '—In the fifth volume I have been very good',[50] and he claims that his resistance has gradually become sterner: 'In this last volume I have done better still'.[51] His hope is that with a sufficient effort of will, some future volume may attain the ultimate and perfect order represented by the pure straight line:

____ [52]

In this he *is* joking. The expectation of future order is, as usual, ironic. Volume VII is a prolonged and entire digression, and Tristram has considerable difficulty, in Volume VIII, in re-establishing the scene at Shandy Hall sufficiently for him finally to introduce Toby's amour with Widow Wadman in the last volume.

But as far as the parts of the book already written are concerned, it is not a bad characterisation. Volumes V and VI are less complicated and less twist-bedevilled than the first four, less concerned with problems of design and form. They are the least considered and the least useful part of the book from the point of view of academic scholarship. As Tristram reminds the reader in Volume VI, Chapter 30, he has been denying himself access to his study. The bounding of the chaise in the first chapter of Volume V has led him to make a vow: 'By the great God of day . . . I will lock up my study door the moment I get home, and throw the key of it ninety feet below the surface of the earth, into the draw-well at the back of my house.'[53] He cannot read his books, he cannot quote his beloved (but digression-making) curses, sermons, documents and histories—'I wish . . . I had the key of my study out of my draw-well, only for five minutes',[54] so that he could quote a proper and not a made-up list of mysogynistic heroes. He does give a list, but it has nothing of the distracting fascination of his usual documentary sources.

So he is left with the Shandy story, and this he gets on with. Between the start of Volume v and Volume vi, Chapter 36, where he begins to orchestrate the coda at the end of the published unit (Volumes v and vi being published together in December 1761) there are only some eight chapters which do not directly illustrate the Shandy characters and their history.

The page left for the reader's illustration of the Widow Wadman's corporeal concupiscence comes at the end of this part of the book—in Volume vi, Chapter 38. As so much of the previous volumes has been given over to just this kind of illustration, it seems a good place for the reader to be able to display his new and subtle appreciation of character-drawing. It is a fine reflection on Sterne's audience that, especially in old library copies, this page is usually occupied by a drawing which does in fact express not only the Widow's physical charms but also her overwhelming interest in amatory matters.

In fact each volume of *Tristram Shandy* has its own individual character. The first volume is mostly introductory, establishing the tone. Volumes v and vi are narrative, vii and viii are very digressive, Volume ix resumes and finishes the story.

This leaves Volume ii, iii, and iv. As I see it, these volumes are the *didactic* heart of *Tristram Shandy*, or rather they contain it. Volumes ii and iii contain a number of the work's central passages and documents—a comparison of Toby and John Locke near the beginning of Volume ii; the sermon and its reading; the Author's Preface—and these will receive attention in Chapters 5 and 6. But these more rhetorical set pieces and the arguments or demonstrations which they put forward are counterpointed, backed up, by some of the smaller events of this area of the book: and these smaller events are the subject of the remainder of this chapter.

For some readers at least, the beginning of Volume iii marks a watershed in the book. Until then, the expectations of progress have not entirely died; the hope of a conventional story has not been educated away. But during Volume iii's first few chapters these expectations tend to evaporate at last.

This new realisation, when it comes, is accompanied by a paradoxical feeling of release from frustration. The terms on which the book is to be taken become clearer. Tristram is going to go on pretending to delude himself that he is eventually going to get his life down on paper, but it is now plain that this is only a delusion, or a pretence of a delusion. Tristram is still hopeful about his prospects at the end of Volume IV: 'it is from this point properly, that the story of my LIFE and my OPINIONS sets out',[55] but everyone has long since realised that his hope is simply a very necessary stimulus to his writing anything at all.

It is not accidental that the beginning of Volume III is where this change is to be felt. Nor is it due merely to the fact that a certain mass of material has built up a certain pressure of scepticism in the reader which comes to a head with the formal re-beginning of another volume or published unit. It has to do with a change in the nature of the book.

The principal change is that this is where the breaking of patterns begins to be felt as something more than an activity which deals only in negatives. Tristram's disruption of Walter's belief in the pattern of necessary correspondence between mind and body in Chapter 4 has already been mentioned: but so many smaller systems of both thought and action break down or have their elements pulled out of shape in this part of the book that this breaking becomes its dominant activity. (In Volume I, only Walterian systems are pulled apart.) Also, the wrecks that are made in each individual chapter begin to be sensed not as discrete events but as miniature analogues of the book as a whole. The collapse of small systems of order inside the book begins to reflect back on to the set pieces, and also on to the larger collapse which is going on at the same time, the perpetual collapse of the order of *Tristram Shandy*. The only pattern left untouched is the basic process of cause-and-effect which governs the events surrounding Tristram's birth—a pattern which will be discussed in Chapter 6.

Toby is the hero of the first part of Volume III. In Chapter 1, his very-nearly-incomprehensible interjection, *'I wish, Dr. Slop, . . . you had seen what prodigious armies we had in Flanders'*,[56] breaks up the conversation between Slop and Walter. This conversation had been threatening (in Volume II, Chapter 18) to turn into a tiff. Tristram draws the reader's attention to the fact that Toby's interjection leads to Slop having to forego the verbal retaliation he had planned against

Walter. Tristram describes this retaliation in terms of *balancing accounts*:

> the safest way in general to take off the force of the wish, is, for the party wished at, instantly to get up upon his legs—and wish the *wisher* something in return, of pretty near the same value,—so balancing the account upon the spot.[57]

But Slop's mind cannot cope with Toby's wayward associations, and begins to move in the fashion which will give it most relief from the conundrum. The directional impetus against Walter is exchanged for random movement. By the end of the chapter he is counting the brass nails on the arm of his chair, and takes no more part in the action until Chapter 9, where his mind at last recovers its balance ('Some little gusts of passion or interest'[58] begin to drive it along once more, as he casts his eyes on the knots Obadiah has tied round his bag). Toby has wrecked the balance, the to and fro, of the scene, and in the process has halted the tiff and restored harmony.

In Chapter 2, it is Walter's posture which loses all proportion and harmony, as he fishes with his left hand for a handkerchief which lies in his right-hand coat pocket. Again Tristram stresses that what is happening is the very antithesis of proper proportion or balance. Had Walter used his other hand, he says, 'his whole attitude had been easy—natural—unforced: *Reynolds* himself, as great and gracefully as he paints, might have painted him as he sat'.[59] These two preliminary breakings, of the 'balanced' conversation and of Walter's harmonious posture, are then used by Tristram in Chapter 5, to make a larger point about the value of breaking pattern. He has led up to this in Chapter 4, where he makes the claim that body and mind do not mutually reciprocate, and illustrates his claim by referring back to Toby's letting go the fly. In Chapter 5 the action of the scene at Shandy Hall continues from where it was left at the end of Chapter 3: Walter has had his face turn red with the effort of trying to reach his handkerchief. Toby has had a military association engendered in his mind by Walter's posture, and concludes from the redness of his brother's face that Walter has seen into his mind and is angry that Toby's Hobby-Horse should be obtaining nourishment from his own discomfiture.

Tristram then uses, in his resolution of the scene, a conventional metaphor in an unusual way. Anyone but Toby, he says, who had seen Walter's face redden and contort,

> —would have concluded my father in a rage; and taking that for granted,—had he been a lover of such kind of concord as arises from two such instruments being put into exact tune,—he would instantly have skrew'd up his, to the same pitch;—and then the devil and all had broke loose—the whole piece, madam, must have been played off like the sixth of Avison Scarlatti—*con furia*—like mad.—[60]

But Toby does not know about this concord and harmony, and replies with a look of 'inexpressible good will'. Tristram makes a very clear distinction, when he stands the metaphor on its head like this, between the two brands of harmony involved. The discord in the scene (what Tristram calls the *concord*) is attributed to a vibrational harmony, the interpersonal association or sympathy of mood. But Toby's mind does not respond to any associations except his own; a mental or emotional tone-deafness. His breaking of harmony becomes an active source of harmony.

Toby breaks things at random. His powers are by no means all positive. He is as likely to infuriate Walter by making his military associations as pacify him by apologising for them. In this chapter, his behaviour is not part of a consciously-directed pattern, but simply represents an aspect of his human nature. It just so happens that his goodwill is strong enough to overcome his military Hobby-Horse when it is a question of a direct conflict between them.

His *whistling* is made into an interesting reflection of this curious lack of direction in him. Toby's whistling is his equivalent of Slop's counting of nails, only more frequently used. In itself it is the opposite of vibrational or sympathetic harmony, in that it is habitually used by Toby as an alternative to verbal retaliation, to 'balancing the account'. But as well as signalling that Toby wishes to break a mood, it also creates one. 'Lillaburlero', the tune he whistles, is an old anti-Catholic tune.[61] Toby, by repeatedly whistling it in the presence of Slop (a Catholic) may well be unwittingly adding to the long list of insults and injuries which Slop feels the Shandys offer him. But again, Toby knows nothing of this: it just so happens that the tune might do this.

At the end of Chapters 6 and 7 Tristram produces an interesting comparison of Toby and Obadiah which reinforces the musical metaphor in Chapter 5 by reinforcing the point that harmony can as easily be the cause of destruction as of concord. At the end of Chapter 6, Toby whistles his tune, with its usual potential double effect. Then at the end of Chapter 7, Obadiah has a whistle. Tristram expresses this whistling as an effort on Obadiah's part to establish harmony in the face of the random jingling made by the instruments in Slop's bag, which Obadiah is carrying from Slop's house to Shandy Hall. To be able to hear himself whistle he ties knots round the bag, using his hat-band for cord. In Chapter 10, Slop will be unable to cope with the intricacies of Obadiah's knots; he will cut his thumb instead of the cord; later he will crush Tristram's nose with the forceps in his injured hand. Obadiah thus plays a small but crucial part in the plot against Tristram: harmony and the desire for it becomes a cause, albeit a remote one, of catastrophe.

Slop cuts his thumb and curses Obadiah. Walter takes this berating of his own servant as a personal insult to himself, and persuades Slop into reading Bishop Ernulphus's curse, against Obadiah. The curse turns out to be 'an excommunication of the church of Rome', and is out of all proportion to the occasion of its use. Walter, in making Slop read the enormous curse in such trivial circumstances, is making a fool of him in the same way as he did when he persuaded him to listen to the sermon, which turned out to be anti-Catholic in sentiment.

Slop knows he is being made a fool of. He thus has another reason for being out of temper when he comes to deliver Tristram. Walter's revenge, as usual, rebounds back on himself.

The argument Walter uses to persuade Slop into reading the curse reveals the same perverse opportunism with regard to proportional argument as he showed in Volume II, Chapter 19, in his justification of his system of body and mind. It emerges quite strongly, during Chapter 10, that Walter is capable of making conscious use of his own love of systematic knowledge, rather than being under its Hobbyhorsical control all the time. He deliberately acts in character in order to make Slop want to read the curse. He stresses that the curse is proportionate, that it fits into a proper place in a well-wrought system of swearing, a system devised and executed by Ernulphus. In fact, the curse is not a fragment but the whole system, being Ernulphus's entire output on the subject (as Walter knows quite well). But Walter assures Slop that Ernulphus's system is designed to provide a curse fit for any occasion; he says

> I have the greatest veneration in the world for that gentleman, who, in distrust of his own discretion in this point, sat down and composed (that is at his leisure) fit forms of swearing suitable to all cases, from the lowest to the highest provocations which could possibly happen to him.[62]

He hints that Slop would be conforming to neoclassical ideals of right proportion in reading the curse:

> A wise and just man however would always endeavour to proportion the vent given to these humours, not only to the degree of them stirring within himself—but to the size and ill intent of the offence upon which they are to fall.[63]

But his intention is to make Slop appear to be a monster. He wants not to establish proportion but to break it. He has temporarily taken over Tristram's role of the breaker of order, and is becoming as successful as he is in undermining the credibility of arguments based on systems of well-wrought proportion.

Perhaps the most interesting fact to emerge from Chapter 10 is that Walter knows he can argue successfully using this form of argument, the promise of right proportion, of design. His persuasion meets with an excellent response from the audience; Slop is entirely taken in by it. Walter seems to be aware of just how pervasive and typical his own outlook, his love of system, is, and to be capable of making this situation work to his advantage.

Chapter 12 continues the discussion about the curse; but this is a tricky chapter, and is not at all what it seems to be.

On the surface it looks simple enough, and quite in keeping

with what Tristram has been doing so far. There is some satire of 'connoisseurs', meaning critics who measure the value of works of art by the degree to which they conform to systems of rules, especially rules involving the keeping of proportion. These critics are equipped with stopwatches, rule and compasses, and with much geometrical cant about angles and pyramids. Tristram scores easy points off these gentlemen, and then goes on to disagree with Walter over the significance of Ernulphus's curse. He can now reveal his father's true attitude to that curse: Walter considers it to be 'an institute of swearing',[64] a codified collection of oaths. Tristram on the other hand simply sees it as good reading, stresses its originality, its vigour and individuality, and thus goes back to breaking up Walter's systems in the same fashion as he did in Chapter 4. This much is easy.

But if Tristram is falling back on to the same methods, he is himself creating a pattern, a pattern of the consistent breaking of patterns: and this he might not want to do.

In Chapter 12 he even goes so far as to associate the breaking of order with a sense of moral righteousness, of himself as preserver of the holiness of the heart's affections in defiance of the 'critics'. In general, he appears to be simplifying the issue and dealing in blacks and whites, not in his usual triplicity of black, white and grey.

The reader does receive his usual textual warning that what Tristram says is not to be taken at face value. When he has finished his harangue of the geometrically-minded connoisseurs, Tristram exclaims:

> I would go fifty miles on foot, for I have not a horse worth riding on, to kiss the hand of that man whose generous heart will give up the reins of his imagination into his author's hands,—be pleased he knows not why, and cares not wherefore.[65]

He goes to the other end of the spectrum of possible readers and posits an ideal reader who is the opposite of the 'connoisseur'. But this is a little disingenuous. Anywhere in *Tristram Shandy*, giving up the reins of one's imagination is an activity fraught with potential danger. Tristram is always liable to make a fool of any reader who does not retain his critical faculties. His manipulation of the horseback metaphor in this quotation is designed to stress that he is not speaking as an author, but as a critical dogmatist. The very presence of the metaphor suggests that there are more complex matters than dogma involved.

Despite what he tells us about his opposition to Walter on the question of Ernulphus's curse, Tristram in fact argues himself into an exact replica of his father's attitude. In so doing he negates or qualifies a great deal of what he has said earlier in the chapter about the 'connoisseurs'.

He declares that he thinks that the curse is 'an original',[66] and declares that this is said in opposition to Walter, who thinks it is 'an institute'. No such contrast exists. Like Walter, what Tristram admires is the completeness and comprehensiveness and *system* of the curse. He says that Ernulphus is

> possess'd more of the excellencies of a swearer,—had such a thorough knowledge of the human frame, its membranes nerves, ligaments, knittings of the joints, and articulations,—that when *Ernulphus* cursed,—no part escaped him.[67]

Tristram even proves the same thing as a connoisseur would prove; that all our oaths are based on a *pattern* of oaths—in this case not on a geometrical pattern but on Ernulphus, who, according to Tristram, is the model or pattern upon which all subsequent oaths have been based:

> all the oaths and imprecations, which we have been puffing off upon the world for these two hundred and fifty years last past, as originals . . . there is not an oath, or at least a curse amongst them, which has not been copied over and over again out of *Ernulphus*, a thousand times.[68]

When he says that Ernulphus's curse is 'an original', we take it as meaning original in the sense of having novelty value and a vivacity of its own. This interpretation reconciles Tristram's statement of opposition to his father with the rest of what he says. But in fact this is an unwarranted interpretation of the word, which Tristram is using in its other, earlier sense of *the* original, the one from which all others derive. His disagreement with his father is only a quibble. They both believe the curse to be a pattern, an 'institute'. Really they both like the curse because it appeals to their natural love of rhetoric and formal utterance. The very thing Tristram has been arguing against has found its way into his expression of his own outlook.

Yet another round has gone to uncle Toby. Tristram's satirical verbal retaliation against the connoisseurs, the writer's revenge, the redirected kick, has merely answered those critics on their own terms. It is a response, not an answer. The latter part of the chapter shows the danger of accepting the terms of your enemies' argument unthinkingly: Tristram dealt much more effectively with the critics when he adopted Toby's attitude of passive resistance in Chapter 4 of this volume.

Chapters 13–19 are in part taken up with preparations for the Author's Preface in Chapter 20. Although the themes of comparison and proportioning of ideas disappear for the moment, Tristram goes on breaking up small patterns of action. Toby's unconscious joke about the squirt ruins Slop's rhetorical flourish of the forceps; Walter meets the brick wall of Toby's insouciant ignorance of the Lockean 'succession of ideas'. Walter's fondness for philosophical speculation in what he sees as a Lockean mode suggests to Tristram that this would be an appropriate place to express some of his own views on Locke. The action runs down, the characters (except Slop) all go to sleep. The stage is left free for Tristram's Preface: but although the Preface does continue the themes and techniques of the earlier part of Volume III, it is best considered along with Tristram's other references to Locke and will be looked at in Chapter 5.

As there are 42 chapters in Volume III, Chapters 21 and 22 are the mid-point of the volume. They are about hinges—the squeaking hinges of the Shandys' parlour-door. Douglas Brooks points out[69] that in raising the question of hinges in the exact centre of the volume, Tristram is making a comparison between physical detail *in* the book and the form and construction of the book itself. Brooks, however, does not consider the jocular irony inherent in Tristram's indication that this volume conforms to a basic symmetrical pattern. It is very like Tristram's progress in Chapter 12; having demonstrated all the pitfalls of arguing or behaving in conformity with conventional ideas of pattern, he then makes one of the patterns against which he has just been arguing.

Tristram puts this playful mid-point symbolism to another use. He separates two different kinds of subject-matter in the two halves of the volume. All the material prior to these chapters consists of a variety of comparatively small and disparate examples of the theme of proportion and relatedness: there is no one example which by itself can control the shape of the book. But immediately after the 'Hinges' chapters the theme of NOSES begins to take shape, and carries the book off into one extended virtuoso digression which lasts well into Volume IV. One theme rises up to relegate all others, including the story of Tristram's birth, into unimportance. The digression becomes the nose on the face of the book: once again Tristram introduces physical detail which mirrors form. Disproportion takes over completely the form and direction of the book. The nose of 'the stranger', in Slawkenbergius's Tale at the start of Volume IV, overwhelms all his other features in just the same way. The tale of Slawkenbergius is thus dependent on the theme of proportion which has been evolving through Volume III. Meanwhile Tristram's incidental use of the idea of proportion and harmony has also changed. It is no longer associated with grand external designs, patterns, models or harmonies or whatever: instead it is sardonically applied to the construction of the book, in Chapters 24 and 39. Tristram carefully demonstrates the conventional order of plot and sub-plot, the skilful design of the Shandy family: and all this as the nasal excursion starts to carry the book gently away from this central story and towards the remote and mysterious fictions of Slawkenbergii Fabella: at twenty-two pages, the longest and most unified 'story' in the whole length of *Tristram Shandy*.

5 Sterne and Locke

Like every other aspect of Sterne criticism, the question of Sterne's relationship with the writings of John Locke has been answered or explained in many different ways.

There are those who say Yes to everything that Sterne proposes to them on the subject. They amplify the eulogistic comments on Locke's *Essay Concerning Human Understanding* which Tristram passes in *Tristram Shandy* into a statement that Locke is Sterne's great philosophic father. Sterne is variously a disciple, illustrator, dramatiser or humaniser of Locke. The *Essay* is viewed as a kind of Sterneopaedia, a compleat education for the author. Hafter has already been mentioned as listing some twenty secondary references which develop this point of view.

Of late, critics have been turning round and saying No to all this, and have been pointing out that while analogies between Sterne and Locke are all very well, they ignore the fact that *Tristram Shandy* does not *feel* like the *Essay*. I do not propose to provide a history of this debate. I think Francis Doherty's perceptive observation that 'The striking thing about the feel of Sterne's work is a sense of bewilderment and riddle, which is by no means part of Locke',[1] is quite enough to indicate that the answer to the question cannot be Yes. But neither should it be No. Having decided that Locke is the wrong-shaped hole for the Sternean peg, both Hafter and Doherty decide that they know a better hole (Hume) and they go to it, leaving the central question unanswered.

The central question is, why does Sterne make Tristram ask the question? Why does he draw attention to Locke—is he covering his tracks, distracting attention from the *real model* of which *Tristram Shandy* is a fictional imitation, or is he acknowledging a genuine debt? Or does the point of the question lie in the fact of its being asked?

Given the enthusiasm of both Locke and Sterne for

empirical and pragmatic methods of enquiry, it might be more appropriate to look at those sections of the text of *Tristram Shandy* where Locke seems to be of most importance, and to try to draw some conclusions on the basis of this. Two areas of the book are of particular interest. Early in Volume II Tristram peppers the text with overt and covert references to Locke while describing uncle Toby's military Hobby-Horse: and the Author's Preface ostensibly takes its subject from Locke's discussion of 'Wit and Judgment' in the *Essay*. But before undertaking analysis of these passages, some more general description of how Tristram might view Locke is in order.

What Tristram understands by 'Locke' is not really quite what the philosophers or Sterne's commentators mean by the word. 'Locke' is essentially a device which Tristram uses to define the nature of other characters, and to define the audience. Thus in Volume II he tries to effect a comparison between Locke and Toby, to confuse their energies one with the other. In the Author's Preface, what is discussed is not so much Locke *per se*, as the interpretation and adapting of his writings in the eighteenth century.

There are two crucial facts which ought to be remembered. Firstly, that Sterne's art involves a great awareness of, and manipulation of, its potential contemporary audience: and secondly, that John Locke is the eighteenth century's favourite philosopher. In fact if one goes by the number of editions, Locke is second only to God—only the Bible was printed more often than the *Essay* in the period from 1690 to 1790.[2]

The diffusion of Locke's ideas, says Kenneth Maclean,[3] was greatest in the period 1730–40; Sterne received his education at Jesus College, Cambridge in the 1730s. The period of influence of Locke's writings is roughly from 1725 to 1765. By 1760, when the publication of *Tristram Shandy* begins, Locke is no longer quite the force he was: like Marx in our own time, he has become 'Polite Learning'.

> A man of fashion at Paris, however contemptible we may think him here, must be acquainted with the reigning modes of philosophy as well as of dress, to be able to entertain his mistress agreeably. The sprightly pedants are not to be caught... by dumb show, by a squeeze of the

> hand, or the ogling of a broad eye; but must be pursued at once through all the labyrinths of the Newtonian system, and the mazy metaphysics of Locke,[4]

wrote Goldsmith in 1759. As with Tristram, Locke is not important to Goldsmith for his own sake but because he can help to define the audience. Tristram's use of Locke is, I think, not different in kind from Goldsmith's, although he goes a great deal further than casual reference. He works him deep into the fabric of the book. His 'interpretation' of Locke begins near the start of Volume II.

I UNCLE TOBY, JOHN LOCKE AND THE SEARCH FOR TRUTH

Tristram begins a new volume in order to tell the reader about Toby's 'perplexities'. Toby gets into difficulties when he tries to explain to his visitors the exact location on the battlefield at Namur where he was struck by the cannonball and contracted his wound. He reads up a great deal of military history in order to be able to point to, and discourse on, the exact spot and surroundings where his personal catastrophe occurred.

The conclusion that Tristram eventually reaches about the origin, the 'cause' of Toby's perplexities, is that ''Twas not by ideas,—by heaven! his life was put in jeopardy by words';[5] and a few lines previously he has told us of 'the unsteady uses of words which have perplexed the clearest and most exalted understandings'.[6] This refers to the specialised terminology of the military textbooks from which Toby's knowledge and eloquence are derived. But Tristram is not being quite candid when he says this, for the uses of words in the military textbooks are anything but unsteady. The books are scientific tomes which aspire to precise technical language. Equally, Toby cannot be realistically classed among 'the clearest and most exalted understandings'. It may be that, as 'Sir Critic' says, Toby is 'no fool', but his character has none the less been established in Volume I as simple, placid, unconcerned with any kind of formal knowledge. He is obviously ripe for perplexity when he does involve himself in such a system of knowledge.

It is Toby's *mind* which is unsteady in this situation, and it is unsteady because his Hobby-Horse, his desire for knowledge about warfare, has suddenly raised its head. His ruling passion at this point is a desire for that knowledge and a desire to express it. Words—printed words—are only the means to this, and they are not unsteady until they get to him (as in Volume I, it is in fact the character and not the external system that is the *shown* cause of the situation).

But it is not just uncle Toby to whom these points can be applied. Tristram also brings John Locke up for consideration, and his reference to 'the clearest and most exalted understandings' could quite well mean Locke.

John Traugott observes[7] that in Volume II, Chapter 2, there is not merely a verbal reference to Locke's *Essay*, but an entire passage stolen—or rather adapted—from that work. The original passage is about 'the cause of obscurity, in simple ideas'—it is about much the same kind of perplexities as those from which Toby suffers. The causes of obscurity, claims Locke, are threefold:

> either dull Organs, or very slight and transient impressions made by the Objects, or else a weakness in the Memory, not able to retain them as received. For to return again to visible Objects, to help us to apprehend this matter: if the Organs, or Faculties of Perception, like Wax over-hardned with Cold, will not receive the impression of the Seal, from the usual impulse wont to imprint it; or, like Wax of a temper too soft, will not hold it well, when well imprinted; or else supposing the Wax of a temper fit, but the Seal not applied with a sufficient force to make a clear Impression: In any of these cases, the print left by the Seal will be *obscure.*[8]

The reader may notice that Locke only manages to illustrate two of the three instances he gives, if that. The trouble is that 'wax' cannot be used to stand for both 'organs' and 'memory' without creating problems. The same action has to represent three different situations, and it has to do this simply by means of variations in phrasing. As Locke's phrasing is not up to this, he arrives in the rather Shandean position of having an obscure and confused explanation of obscurity and confusion.

On this Tristram pounces, and emphasises its character by exaggerating it and making it more dramatic—'Dolly' trying to seal her love-letter to 'Robin', and being frustrated by her Mistress ringing the bell to call her. All this has been brought in to illustrate the cause of Toby's confusion, but Tristram is jocularly scathing about it when he has run through it: 'not one of these was the true cause of the confusion in my uncle *Toby*'s discourse'.[9] It is at this point that Tristram mentions the unsteady uses of words as the true cause of Toby's confusion: a judicious piece of arrangement means that this now refers much more directly to Locke's own unsteadiness than to its ostensible reference, the military textbooks. Not, of course, that Locke is in any way the *cause* of Toby's mental behaviour: as usual, Tristram's promise of an enquiry into the 'first causes' of human action remains unfulfilled. All he has done is to make a sly comparison between Toby's mind and Locke's. In fact the illustration is brought in largely to dazzle the reader and confuse *him* with its distracting irrelevance—and what Tristram is doing to the original passage in the *Essay* is not to follow it, but to caricature it.

Locke does not come off from this very well, despite the fact that the cause Tristram claims to find for Toby's perplexities is a cause also examined by Locke in other parts of the *Essay*, the imperfections of words.[10] Locke is made to appear very much like Toby, in that the words in his passage were not unsteady until he took hold of them. So when Tristram, in the same chapter, describes Locke's *Essay* as 'a history-book . . . of what passes in a man's own mind',[11] the remark has a double edge, given that Tristram will then go on to show that what happens in a man's own mind is always in danger of some confusion in expression. It is a point which is of some relevance to the *Essay*: it is well-known that Locke's work is full of confusion between the content and the style, of condemnations of figurative language which are themselves rounded out with fine figurative flourishes,[12] and of definitions of one faculty of the mind by means of the manifestation of its opposite.[13]

Tristram's method here is very like his method in Volume I, telling the reader something while showing him something different. However the point here is very much for the initiated. Unlike the examples in Volume I, the evidence for the alternative 'shown' viewpoint is not freely available in the text, but resides in external specialised knowledge. The reader needs to know the source of the 'sealing-wax' passage before Tristram's platitudes about words become part of any larger pattern of thought.

In Chapter 3 Tristram extends the comparison between Locke and Toby. He does this by using the same techniques as he did in Chapter 2; by using esoteric data, and by providing certain specific statements which the reader is made to feel as generalisations. In Chapter 2 these techniques were used simultaneously, one extract of Locke being pressed into service as representative of the whole opus and, for those who know its origin, helping to determine Locke's character in the book. In Chapter 3 these techniques are used separately.

Toby's search for truth and knowledge is a fairly specific affair, yet Tristram chooses to make this one search stand for many others, in fact for all such searches. He does this by means of his semi-ironic interjections: '—Endless is the Search of Truth! . . . intricate are the mases of this labyrinth!'[14] He is worried for Toby's health as Toby becomes feverishly embroiled with his Hobby-Horse. If the reader has any feeling that Locke (whose interest in the 'search of truth' has been demonstrated by his involvement in the previous chapter) is present in Tristram's mind at this point, then he will be worried not just for Toby's health but for Locke's as well.

In fact, the esoteric information in this chapter has to do with Locke, and in particular with a connection between him and Toby's studies. Once he has mastered the techniques and the terminology of the science of fortification, Toby begins to specialise a little. The branch of military science which he chooses is, not surprisingly, ballistics. He wishes to understand the precise details of the way in which the cannonball arrived in his groin. Tristram disapproves of the committed nature of Toby's study: he fears that the activity will exasperate his symptoms and retard his recovery from the wound. Continuing in his rhetorical-interjectional manner, Tristram cries 'stop! . . . stop!', anxious that Toby should call a halt to his dangerous Hobbyhorsical search.

Carol Kyle, in a note in the *Philological Quarterly*,[15] has pointed out that there exist occult resemblances between this passage and others in *Tristram Shandy*, and a passage of

Locke's *Essay*. Tristram, in Volume VIII, Chapter 25, uses the simile of a cannon to describe the eyes of the Widow Wadman, when she and Toby are engaged in actions preliminary to the non-consummation of their amour. It is a tableau: the action is suspended while Toby gazes into her eyes, searching for a purely fictitious speck of dust, while they shoot amorous fire at him. Into this tableau Tristram drops his simile.

> An eye is for all the world exactly like a cannon, in this respect; That it is not so much the eye or the cannon, in themselves, as it is the carriage of the eye—and the carriage of the cannon, by which both the one and the other are enabled to do so much execution.[16]

Tristram is proud of this comparison: 'I desire . . . that whenever I speak of Mrs. Wadman's eyes . . . that you keep it in your fancy',[17] and justly proud, for it is very exact. The Widow's eyes are as interested in Toby's groin as was the projectile fired by the original cannon. Those eyes are referred to again in Volume IX, Chapter 16, another tableau scene, where Toby and Trim hesitate before the Widow's front door for a full minute, Trim's hand on the knocker. The Widow sits in her bedchamber, 'with an eye ready to be deflowered again'.[18]

Locke also uses the example of a cannon to illustrate the idea of a suspended moment of time. His use seems a little paradoxical, in that he is actually describing what happens in the mind when ideas follow each other too quickly to allow succession to be perceived. He remarks (in Book II, Chapter 14, para. 10) that a cannonball passing through a room doubtless strikes one wall before the other, and spends a certain length of time in crossing the room, but that to human faculties this seems only a single moment or instant. As with Tristram's description of the Widow's eyes, Locke presents a tableau with one moving object, the projectile.

In Volume II, it is Toby's mind which moves too fast. Toby almost seems to derive his impetus, the momentum of his thoughts, from the projectiles that he studies. If he could have felt Tristram's simile in Volume VIII, no doubt the Widow's artillery would have stimulated Toby's mind in much the same way, and achieved its effect (equally, if he had read the

Sorbonne doctors' deliberations, his Hobby-Horse might have trotted down a different path).

By itself, of course, this highly esoteric material does not do more than suggest a faint similarity between Toby's mind and the mind that Locke describes. But Tristram also uses a strong echo of a much more accessible Lockean phrase: the 'Search of Truth' is an ironical reminder of the mind's 'searches after Truth'[19] in the first paragraph of Locke's 'Epistle to the Reader' at the beginning of the *Essay*.

Tristram's association of Toby's quixotic energies with Locke, and through Locke with socially acceptable energies, continues through Chapters 4 and 5. On the one hand, he establishes Toby as a full Quixote-analogue by making a comparison in Chapter 3 between Toby's library of military books and the original Don Quixote's library of chivalric romances. This comparison is then reinforced in Chapter 5 by the introduction of Trim, who is to some extent the Sancho Panza to Toby's Quixote.

At the same time Tristram emphasises the fact that Toby is representative of society in general rather than a freak of nature. In Chapter 4 he does this by way of one of his many semi-Lockean tags:

> The desire of life and health is implanted in man's nature; —the love of liberty and enlargement is a sister-passion to it: These my uncle *Toby* had in common with his species.[20]

This is a diffuse echo of Locke's definition of man's property in the 'Second Treatise on Govenment': 'his Property, that is, his Life, Liberty and Estate'.[21] For good measure he has another Locke-tag a few lines later on: 'The succession of his ideas was now rapid'.[22] These details make Tristram's language more public than it has been before, and emphasise that he wants the reader to see Toby as something much more than an individual Quixote. His method is in fact the obverse of the one he used to persuade the reader of Walter's typicality. He insists that Walter is a complete individualist, but shows us at the same time how close he is to the conventional science of his time. Toby, says Tristram, is not at all a freak but is quite representative of his society—but at the same time he develops the quixotic and individualistic elements in Toby's nature.

Locke has not emerged from these chapters with a great deal of credit. Tristram seems to be suggesting that the Lockean search for truth is the source of Toby's energy, or an analogue of it. If this is so then Locke becomes merely the archetype of systems-builders, and his philosophy only the largest of the Hobby-Horses in the book. This is a rather serious charge to make against the eighteenth century's favourite philosopher: the question of why Tristram should want to make it is of some importance. He seems to be saying that Locke has not noticed the quixotic elements present in his system of philosophy, and that a *natural* comparison exists between Locke's mind and Toby's. It is worth pressing this comparison a little harder than Tristram does, because when Locke's thought is considered generally, it becomes clear that these quixotic elements have the closest connections with uncle Toby's character, and with *Tristram Shandy* more generally. These connections can best be explored by looking at Locke's own ideas about the nature of man's mind.

Referring to the eighteenth century's practical interest in education, and to the popularity of Lord Chesterfield's letters to his son (which were published in 1774) Kenneth Maclean says that 'This new stress on the education of the young . . . may well have been the result of Locke's philosophy, which had cast aside all innate ideas and made experience requisite for all knowledge.'[23] He goes on to say, *a propos* of Locke's notion of the 'Tabula rasa' of the newborn mind, that 'since it is learning rather than a native capacity that generally separates one man from another, the moral issue behind Locke's attack on innate ideas, and in the background of the entire *Essay*, is the doctrine of *work*'.[24] There is often a strong sense, in Locke's writings, that it is the activity of the mind (and body) which is important for its own sake, rather than for the value of the objects on which that energy is expended. Thus in the 'Epistle to the Reader', the mind's 'searches after Truth, are a sort of Hunting and Hawking, wherein the very Pusuit makes a great part of the pleasure'.[25] The labour theory of value is central to all Locke's works. It is as crucial to his arguments about property in the 'Second Treatise on Government' as it is to the *Essay*. His equation of work with happiness is especially noticeable: 'for 'tis Labour indeed that *puts the difference of value* on every thing . . . *labour makes* the far greater part of *the value* of things we enjoy in this world'.[26] The idea that every individual has his basic property in his own body and in his ability for labour is a widely-accepted one by the late seventeenth century.

The relevance of this attitude to a study of Sterne lies both in its being received opinion in the eighteenth century and in what can happen to it when it is forcefully expressed and claimed as a law of behaviour:

> Human life consists in the attainment of every possible sort of purpose, high, low, important, unimportant, etc., to which is applied every degree of human energy. Attention is called to the fact that in this attainment there exists no constant relation between the amount of energy spent and the value of the object: now and then on absolutely trivial purposes there is expended an enormous amount of energy, and vice versa. This is often observed in individuals who work with the same ardour for simple as well as for great things. The conclusion follows that it is necessary to distinguish between the act of striving and the meaning and value of the object, and that the essence of the matter consists in the striving—the thing striven for is of secondary importance.[27]

This is interesting. Uncle Toby's Hobbyhorsical energies, and energies like his, are being described as identical in value and function to the central social and economic energies of mankind. It is the 'striving', the work, that is essential to man's nature. The illustration that the writer finds for this idea of striving-as-normative is the man who expends energy on amassing collections of objects—stamps or butterflies or whatever. The man with a *Hobby* or obsession exhibits a trait that supposedly represents the central socio-economic motivations of his society.

The quotation is in fact from Pavlov, from the *Lectures on Conditioned Reflex*. Pavlovian behaviourism, indeed behaviourism from Descartes to Pavlov, is continuously prone to set up standards of conduct in which there is little or no distinction between the eccentric and the normative aspects of striving.

Pavlovians even burst out into detailed descriptions of the

evolution of quixotism in order to justify their own activities. Words take the place of reality:

> Before the appearance of the family of homo sapiens the contact of the animals with the surrounding world was effected solely by means of direct impressions produced by its various agents which acted on the different receptor mechanisms of the animals and were conducted to the corresponding cells of the central nervous system. They were the sole signs of external objects. In the future human beings there emerged, developed and perfected, signals of the second order, in the shape of speech—spoken, auditory and visible. Ultimately these new signals began to denote everything taken in by human beings directly from the outer, as well as from the inner world; they were used not only in mutual intercourse, but in self-communion. This predominance of the new signals was conditioned, of course, by the tremendous significance of speech, although words were and remain but second signals of reality. We know, however, that there are large numbers of people who, operating exclusively with words, and failing to base themselves on reality, are ready to draw from these words every possible conclusion and all knowledge, and on this basis to direct their own life as well as the life of others.[28]

The reader may be aware that Pavlovianism itself exploits and encourages mankind's potential for quixotism. Psychotherapy, as practised by Pavlovians, involves the deliberate inversion of the two signal systems of reality in the patient—secondary above primary, words above things—in the hypnotic states of suggested sleep known as the 'paradoxical' and 'ultraparadoxical' states. It is here that the 'cure' based on hypnotic verbal suggestion can be effected.

It would also be interesting to have Sir Richard Blackmore's comment on the following, a description of Pavlov by one of his disciples:

> During his whole professional career the thing that marked Pavlov from the ordinary investigator was this strong, passionate yearning, this consuming zeal that drove him along in an intense, unremitting search for scientific truths.[29]

What matters, it seems, is not the windmills but the tilting, not the truth itself but the search for it. It would be unwise to claim that the Pavlovians and the medical and philosophical writers of the late seventeenth and early eighteenth centuries have more than a general connection. Nevertheless it was Descartes who originated the concept of the *reflex*, which only finds its final development in Pavlov's work, and, as we have seen, the scientific attitude to the study of man is well advanced by the start of the eighteenth century.

Given Sterne's admitted interest in mental conditioning and reflex response, it is intriguing to find that his supposed philosophical mentor, Locke, has this common ground with the behaviourists. It appears that there is some point in Sterne making a covert comparison of Locke and Toby. What Locke does is to set up a situation which licenses quixotic energy by saying that it does not matter what you expend your energies on so long as you expend or indulge them.

In fact the medical tradition which was examined in Chapter 3 very nearly manages to attain to the notion of a *conditioned* reflex, a passive and necessary response to a stimulus which can be controlled from without. The following is an extract from the *Essay on the Vital and other Involuntary Motions of Animals* of Robert Whytt, written in 1751 (Whytt was an Edinburgh professor of medicine who specialised in the theory of nervous diseases: he was well known enough to have a complete new set of his works on sale in 1768, in the same York auction at which Sterne's library was sold).

> We consider, that not only an irritation of the muscles of animals, or parts nearly connected with them, is followed by convulsive motions; but that the remembrance or *idea* of substances, formerly applied to different parts of the body, produces almost the same effect, as if those substances themselves were really present. Thus the sight, or even the recalled *idea* of grateful food, causes an uncommon flow of spittle into the mouth of a hungry person; and the seeing of a lemon cut produces the same effect in many people . . . the *idea* of a *stimulus* has, in many cases, almost the same effect as the thing itself . . . very many remarkable changes and involuntary motions are suddenly produced in the body by the various affections of the mind.[30]

Whytt's science is still, in the 1750s, controlled by the same analogies as were invoked by the earlier writers. He tries to account for the above findings by positing the existence of a 'sentient principle', an immaterial force which regulates the whole animal organism. His name for this force, in a later work,[31] is *sympathy*—basically the same medical phenomenon as was described by Galen and Hippocrates (he notes their use of the concept, in a footnote)—and what transforms the idea from an antique oddity into an acceptable scientific principle is, as usual, the invocation of the same idea in Newton, to which he resorts in the Preface to each work. Thus in the Introduction to the *Essay on the Vital Motions*, he admits that he does not know what the substance in the nerves is which makes the muscles move, but that

> though the laws of motion and gravitation be fully understood, and demonstrated by philosophers, yet the first cause of motion, the manner in which it is communicated to bodies, and the nature of gravity itself, have never been explained.[32]

Gravity and conditioned reflex: gravity and Pavlovianism—which, curiously enough, is the form in which the problem of action at a distance from the passively responding character has been treated by a twentieth-century novelist, as the reader will discover if he should pick up Thomas Pynchon's novel, *Gravity's Rainbow*.

In short, Walter and Toby, with their Hobby-Horses, their obsessional energies and wayward associations of ideas, exist in a world which is interested in them as case-studies as well as characters in a novel. When Tristram bundles Toby and Locke together so skilfully and makes sly comparisons of their energies, the eighteenth-century audience might find that as well as looking at Toby as an interesting phenomenon, it is also having to cope with one of its own most representative figures as a suitable case for treatment.

It certainly seems wrong to insist, as Arthur Cash does, that Locke's empiricism, 'the empiricism of the age of science',[33] is 'at the root of *Tristram Shandy*', if only because the enthusiasm of that kind of empiricism is such a rich vein for Tristram to mine, both in the character of Toby and in his own discourse.

Whenever he is determinedly sensational or empirical, in the sense of relating mental events to sources in the physical world, he adopts that enthusiasm and displays his own Hobbyhorsicality:

> I wish you saw me half starting out of my chair, with what confidence, as I grasp the elbow of it, I look up—catching the idea, even sometimes before it half way reaches me—
>
> I believe in my conscience I intercept many a thought which heaven intended for another man.[34]

II THE AUTHOR'S PREFACE

Tristram's 'Author's Preface', so appositely placed in Volume III, Chapter 20, is about the relation between wit and judgment, and on a different level, about Locke and Locke's audience. This second subject leads to a more general question, of why Sterne should think that Locke's philosophy is of value if he has such reservations about it. It emerges that Sterne and Locke share the same basic attitude to arguments from pattern and design, and that Locke's discussion of the faculty of *judgment* in the *Essay* is where this attitude is most forcefully expressed.

The Author's Preface is about many other things as well as wit and judgment and Locke—mostly it is an excuse for a set-piece display of seemingly uncontrolled stylistic and mental exuberance and wit from Tristram. But it is also very coherent.

When Tristram takes up the theme of the relation between wit and judgment, he is dealing with a subject with which a large proportion of his contemporary audience is familiar. In terms of its effect on the audience of serious literature, Locke's elevation of man's faculty of 'judgment' above that of 'wit' was his most significant general pronouncement. Robert Alter says that the 'deleterious effect' of Locke's subordination of wit to judgment is 'well known',[35] and goes on to note the adoption of a similar attitude in the poetic theorists from Addison to Johnson, and hence in the literature of the age. Alter even thinks that as long as seventy years after the publication of Locke's *Essay* this credo stood in need of a definite rebuttal by Sterne: 'Perhaps the broadest aim of Sterne's novel is to rehabilitate wit after more than half a century during which it had played a subservient role to judgment in British thought.'[36] What is curious about this view of the relative importance of the two faculties is that everyone shares it except Locke and Sterne. It is certainly not expressed in Locke. It is, rather, the opinion that the eighteenth century wanted to find in him, and what they wanted to use the authority of his name to justify or back up. To this end they rearrange his attitude, they put the emphasis in a different place. This alteration of Locke is partly what Sterne is interested in looking at in his Author's Preface.

The discussion of wit and judgment in Locke's *Essay*, and the supposed source for the opinions of Triptolemus and Phutatorius in the Author's Preface, comes from Book II, Chapter 11, 'Of Discerning'. Here Locke says:

> If in having our *Ideas* in the Memory ready at hand consists quickness of parts; in this, of having them unconfused and being nicely able to distinguish one thing from another, where there is but the least difference, consists, in a great measure, the exactness of Judgment and clearness of Reason which is to be observed in one Man above another. And hence perhaps may be given some Reason of that common Observation, That Men who have a great deal of Wit, and prompt Memories, have not always the clearest Judgment or deepest Reason. For *Wit* lying most in the assemblage of *ideas*, and putting those together with quickness and variety, wherein can be found any resemblance or congruity, thereby to make up pleasant Pictures and agreeable Visions in the Fancy; *Judgment*, on the contrary, lies quite on the other side, in separating carefully, one from another, *Ideas* wherein can be found the least difference, thereby to avoid being misled by Similitude, and by affinity to take one thing for another. This is a way of proceeding quite contrary to Metaphor and Allusion, wherein for the most part lies that entertainment and pleasantry of Wit, which strikes so lively on the Fancy, and therefore is so acceptable to all People; because its Beauty appears at first sight, and there is required no labour of Thought to examine what Truth or Reason there is in it. The Mind,

> without looking any further, rests satisfied with the agreeableness of the Picture and the gayety of the Fancy; and it is a kind of Affront to go about to examine it, by the severe Rules of Truth and good Reason, whereby it appears that it consists in something that is not perfectly conformable to them.[37]

Locke in fact refrains from making any direct value-judgments about the two powers. He does not denigrate wit, he merely says that it is something different from judgment. It is true that he assumes a connection between judgment and reason near the beginning of the quotation, but his qualifications of this attitude fall over one another's heels: 'In a great measure . . . perhaps . . . not always . . . most'. In doing this, he also qualifies the passage's implication that wit is to be associated with short-term pleasure and judgment with long-term wisdom. He knows that as a serious philosopher he should be upholding something serious, yet his interest in 'wit', his fascination with whatever it is that so many other people find fascinating, shines through the passage.

Tristram claims to differ widely from Locke on this subject; yet the metaphor he uses of wit and judgment as 'the two knobbs I'm speaking of, upon the back of this self same chair on which I am sitting'[38] places them in exactly the same spatial relation as they appear in Locke; wit is 'quite on the other side' from judgment.

In the last part of the Author's Preface, Tristram uses the opposition which he claims to have created between Locke and himself, to make Locke appear something of a fool. Locke is last seen riding off into the distance, joining the 'great wigs' in their Hobbyhorsical hunting of the vermin *wit*. But this opposition is a false one; at least, it is false unless Tristram is not talking about the real Locke, but Locke as interpreted by the 'great wigs' themselves, by the critical audience of which Triptolemus and Phutatorius are representatives.

As usual, there are some small hints from Tristram as to what he is really engaged in. One of his hints is his saying 'I need not tell your worships'[39] that Locke denigrated wit and praised judgment. He need not, because such is the state of received opinion. Another is where he introduces the main subject of his Preface:

> and that is, How it comes to pass, that your men of least *wit* are reported to be men of most *judgment*. —but mark, —I say, *reported to be*, for it is no more, my dear Sirs, than a report, and which like twenty others taken up every day upon trust, I maintain to be a vile and a malicious report into the bargain.[40]

This could mean that he himself is reporting Locke's opinion; on the other hand it could mean that it is a vile and malicious report of Locke's opinion by other people. This second possibility becomes more plausible when the critical symposium at the beginning of the Author's Preface is considered. Triptolemus and Phutatorius think that 'wit and judgment . . . never go together; inasmuch as they are two operations differing from each other as wide as east is from west.—So, says *Locke* . . .'[41] But Locke does not say 'never', he says 'not always', which is much less dogmatic. This group of Locke's followers is over-emphatic and unfaithful: they read almost as much into Locke as Walter will try to read into Erasmus on long noses in Volume III, Chapter 37. They reduce Locke's speculations to black and white, and form a fixed system of rules from this residue. Tristram is of course dealing in blacks and whites himself, in that he is not concerned with proving that this attitude to Locke prevails in the real world. He merely sets up a symbolic or cliché audience, and sets out their idea of a cliché Locke.

When Tristram pretends to be sarcastic about Locke at the end of the Preface, it is not to the real Locke that he is referring, but to this cliché Locke. He is very precise in his irony when he talks about the activities of this figure. Two Lockean phrases are used in his argument against Locke. The 'great wigs', as well as using their wigs and their grave faces against the wits, are made to use 'other implements of deceit'[42] to advance their cause. Locke himself uses the phrase 'that powerful instrument of Error and Deceit'[43] to refer to the eloquent arts, 'artificial and figurative application of Words . . . Wit and Fancy . . . Arts of Deceiving'.[44] It seems that the 'great wigs', who manage to 'deceive' poor Locke with their verbal hue and cry against wit, are making use of wit's own weapons, the very quality they wish to pursue. They are using methods which Locke declares he opposes.

Also, Tristram suggests that Locke was deceived by the wigs because he 'took the fact for granted',[45] meaning that he did not wait to examine the truth of their belief that judgment is superior to wit. This phrase is a repetition of one already quoted, 'like twenty others taken up every day upon trust'. In suggesting that Locke acted precipitately over this question, Tristram is of course suggesting that he acted without judgment, without the necessary pause and deliberation. So Locke is made to act contrary to the principle he himself set up to deal with the specific problem the wigs put before him. Once again it is stressed that the '*Magna Charta* of stupidity'[46] is a thing of the wigs' own devising.

This discussion has, I hope, shown that Sterne does not think that Locke's treatment of wit and judgment is pernicious in itself. However it has done nothing to suggest why he thinks it worth defending against its adulterators. This can now be done by considering what Locke says in a wider and more sensible context.

The faculty of *judgment* is by no means under a consistent definition in the *Essay*. In fact Locke succeeds in virtually contradicting his own first definition (the one referred to already, the nice ability to separate out, distinguish and consider ideas coolly) by a second one which occurs in Book IV, Chapter 14, 'Of Judgment'. It is in this chapter that Locke makes his legendary elevation of man's faculty of judgment to a pre-eminent position. This in no way affects the argument which has been applied to the Author's Preface, because the definition of judgment in the later chapter makes it appear more akin to the faculty of *wit* as described in Book II, Chapter 11, than to judgment as it there appears. As before, a lengthy quotation will be given: Locke does not like to express a single idea in less than about three hundred words.

> The Faculty which God has given Man to supply the want of clear and certain Knowledge, in Cases where that cannot be had, is *Judgment*: whereby the Mind takes its *Ideas* to agree, or disagree; or, which is the same, any Proposition to be true, or false, without perceiving a demonstrative Evidence in the Proofs. The Mind sometimes exercises this Judgement out of necessity, where demonstrative Proofs, and certain Knowledge are not to be had; and sometimes out of

Laziness, Unskilfulness, or Haste, even where demonstrative and certain Proofs are to be had. Men often stay not warily to examine the Agreement or Disagreement of two *Ideas*, which they are desirous or concerned to know; but, either incapable of such Attention, as is requisite in a long Train of Gradations, or impatient of delay, lightly cast their Eyes on or wholly pass by the Proofs; and so, without making out the Demonstration, determine of the Agreement or Disagreement of two *Ideas*, as it were, by a view of them as they are at a distance, and take it to be the one or the other, as seems most likely to them upon such a loose survey. This Faculty of the Mind, when it is exercised immediately about Things, is called Judgment; when about Truths delivered in Words, is most commonly called *Assent* or *Dissent* . . .

Thus the Mind has two Faculties, conversant about Truth and Falshood:

First, Knowledge, whereby it certainly perceives and is undoubtedly satisfied of the Agreement or Disagreement of any *Ideas*.

Secondly, Judgment, which is the putting *Ideas* together, or separating them one from the other in the Mind, when their certain Agreement or Disagreement is not perceived, but *presumed* to be so; which is, as the Word imports, taken to be so before it certainly appears. And if it so unites or separates them as in Reality Things are, it is *right Judgment*.[47]

In this passage, judgment involves the combination of ideas just as much as their separation and examination. Locke especially stresses that this covers those instances in which the mind joins ideas in a rapid and superficial way—a 'loose survey'—which in Book II, Chapter 11 was ascribed to, or associated with, the quality of wit. There is even a strong similarity between what he says here about judgment, and his description of the principle of the association of ideas in Book II, Chapter 33 of the fourth and subsequent editions of the *Essay*, 'Of the Association of Ideas'; and here Locke sees association (some association) as evidence of madness in the mind. His description, in Book IV, of wrong judgment as faulty relations made by a lazy mind between ideas, reminds the reader that Locke's description of false association is only that there is a 'Connexion of *Ideas* wholly owing to Chance or Custom'.[48] False association is simply wrong judgment, induced by the mind's dependence on chance and custom, its inability to go deeply into the relations of ideas every time a particular configuration of ideas crops up. However this *wrong* judgment is not an independent faculty but an aspect of the same quality as can lead man to that limited truth which is often his only knowledge of how things really are. Even though 'judgment' is man's access to right thinking, it is essentially a casual thing. Because of man's inherent laziness and imperfection, it is as likely to be wrong as right. It is not, of itself, a virtue or a good thing, merely a neutral, though powerful, part of man's nature.

What stops Locke from making a *system* out of his thoughts on association and the conjunction of ideas is that he does not conceive of human psychology wholly in terms of an aspiration towards perfection. Man can never aspire to a pattern of absolute knowledge, not while he remains in 'that state of mediocrity and probationership [God] has been pleased to place us in here'.[49] Locke does not set up the goal of paradise on earth. That he does not do this is a fact of some significance. Later associationist theorists, notably David Hartley, make this goal very clearly part of their arguments: association can lead man to divine and absolute knowledge. Armed with Locke's ideas, and with their unshakeable belief in analogical argument which they claim to inherit from Newton, they evolve the concept of a necessary response to God, in which the association of ideas plays a crucial part. From Locke's casual faculty of association, they develop a system of reflex religion. That Locke ignores or does not care for this pattern is, I suggest, what Sterne sees as his great virtue.

There are one or two points in the text of the Author's Preface which help to substantiate this argument. One of these comes early in the Preface: Tristram actually mentions the paradise on earth which would be the result of all men being filled up to the brim with judgment: 'a paradise on earth, if there was such a thing to be had'.[50] Tristram later takes care to acknowledge that this early 'exordium' was only rhetoric, and thus definitively to disallow the idea of this earthly paradise.

Elsewhere in the Preface, Tristram lets fall one small

indication that he shares Locke's values as regards the true relations between man and God. This is the short comment in which he directly associates the idea of right proportion with the sense of man's perpetual intellectual twilight. He is talking of the sun and moon:

> of these two luminaries, so much of their irradiations are suffered from time to time to shine down upon us; as he, whose infinite wisdom which dispenses every thing in exact weight and measure, knows will just serve to light us on our way in this night of our obscurity.[51]

This is something Locke expresses strongly in his chapter 'Of Judgment':

> as God has set some Things in broad day-light; as he has given us some certain Knowledge, though limited to a few Things in comparison . . . So, in the greater part of our Concernment, he has afforded us only the twilight, as I may so say, of *Probability*.[52]

Only when there is no external pattern visible do Tristram's claims of right proportion stand up. Even as he is making this remark about 'exact weight and measure' he is having to destroy another pattern, from which he has been trying to argue. This is the British weather, which, three paragraphs earlier, he has claimed exerts a consistent influence upon the British temperament. He has decided that as we live in a 'warmer and more luxuriant island', we have a great deal of both wit and judgment: 'the *height* of our wit and the *depth* of our judgment, you see, are exactly proportioned to the *length* and *breadth* of our necessities'.[53] But then he has promptly had to contradict himself, when he realises that the British weather is anything but a consistent pattern:

> sometimes for near half a century together, there shall be very little wit or judgment, either to be seen or heard of amongst us . . . then all of a sudden the sluices shall break out, and take a fit of running again like fury.[54]

The only pattern he is left with is God's pattern, the 'measure and number and weight'[55] to be found in the Creation. Unlike so many other writers, he is unwilling to put this pattern, these designs, to work. It is the only pattern for which he has any real respect; like uncle Toby in Volume III, Chapter 41, his respect is manifested in his unwillingness to argue from it.

Putting the two Locke-sections of *Tristram Shandy* next to each other in this way suggests that Tristram's presentation of Locke is based on a consistent self-contradicting. In Volume II Locke appears to be referred to approvingly; but this approval is qualified by the underlying comparison between Locke and Toby. In Volume III, Locke seems to be ridiculed; but on a close inspection, he can be shown to come off quite well. In each case, the counter-reading hints at a more accurate awareness of Locke's values and character as a thinker than does the more conventional wisdom displayed on the surface of Tristram's prose.

6 Sympathy and Sentiment

Large claims have been made for Sterne's sentimentalism. R. F. Brissenden says that without it, *Tristram Shandy* would not be a real novel: 'What transforms *Tristram Shandy* from an exercise in learned satire or dramatic rhetoric or obscure bawdry is primarily its sentimentalism.'[1] John Traugott even goes so far as to claim that sentimentalism is incorporated into Tristram Shandy for its value as a way out of the Shandys' communicative impasse:

> Solipsism and sentimentalism—these are the two faces of Sterne's coin. This is the way he defines the fall—as solipsism, and the way he redeems the fallen—by sentimentalism.[2]
>
> Sterne's sentimentalism is his greatest glory.[3]

On the other hand, there are commentators who stress that Sterne, especially in the *Sentimental Journey*, often seems to be satirising sentiment. Sterne arranges sentimental 'traps' for the preconditioned reader to fall into. Between these two camps are other critics who hedge their bets (as well as providing the best approach to the problem) by saying that Sterne's attitude to sentimentalism is equivocal in the highest degree.

As with the question of Locke, I do not want to provide a complete discussion of the problem. Rather I should like to try to define Sterne's approach to it by relating it to the main argument of previous chapters of this book, the argument about the constructive breaking of pattern. Much the same procedure will be adopted in the final chapter, in respect of the *Sentimental Journey*.

The central sentimental episode in *Tristram Shandy* is the sermon, in Volume II, Chapter 17: central because it raises so many more questions than it answers. There are other sentimental set-pieces in the book, notably the Le Fever story in Volume VI—and of course the characters, especially Toby and Trim, quite often act or speak in a sentimental way. But I do not think the Le Fever story is really *about* sentiment—it panders a shade more grossly to the sentimental reader's taste than is usual in *Tristram Shandy*, and is the only place in the book where a positive and enthusiastic benevolence in a character (Toby) has a positive and encouraging result—Le Fever's son receives constructive help. The sermon is a much more thorny and complicated affair. Before looking at what happens in Volume II, though, there needs to be some explanation of why sentimentalism appears in Sterne's works not as a doctrine but as a problem.

When a commentator advances the opinion that *Tristram Shandy* and *A Sentimental Journey* have sentiment accepted into them as a force for positive good, he often finds that he can support his argument by saying that Sterne accepted a sentimental background, and went along with a climate of thought which stressed the benefits of sympathy and fellow-feeling in both personal and social relations. For instance, Brissenden says that

> Whether Sterne intended it or not, *Tristram Shandy* may be read as an illustration and verification of sentimentalism—of the psychological and moral theories advanced by Shaftesbury, Hume and Adam Smith.[4]

Traugott echoes this:

> Though the phenomenon of sentimentalism in Sterne's age may well be an intuitive development of a new principle of cultural coherence at a time when the mystique of Church and State was being rapidly attenuated, selfconscious applications of the concept ranged from the puerile elevation of vague benevolistic feelings to a religious principle to Hume's carefully defined doctrine of sympathy.[5]

It is certainly tempting to see such backgrounds as materials which play some causal role in establishing the taste for literature of a sentimental kind. However it does not explain why the best works of this type—the ones that read best today—are sentimental *comedies*, the novels and plays of Goldsmith, Sheridan and Sterne, which go beyond acceptance of a tradition and seek also to qualify it, to put it into perspective. The acceptance of traditions, and the acceptance of sentiment, leads to Henry MacKenzie's *Man of Feeling*, not to the sentimental comedies.

The general aim of the sentimental comedies is to point out the ways in which benevolence and sentiment can become comical when they are overindulged—rather as Shakespeare's *Timon* shows how a man can turn generosity into a fault by not realising that he has given away all his property. If you exaggerate a virtue, it becomes a potential vice, or ridiculous. It is a fine rhetorical technique, pushing something to extremes to show that no idea is good or moral in itself, but only in the way it is used.

But this is not quite the way Sterne works. Although there are strong links between his novels and other sentimental comedies, his books differ in that they hint at a much more precise knowledge of the character of the background from which literary sentimentalism has developed.

It seems to me that some of the characteristics of plot which the physical sciences, the idea of gravity and the post-Newtonian associationist psychologies and physiologies take on when viewed through the peculiar filter of *Tristram Shandy*, also appear in the background to Sterne's sentimentalism. In the *Sentimental Journey*, they develop around the systems of morals and of aesthetics which have traditionally been regarded as the sources of the book, the works of the Latitudinarians and Cambridge Platonists, and of Shaftesbury and Hutcheson. Both the *Journey* and *Tristram Shandy* explore a tension which exists between this cultural background and the more scientific background to sentiment. The cultural tradition insists that sentiment is a directional, positive force: the scientific tradition, try as it might to acquire or support the benevolent and upward-seeking qualities of the moral and aesthetic writers, lays bare the radical amorality of sentiment and sympathy. It is a tension of this kind, between claimed directionality and shown neutrality of power, which constantly underlies Sterne's attitude to sentimentality. The wider cultural background will be discussed in the next chapter, in relation to the *Journey*. As the scientific background has already been partly described in Chapter 3, and as it is of more interest to *Tristram Shandy*, this is a good place to invoke it.

The frequency with which the word 'sympathy' appears in the writings of medical writers of the early eighteenth century is, of course, a symptom of their post-Newtonianism. Originally this is sympathy in the purely scientific sense of a harmony and correspondence between man and the physical macrocosm: but this analogy is parent to other sciences.

For instance, although Robert Whytt uses 'sympathy' in its Galenic sense of a harmony among the different parts of the body, thus:

> Our bodies are, by means of the nerves, not only endowed with feeling, and a power of motion, but with a remarkable sympathy, which is either general and extended through the whole system, or confined, in a great measure, to certain parts[6]

he also uses it to explain man's susceptibility to suggestion from external stimuli:

> now it appears that there is a still more wonderful sympathy between the nervous systems of various persons, whence various motions and morbid symptoms are often transferred from one to another, without any corporeal contact or infection.[7]

The doctrine of the association of ideas in the eighteenth century depends on the premise that there is a natural sympathy between some ideas, so that one of them 'upon its appearance, naturally introduces its correlative'[8]—to re-quote David Hume. The same premise of sympathy is applied to social relations. For instance Hume, in the *Treatise*, goes on to infer from the association of ideas 'a like association of impressions',[9] impressions meaning, in this case, something close to emotions. From this he develops his theory of an innate 'moral sense', or, as he calls it in the *Treatise*, 'sympathy'.

But because this sympathy is derived from the principle of association, it must always be limited to the automatic transition of feeling from one person to another. Something which emerges most strongly from the *Treatise* is the inadequacy of any system of ethics or morality based on a vision of this kind of harmony. Humean man can never feel sympathy *for* someone, only sympathy *with* them. David Mercer says that

> As far as the genesis of sympathy goes . . . it appears that there is no question for Hume of sympathy involving an agent's imaginative realisation of another's feelings. His notion of sympathy seems more akin to the instinctive response which is emotional infection than to the exercise involving imagination and self-consciousness.[10]

The background to the idea being what it is, this could hardly have been otherwise—unless the writer has been conditioned by the presence of the argument from design into assuming that sympathy must be a naturally positive force. Hume is in a way very untypical of the thought of his age, in that he knows exactly how far his principle of 'sympathy' can legitimately be taken. He recognises it as a law of behaviour, not a moral value in itself. This awareness is well expressed in a letter of Hume's to Adam Smith, in which he discusses Smith's *Theory of Moral Sentiments.*

> I wish you had more particularly and fully prov'd, that all kinds of Sympathy are necessarily Agreeable. This is the Hinge of your System, and yet you only mention the Matter cursorily in p. 20. Now it would appear that there is a disagreeable Sympathy, as well as an agreeable: And indeed, as the Sympathetic Passion is a reflex Image of the former, it must partake of its Qualities, and be painful where that is so.[11]

In *Tristram Shandy*, there seems to be a clear separation of this kind of sympathy from true or cognitive sympathy. On the one hand there is the reflex association of mood between, say, Slop and Walter. Slop is ridden off his horse by Obadiah; is angry; curses Obadiah. Walter becomes angry; makes a fool of Slop (to 'balance the account', one might say); Slop and Walter begin to glare at each other . . . and Toby breaks the pattern. Toby's sentimentality is quite closely defined by the episode in which he lets the fly go (in Volume II, Chapter 12).

He does not let it go out of sympathy, not out of this kind of sympathy. The proper sympathetic response to being annoyed by a fly is to be annoyed, and to flatten the fly. That Toby lets it go is due to a sympathy which is well out of the reach of association, and which is even actively opposed to it. His sentimental values are a good answer to the ethics of the necessary response. He breaks up harmony, as Tristram says in Volume III, Chapter 5: but this harmony or 'concord' he breaks is merely sympathetic association of mood. In breaking this circle of reflex emotion, he creates peace. The irony is that he has no idea that this is what he is doing, because being deaf to this harmony, he cannot be engaged in such a circle, and cannot feel its power. His own powers are accidental.

This raises some questions about Walter's responses to his brother's disarmingly sentimental moments—to the look of 'inexpressible good-will' in Volume III, Chapter 5, or the 'gleam of sunshine' in Volume IV, Chapter 2. Is Walter's response cognitive? Is it valuable enough to be called a redemption from the 'fall' of solipsism? Or is it in fact just another passive association of mood, a sympathetic response to Toby's benevolent beam?

In fact, Sterne makes Walter's reactions much more complicated and subtle than this. If one considers, for example, the scene in the early chapters of Volume IV: Walter on the bed in silent misery over the catastrophe of the crushing of Tristram's nose, with Toby sitting beside him. When Walter feels the force of Toby's sunny smile his grief melts in an instant and he appeals to his brother for consolation. But as Toby does not share Walter's grief (a nose is no more than a nose to Toby) all he can do is to provide a military association—Walter falls back on to the bed. Toby and Trim then follow up this association, and tell the story of the grenadier whipped for stealing ducats. Walter is taken completely out of himself by this story and by the sentimental manner of its telling, and his mind is composed enough at the end of it for him to address Toby rhetorically on the subject of affliction. So in a sense he *has* been brought out of his private world. This is what Toby wanted to do—console his brother. But this communication is not achieved sentimentally, through Toby's feeling for Walter: it is achieved through Walter's reactions to the irrelevant sentimental story. The story first forces him to blush; then to smile; then to look grave. At first he finds Toby's feelings embarrassing (Toby unwittingly implies that Walter is grieving over nothing): then he finds him amusing: then he remembers that Toby's story is really irrelevant. The episode switches fluently between sentiment and a delicate humour, between the communication of feelings and the privacy of the characters' personalities. This fluency is characteristic of Sterne's control of sentiment when he is dealing with the relationship between the Shandy brothers rather than making a set-piece out of something like Toby and the fly, or Le Fever. It certainly goes far beyond either accepting sentiment as a general positive force, or satirising it as mere reflex: and it seems that it is Sterne's awareness of the different kinds of sympathy that enables him to pay his characters this compliment.

When eighteenth-century writers fail to set up this distinction between two kinds of sympathy, they often make statements which, although they are 'sentimental' in the widest sense, are inadequate and even logically false: 'A fellow-feeling makes one wondrous kind',[12] says David Garrick; but it need not. It all depends what the other fellow is feeling. Rousseau makes the same mistake in the *Origin of Inequality*: 'Compassion must be, in fact, the stronger, the more the animal beholding any kind of distress identifies himself with the animal which suffers.'[13] As before, it does not follow. Cruelty can be a fellow-feeling as much as compassion; an identification with the distress of a sufferer may as easily take the form of sadism (de Sade's writings are nothing if not feeling). If the other fellow is feeling vicious, you may have a situation such as Faulkland, in Sheridan's *The Rivals*, describes when he expresses his fears about the effects of a country-dance:

> If there be but one vicious mind in the Set, 'twill spread like a contagion—the action of their pulse beats to the lascivious movement of the jigg—their quivering, warm-breath'd sighs impregnate the very air—the atmosphere becomes electrical to love,and each amorous spark darts thro' ev'ry link of the chain![14]

Faulkland, true to his character in the play, is being neurotic.

Another less worried person would describe these effects as natural. But he does manage to make the point that what happens is not under the control of the individuals in the group, nor does it belong to the positive kind of sentimentalism which he would like it to stand for. Miss Sukey Shandy, in one of the many contemporary imitations of Sterne's book, also manages to convey the fact that, in a very special way, sympathy between people makes the good society possible:

> sympathy is a favourite subject of mine. When two lovers fix their eyes on each other, they must undoubtedly receive mutually a subtile matter from this meeting of their visual rays, which, thrilling through the nerves, pervades the whole nervous system, and often produces sensations more exquisite than are felt in the very act of enjoyment. This, whether the general hypothesis be true or false, I experienced whenever I saw the young Celadon, who made the first impression upon my heart; and these sensations were by no means strongest in the optic nerves.[15]

One would like to think that Miss Sukey was the original young lady who removed the hyphen from that line of Garrick's.

THE SERMON AND ITS CONTEXTS

It may seem strange to go straight from such frivolities as Miss Sukey Shandy to a discussion of that apparently serious document, the sermon in *Tristram Shandy*. None the less, some of the lessons that the sermon teaches are not dissimilar to the point which that young lady so delicately made about the twin personalities of sympathy.

The fascination of the sermon lies in the sheer variety of ways in which it makes its effect, and in the fact that its lessons, though they are taught in several ways, are all variants of the same lesson. It is the finest of Tristram's Chinese boxes: each of its levels illuminates the others. What these levels have in common is that they all stress the amoral nature or effects of some higher authority which is invoked for its moral qualities. Each shows an untrustworthy macrocosm, and shows also the quixotism of a correspondence made between a higher power which is invoked for its qualities of order and certainty, and the idiosyncratic world of men. But trying to sum up the sermon in a sentence is very hard. It is better to treat things one at a time.

There are three ways of looking at the sermon in *Tristram Shandy*.

Firstly, as a document which is important for its own sake and is to be considered separately, for what it says. Seen in this way, the sermon is an excrescence on the fabric of the book, a large lump of extraneous matter. This it certainly is, and this is how it is most likely to be seen on a first reading.

Secondly, as a device used by Tristram to illustrate his characters, or to further their development. This involves treating it in its immediate context of being read by Trim to Walter, Toby and Slop, and seeing it primarily as a reflecting device.

Thirdly, as an integral part of the mighty engine of Tristram's plot. This involves considering the sermon in a much larger context, as part of a process of causation which ends in the misfortunes of Tristram's birth, and thus considering it as integral to the novel's development as a whole. I would now like to look at each of these aspects in turn.

I *The Sermon: 'The Abuses of Conscience'*

Technically speaking, the sermon (and indeed the contexts in which it is delivered) is worked by the device of irony through self-contradiction.

Tristram—or rather Yorick—or rather Sterne, because it is after all a real sermon designed for duty in a Yorkshire church—begins by showing the audience the device quite clearly, in its unironic form of rhetorical self-contradiction. The first three paragraphs state as received truth the fact that mankind can see and know the depths of their own characters, and that man's conscience must therefore be an adequate law unto itself. The reader is not surprised to find this statement rhetorically contradicted very quickly, as it has been set up in order to be knocked down again, or at least to be heavily qualified.

He is not surprised because he remembers the difficulty

Tristram has previously experienced in 'coming at' specific characters (bewailing the lack of 'Momus's glass in the human breast' in Volume I, Chapter 23) and he remembers also Tristram's refusal to discuss his own character, and indeed to describe systematically anyone he cares for. In short, the reader has seen this discussion under different guises several times before the sermon is reached. So he ought not to be surprised when the sermon moves on to describe the impossibility of full self-knowledge and self-awareness, and on again from there to an appeal that the individual should put himself under the guidance of the universal laws of 'religion and morality'. He should submit to the common forms of conscience, the settled laws: the sermon finishes with a legal simile along these lines:

> No, God and reason made the law, and have placed conscience within you to determine . . . like a *British* judge in this land of liberty and good sense, who makes no new law, but faithfully declares that law which he knows already written.[16]

An absolute authority, a higher power, is invoked. Arthur Cash goes so far as to call the sermon's final paragraph 'classical'. 'Sterne is advocating the ethics of "right reason" so closely associated with the classical values.'[17] Sterne's words even have a Miltonic ring about them: they were perhaps suggested by these lines from *Paradise Lost*:

> And I will place within them as a guide
> My umpire Conscience, whom if they will hear,
> Light after light well us'd they shall attain,
> And to the end persisting safe arrive.[18]

But in fact Sterne is up to his old tricks again, telling and showing the reader different things. The process of contradiction has now become invisible, lurking beneath the surface of the text. A great deal of the material with which these 'classical values' are illustrated is nothing more than a 'flap upon the heart' of the listener, an emotive demand that the audience, as individuals, should feel in a certain way about the figure of the prisoner in the Inquisition's dungeon—

should feel emotional sympathy. Sterne, in short, does not practise what he is preaching. He preaches the absolute laws of morality: he practises emotional bullying via the doctrinaire anti-Catholicism of his rhetoric. It is really an amoral sermon. Its apparent argument is paralleled or denied by the call to respond to the words in an unthinking, reflex, sentimental way. It is this tension which is brought out, rendered visible, in the close context.

There is a strong suspicion that in the sermon and the scene surrounding it, Sterne is toying with the meaning of the word 'conscience', and of the title-phrase, 'The Abuses of Conscience'. The word has some ambiguity about it in the eighteenth century, an ambiguity which in later times is only present when 'conscience' is used with some sense of its French meaning being present—as when Conrad uses it in his phrase about Henry James, 'the historian of fine consciences'.[19] In French the word means 'consciousness', and this is also an obsolete English meaning. The third definition that Samuel Johnson gives of 'Conscience' in his *Dictionary* (in 1755) is

> Consciousness: knowledge of our own thoughts or actions. —'Hector was in an absolute certainty of death, and depressed with the *conscience* of being in an ill cause'. Pope.[20]

The sermon, as well as being a description of the abuses of conscience which the characters (the Inquisition) perpetrate, is a description of the abuses perpetrated by the writer on the consciousnesses, the sensibilities, of the audience. More evidence of these abuses comes to light when the close context is considered.

II *The Close Context*

The reading of the sermon emphasises the divisions and contradictions in its text. Brissenden claims that the discrepancy is between the sermon's message—that 'it is not merely enough to act and believe in accordance with your own heart and conscience, good though you may think these are'[21]—and its effect on the audience, or rather on its speaker, Trim. But the 'content' of the sermon is not just its message. It is also in the built-in stage-effects, the scene of the Inquisition's prison to which Trim responds so quickly. Trim does not get anything out of the text that was not put there by Sterne. His sentimental reaction to the sermon emphasises the sentimental aspect of what he reads.

Another element of his behaviour emphasises just how thoroughly this side of the sermon contradicts its ostensible 'message' and its classical values. This is his posture, carefully described by Tristram before Trim starts to read. It is a natural, graceful posture (though unsuitable in every respect for rhetorical delivery, according to W. J. Farrell[22]), but regulated (by Tristram) with infinite precision: 'He stood before them with his body swayed, and bent forwards just so far, as to make an angle of 85 degrees and a half upon the plain of the horizon',[23] and the regulations are the 'common forms' of the approved aesthetic law: 'but so as to fall within the limits of the line of beauty'.[24] The grace of Trim's posture gradually dissolves as the Inquisition-scene builds up: he blushes, breaks into tears, drops the sermon, claps his hands together, stamps his feet and gives up. By the time the final paragraph is reached, his posture has been completely shattered. He is in no position at all to heed the classical values of that paragraph.

Trim's distress is paralleled by the distress of the figure in the sermon, the prisoner. The two men are linked by Trim's brother Tom, whom the reader suddenly discovers is also languishing in an Inquisition prison. The similarity between the three men lies in their enforced passivity. In each case that passivity has a strong tendency to become suddenly and unwittingly active, even malevolent, as soon as it comes into contact with other elements of the scene. The sentimental distress of the two prisoners wrecks Trim's composure and destroys the balance of his mind and body: and in its turn, Trim's sentimental distress as he reads becomes part of a systematic plot. This is a plot against the character of Dr Slop. In this process of sentimentality turning into an active but unwitting conspiracy lies the self-contradiction of the close context.

Slop's problem is really circumstances (in fact he has trouble with them all through Volume II). Here, 'circumstances' manifests itself in Trim's just happening to have a pathetic brother in Portugal in the Inquisition's prison, and in Tristram's just happening to bring him to Trim's mind at this point. As a result of these circumstances Trim's sense of frustrated helplessness increases, and he loses his temper at the behaviour of the Roman Catholic church, which of course is controlling the Inquisition. As feeling rises against Catholicism in general it must also rise against Slop, who is the nearest representative of that faith. Slop, as Walter perceives, is 'incensed' by Trim's response to the sermon: not only does it portray his own church in a bad light, it also reflects discredit on him personally.

The sermon works against Slop in several ways, making him appear both unfeeling and stupid. But although this seems a one-way process, it also reflects back on to the sermon and demonstrates its inadequacy in the present situation. By any standards that the sermon can set up, Slop is a failure as a character. He is put ideologically and emotionally in the wrong by being forced to uphold the Inquisition. That he does so demonstrates (or so the sermon has it) his lack of the right principles and laws. He is also put pragmatically in the wrong by his fruitlessness, his inability to do things right, to open his bag, to deliver Tristram properly: for the sermon says, '*By their fruits ye shall know them*'.[25]

But the fault is hardly his own. He upholds the Inquisition before he or anyone else is aware that the sermon paints such an emotive picture of its effects; and from the first moment that the reader sees him (crossing himself) he has behaved and spoken (when he has had the chance) in accordance with the established laws and principles of his church, yet never in a fanatical way. His principles are not really at fault. Brissenden says of the sermon,

> the wretch who perishes in the *auto da fé* perishes because of a principle: 'this principle, that there can be religion without mercy'—he is killed, in short, because of the intolerance of a system, because he gets under the hooves of a particularly hard-driven Hobby-Horse.[26]

The paradox is that Slop, who comes under such heavy oblique fire in this situation, drives no horses. Earlier chapters of Volume II (Chapters 9 and 11) show him as a man much more ridden against than riding. There is an obvious physical example of this in his encounter with Obadiah at the corner of the garden-wall: but he is also ridden against by Tristram. It was Tristram after all who set up the time-scheme whereby Slop and Obadiah should just happen to meet there. It was Tristram who took pains to draw his brief satirical portrait of the doctor in Chapter 9, and wreck his character by 'coming at' it so directly. And in Chapter 11, it was Tristram who directed another crass causality of coincidence against him. This chapter is the only place in the entire book where Tristram promises the reader 'hidden causes' and then goes through with his promise: 'truce, good Dr. *Slop*!—stay thy obstetric hand;—little do'st thou know what obstacles;—little do'st thou think what hidden causes retard its operation!'[27] Slop has in fact left his bag, with all his instruments, behind. The whole episode is based on a coincidence: Slop has only ridden out on speculation, 'taken a ride to *Shandy-Hall* . . . merely to see how matters went on',[28] without being aware that Mrs Shandy is in labour. He rides into a situation where every kind of circumstance is against him. He is almost a pure passive agent. What the reader is made to watch is merely what happens to him. The contrast between the Shandys and Slop is absolute, in that his character has nothing to do with what happens to him, nor with our opinion of him. If we were in any position to notice, we would say that his riding out 'to see how matters went on' spoke for his good character. All we in fact register is that he has left his bag at home. For the moment Tristram is only interested in establishing this contrast, and in the crassness of the causality which is to surround Slop, which he will use to different effect in the scene of the reading of the sermon.

Both the closer and the wider contexts turn the sermon's maxim of '*By their fruits ye shall know them*' into an irony. Slop actually believes that he is in control of events, but the book as a whole shows the reader that what happens is completely out of his hands, except in the strict literal sense.

Trim is not 'wrong' to feel or to express himself as he does, but what he does to Slop (and the fact that he does not realise he is doing it) emphasises the ultimate *in*delicacy and even unfeelingness of his apparently feeling response. It also demonstrates the inadequacy and even tyranny of the sermon in demanding this strong emotional response from all its auditors.

III *The Wider Context*

In its turn, Slop's enforced passivity as he sits and suffers, watching Trim orate the sermon, becomes part of a larger active system, directed against yet another helpless character. Tristram as unborn child is the ultimate sentimental character, because he has absolutely no power to fight back at anyone. The sermon is a definite link in the plot against Tristram-as-foetus.

This plot begins with the characters of Walter and Toby, and with the pure coincidences—Obadiah's unseating Slop, Mrs Shandy's inopportune labour. Walter's character dictates that the sermon shall be read, and the reading of the sermon adds insult to Slop's injuries. Circumstances pile up, the furious doctor cuts his thumb, curses Obadiah: Walter makes Slop read the curse of Ernulphus. As a consequence (though it is never stated that it *is* a consequence) Tristram has his nose crushed by the irate and exasperated (though the reader is never shown Slop delivering Tristram) man-midwife. This is where the sermon's flap upon Trim's heart has helped to get the book. On each of three levels sentiment has become a conspiracy. Either the moral message has been encased in an amoral medium, rhetoric, or a feeling response has turned out to be unfeeling, or virtuous and distressed characters (Slop is both virtuous and distressed) are made to perpetrate acts of violence.

After writing the sermon-scene, Tristram explains Walter's ideas about sympathetic correspondence between body and mind, in Chapter 19. It is not surprising that Tristram goes on to qualify his father's theories: he has just written a scene in which he has demonstrated to the reader the pitfalls inherent in a different type of automatic sympathetic response. Walter is really insisting, wth his theories, that everyone is as much at the mercy of his emotions as Trim was while he was reading the sermon. Perhaps this explains (on a naturalistic level) why Walter tends to mistrust emotions and to place his faith in systems of ideas instead.

When R. S. Hafter was discussing Sterne's 'ambiguity', he came to the conclusion that Sterne does not 'charge his prose with multiple levels of meaning' (Chapter 1, note 32 and ref.).

In a sense this is quite true. All that Sterne does as far as the actual writing, the style, is concerned, is to engage in correspondences—pun, metaphor, double entendre and so on—which offer the reader alternative interpretations available on the same level. Yet there is no doubt that *Tristram Shandy* is somehow 'charged', that it manages to go beyond mere ambiguousness. (James Joyce, when he was trying to explain the nature of his ambitions in writing *Finnegans Wake*, gave *Tristram Shandy* as an illustration of what he wanted to achieve: 'I am trying to build many planes of narrative with a single esthetic purpose... did you ever read Laurence Sterne?'[29]. This charge is given to the book by the correspondences between text and background which inform the writing. All the moods, themes and events of *Tristram Shandy* can, should the commentator wish, be discussed separately, as distinct and autonomous. Sentiment in the book can be taken on its own or referred outward to a sentimental background; but there is a single background which is relevant not merely to sentiment, but also to the cannonball that strikes Toby in the groin; to John Locke; to the characters' wayward associations and obsessions; to the theme of consolation; of literary correspondences; to the sources of action and motivation in the book; even to the *form* of the book. A large number of the phenomena of *Tristram Shandy* seem to have a point of reference in this single intellectual area. But a great number of them also have another common point of reference, in that they form part of an exploration of a purely novelistic problem, the relation between plot and character. Everything goes forward on these two levels at the same time; the background is metamorphosed into the elements—not the story—of a novel. And of course the *story* is something different again. *Tristram Shandy* contains many different books, including a story about the eccentricities and tribulations of a group of Yorkshire characters—just as *Ulysses* (to go back to Joyce) contains among all its other elements, what would be (could Joyce have told it differently) a rather straightforward and interesting story about a younger man and an older man who are in some sense looking for each other, and who in some sense find each other.

7 *A Sentimental Journey*

The case to be presented about *A Sentimental Journey* can best be introduced by way of noticing a paradox which emerges when the *Journey* and *Tristram Shandy* are considered together.

Tristram Shandy is written as if it were a documentary, a retrospective approach to certain characters, Walter, Toby, and so on. Tristram accepts their reality, accepts that they are not fictions nor figments of his own imagination. 'He is their Boswell,' says Edwin Muir.[1] Yet *Tristram Shandy* in no way reflects this sense of a common reality. It reflects its narrator, Tristram. It is not well designed to show off its characters, who appear almost by accident, a glimpse at a time. The book is wayward, perverse, and solipsistic.

A Sentimental Journey, on the other hand, appears to be written in an impressionistic way by a man who has little visible concern to tell a definite story, or to give the reader any sense of an objective reality. Yorick's interests are ostensibly the description of, and participation in, various separate sentimental incidents. All that these incidents have in common is that they seem to be open to Yorick's sentimental interpretation of them. Structurally there is little to connect them—except Yorick's personality. The *Journey* ought to be as elastic in form as *Tristram Shandy*; yet it is not. In this book things tend to follow from one another in a clear and connected way, obeying the finest laws of the traditional novel. The principle of cause-and-effect is not used to tease the reader to the extent that it is in *Tristram Shandy*. There is also a strong sense of a communal, linear time-scheme present through much of the book: Yorick begins at the beginning in Dover, goes carefully through the middle and finishes simultaneously at the end of Volume II, the end of the story, and the end of the 'fille de chambre'. He digresses only to apostrophise or to tell short illustrative stories.

This paradox leads immediately to a crucial question. What

should be the reader's attitude to Yorick's apparently competent presentation of reality? Should Yorick be accepted as an adequate narrator? Can his undoubted eccentricities, his egoism and his enthusiasms, be dealt with from within his own frame of reference, or do they require a more radical treatment?

It has frequently been observed that the *Journey* brings out Yorick's 'vanity', the egoistic or self-generated nature of his search for the sentimental scene or person. He tends to transform everything he meets into a sentimental object, irrespective of whether or not they are definitely and certainly sentimental. From this, one may infer that he is solipsistic and egocentric. Thus Cash says of the first scenes of the book,

> Yorick is in a mood to think the entire world made up of 'kind-hearted brethren', albeit many 'fall out so cruelly' through a love of material goods. Obviously, Yorick is infatuated with the idea of courtesy and kindness . . . Yorick sets out on his travels possessed of that not-uncommon vanity by which, seeing benevolence indiscriminately in all humanity, he can assume it in himself.[2]

And he says that Yorick is 'smug'. John Stedmond criticises Yorick in the same way, saying that he 'flirts with the idea of philanthropy',[3] that his continual pose as the 'man of sensibility' indicates that he is trying to live up to a 'self-imposed ideal', an obsession with benevolence.

This attitude to Yorick is more or less universal. He is taken very much at face value, and criticised for his limited and imperfect vision. But in a sense it is Yorick who comes out on top in this exchange of views. His ability to persuade his readers that he can be criticised in this way, is Sterne's triumph.

Gardner Stout repeats the same criticism, but at the same time he almost gives the game away. He says that

> Yorick's benevolent impulses are the counterpart, in an 'Age of Sensibility', to Don Quixote's chivalric ideals; and he gives them free rein in the justified faith that they are in harmony with the divine SENSORIUM of the world. As a result, the Sentimental Traveller posts into quixotic dilem-

mas which dramatize the comic frustrations of sentimental knight-errantry. These dilemmas arise partly from the conflict between benevolent idealism and the Shandean realities of an imperfect world. But they also arise from the fact that, unlike Don Quixote's exalted motives, Yorick's benevolent impulses are themselves radically imperfect.[4]

Stout compares Yorick to Don Quixote half in jest, as if it were no more than a good and exact comparison. But if we look back to *Tristram Shandy*, we find Sterne equipping him with several attributes of Cervantes' character. He rides a horse as decrepit as Rocinante. He is careless of what others think of him, and is unperturbed or unaware of the effect he has on others. So his 'vanity' in the *Journey* seems to be an essential part of his character.

He is not exactly a quixote, in *Tristram Shandy*: there are other characters who take over the role of quixote in that work, notably Toby and Walter. However, in the *Journey* Yorick's Hobby-Horse, benevolence, is specific and consistent enough to draw attention to its pedigree. His obsession is the obsession of a quixote with his texts. Both the essential ingredients for quixotism are present: the replacement of reality by a fixed code representing a limited aspect of reality (benevolence, sentiment, and their expression in print), and the tilting, the energy or eagerness involved in the enthusiastic pursuit of that particular windmill which the quixote sees as giant.

Suppose Don Quixote, instead of merely reading the chivalric romances in his library and interpreting the world in their light, had written his own book. How could the reader have know that it was written by a madman? Don Quixote, after all, could charm his audiences with wonderful sane discourses on real knights and real historical wars.

So perhaps the reader should beware of taking the charming and deceptive sanity of the book at face value. As it is Yorick who is giving us the book, it is more important to acknowledge that he is a quixote than that he is quixotic about anything in particular. It means that naturalistic criticism of him is rather like criticising Don Quixote for being under the control of the romances. If Don Quixote's motives are exalted, they are exalted because his texts tell him that this should be so. If Yorick's motives are imperfect, this must be because they have been dictated by his texts.

It is a curious fact about eighteenth-century fiction and drama, that the theme of the quixotic character emerges and develops at about the same rate as do the trends towards sentimentality: the sentimental comedies of Sheridan and Goldsmith contain characters (Mrs Malaprop being the most definite) whose function is to be overwhelmed by books or by the literary qualities of language ('allegory' for 'alligator', 'illegible' for 'eligible' and so on). The sentimentalist school of novels is accompanied by the named quixotic genre which grows out of Fielding's play *Don Quixote in England* (1734) and Charlotte Lennox's *The Female Quixote* (1752)—this eventually encompasses the many examples mentioned in Chapter 1, as well as Smollett's *Launcelot Greaves* and all the Cervantic characters in Fielding's novels.

All that Sterne does is fully to integrate these two traditions. The *Journey* is of course like the sentimental comedies in some ways—the notion (or the abuse) of universal benevolence is examined as critically in Goldsmith's *The Good Natur'd Man* as it is in Sterne—but no other example manages to involve the reader of the book in the quixotic equation. And no other writer is so much in control of his sources, and knows so well the history of the situation.

Yorick does not directly name his texts, mainly because this would make the book more transparent than Sterne wants to have it. However a likely place to find them would be in those sources which are generally reckoned to constitute the background to both *A Sentimental Journey* and Sterne's sermons. It has long been accepted that the *Journey* is in some way a development from the writings of the Latitudinarian divines of the late seventeenth century (who preached doctrines of universal love and natural benevolence in reaction against the reprobatarian fiercenesses of the Puritan preachers: 'Parson Yorick their successor', says R. S. Crane[5]), from the Cambridge Platonist school, from the third Earl of Shaftesbury and the 'Moral Sense' writers whose ancestor he is. These writers are also accepted as an important element in the background to Sterne's sermons—which were published as *The Sermons of Mr. Yorick.* The sources of the sermons thus become the quixotic raw material. It is sources of this nature which determine that Yorick's quest should take the form it does, a search for correct sentimental behaviour and for the virtue (or virtu) this represents.

Some hints as to Sterne's reasons for wishing to show the sentimental background in this rather derogatory light were put forward in the previous chapter, and in Chapter 3. They will be substantiated in the latter part of this chapter. It may at first seem rather unlikely that Sterne should wish to make comedy out of this background. He is after all a liberal, tolerant and humane writer (most of the time), and this background represents the mainstream of liberal, tolerant and humane writing in the early eighteen century. There is no doubt that Sterne-as-priest believes in a great many of the things that these writings stand for.

However Sterne-as-novelist has different values from Sterne the priest. In particular he has a far more critical attitude towards the inadequacies and inconsistencies in the background to his own sermons, especially as they manifest themselves in naïve attitudes towards ideas involving metaphysical correspondence. It is almost true to say that *A Sentimental Journey* is written *against* the sermons.

If a professional philosopher (John Laird) is consulted on the question of Sterne's sermons, one finds that he is not very impressed:

> the general framework of Sterne's pulpit orations is so correct, so easily satisfied with its correctness, and so incurious of its grounds that philosophy is not its name . . . But if the philosophy in Sterne's sermons was not very strong, their benevolence was.[6]

It is hard to see how anything so smooth and 'official' (Laird) as the sermons could directly inform Sterne's fiction. There are other radical differences between the two forms, for instance in their attitudes to character. Sterne-as-priest uncritically takes up the notion that there is a perfect correspondence between souls and bodies, and that this lets the observer see into a man's soul.

> Nature has assigned a different look, tone of voice, and gesture, peculiar to every passion and affectation we are

> subject to; and therefore, to argue against this strict correspondence, which is held between our souls and bodies,—is disputing against the frame and mechanism of human nature . . . The mind will shine through the veil of flesh which covers it, and naturally expresses its religious dispositions.[7]

Sterne-as-novelist takes very direct issue with everything expressed here, in the 'Momus's glass' passage in Volume I, Chapter 23 of *Tristram Shandy*, as well as in the general attitude of 'riddles and mysteries' he establishes when trying to fathom character. And the belief in strict correspondence between mind and body is Walter's belief (in Volume II, Chapter 19)—not Tristram's or Sterne's.

But the most important aspect of the relationship between the *Journey* and its background is that Sterne does not draw excessive attention to it. *A Sentimental Journey* is not *The Sentimental Quixote.* What is comic in the book does not come from what is sentimental in it. The positivist nature of Yorick's sentimentality is only a single aspect of his more general enthusiastic optimism about life. His sentimentalism only becomes naive when his use of *words* is seen by the reader as being naïve.

Yorick is a great reader, an inveterate interpreter. His book, the *Journey*, is as much about the problems of reading as *Tristram Shandy* is about those of writing. Yorick rarely presents himself as the writer or narrator of *A Sentimental Journey*: he provides a record of his reading of the world—of his interpretation of events. The reader in turn has to interpret Yorick's text. But this is an activity fraught with difficulties. Yorick is possessed of a great confusion between reality and verbality, between things, events, and things and events as told in words, and this confusion is preserved everywhere in the text. There is no viewpoint on Yorick, no second omniscient narrator. The world is Yorick's text: he feels impelled to provide a 'commentary' on it, to 'translate', as he puts it, the gestures and actions of men into phenomena which are comprehensible in terms of his own system of benevolence. When he goes to the theatre in Paris, he does not watch the play. The audience, for him, are the actors, the real world aesthetic. All nature becomes his book.

The reader is never told that Yorick's reading of this book is wrong, or even partisan. However most of the scenes in the *Journey* admit of other readings than Yorick's. What the reader makes of the book will depend, of course, on the nature of the reader. He can read one thing into it, or another: but basically the text of the *Journey* is neutral. It says one thing, and at the same time implies satire of it. But at bottom it is neither one thing nor the other. It is about the reader being forced to read, to make his choice.

Q. D. Leavis was probably the first to complain that the history of responses to *A Sentimental Journey* is a history of very partial responses.[8] This is quite true; I think it is Sterne's intention that it should be true. And Thackeray's complaint about Sterne, that he can always feel him looking in his face to see his reaction— 'He is always looking in my face, watching his effect, uncertain whether I think him an imposter or not'[9]—is perhaps not so much a complaint as the reaction of an exceptionally shrewd reader.

In attempting to describe the *Journey*, I shall look first at the text itself: some of the points which emerge will then be applied to the background, to see if any analogy between text and background can be suggested. But it may be wise, before beginning, prematurely to outline the nature of this analogy.

As was noted in the previous chapter, there is, in the background to the *Journey*, a confusion between directionality and neutrality—between an optimistic and positivist world of moral and religious thought, and a physical, scientific world which aspires (or should aspire) to neutrality and objectivity. In the text of the *Journey* one finds a similar confusion between the positivism of Yorick's interpretation—his readings *into* his text, into the external world of events and behaviour—and the underlying neutrality of the reading experience, the radical amorality of the suspension of disbelief. The sentimental concerns of the book are explored through the deployment of this more purely literary technique. However this is a great deal easier to demonstrate than to explain.

I TEXT

It does not take long for Yorick to start feeling 'benevolent'.

He leaves for France; he arrives in Calais; he has a good dinner of a 'fricasee'd chicken' and Burgundy wine, and benevolence rises up. Even the contemplation of the 'Droits d'aubaine',[10] the French king's right to seize the goods of those who die while travelling on his land, cannot stop him from feeling well-disposed towards the king. Yorick does not say that it is the chicken and the wine that have made him so jolly. He merely mentions them. It is just a small preliminary hint that his feeling could have a physical origin.

Then two little ironies occur. First of all Yorick brings out his memories of recent philosophy and says that because he is feeling so good and so benevolent (he is already thinking of bringing out his purse as well as his philosophy) he cannot possibly be a *machine*. He conjures up his own hypothetical 'physical précieuse', a French blue-stocking who would argue (following fashionable but scandalous models such as La Mettrie's *L'Homme Machine* (1747)) that men run on mechanical principles—and he confounds her argument before he has even allowed her to open her mouth. But by just happening to choose unfortunate phrasing, he demonstrates his unawareness of the terms of the argument. That his body is working smoothly— 'Every power which sustained life, perform'd it with so little friction'[11]—is, if anything, evidence that he *is* a machine, in the sense of being a collection of parts working to sustain the motion of the whole. The slip of phrasing raises many questions about the nature of Yorick's feelings.

The irony is carried over into Yorick's encounter with the mendicant monk, who enters the room when Yorick's desire to prove his benevolence in terms of hard cash is running high, yet who receives nothing. As so often, Yorick manages to leave an essential piece of information just below the surface of the prose. The monk is 'of the order of St. Francis'.[12] The Franciscans are a Catholic order. We know from *Tristram Shandy*, from the presentation of Dr Slop, the kind of prejudice an Anglican priest might be expected to have against a Catholic monk. Yorick claims that his response to the monk is a whim, a spur-of-the-moment random decision. But as before, his words conspire against him: he says, 'I was predetermined not to give him a single sous'.[13] The irony is that Yorick, who has just been happily claiming that his post-prandial self-approving joy shows him to be above the power of mechanism, now responds by conditioned reflex, in perfect instinctive tune to an old prejudice. He once more demolishes his own philosophical grounds, by his carefree reference to something of crucial importance. In the course of trying to present his response as a whim, he says 'there is no regular reasoning upon the ebbs and flows of our humours; they may depend upon the same causes, for ought I know, which influence the tides themselves—'.[14] By which he means that our humours may depend upon the movement of the moon, to which he now proceeds to declare his allegiance. Had he been speaking as author there would have been nothing wrong with this: his declaration would then have paralleled Tristram's Dedication to the moon in *Tristram Shandy*, as acknowledging a source of poetic inspiration. But the moon is not allowed to be that kind of moon. There is, by 1768, a great deal of reasoning on the moon which controls the tides, and on the laws of gravity which enable it to do so. There is also much reasoning which uses the analogy between the physical and the human orders to apply that knowledge to man's humours. Yorick's statement, taken logically, is a flat self-contradiction. At the bottom of what he says is the pronouncement that a great deal of regular reasoning can be done upon the ebbs and flows of our humours. This, of course, is exactly what he has been trying to lead the reader away from.

Having unwittingly given the reader this small diagram of his own internal scene, Yorick sets off on a long series of readings of the world around him. He begins with the object closest to hand, the monk. As in the philosophical remarks which form the prelude to the book, one part of what Yorick says contrasts with and points up the rest. He begins by making the monk common property between himself and his readers: 'The rest of his outline may be given in a few strokes; one might put it into the hands of any one to design.'[15] This is in deliberate contrast to what happens in the next chapter, where Yorick appropriates the monk wholly to himself. He interprets the monk's physical gestures and movements (which are in point of fact completely equivocal) in the light of his own personal reading of the monk, his own conception of him. To give one example: Yorick, finding excuses for not giving him any money, mentions the '*great claims*'[16] made hourly on the world's charity. The monk glances briefly downwards. He might be shy/embarrassed/disappointed/sorry/angry that Yorick is not going to shell out. But Yorick, who (one might conjecture) is feeling guilty about his own reasons for not wanting to part with his cash, interprets the monk as continuing to importune, to press his claim. The monk could have been dismissed with a shake of the head, but Yorick prolongs the scene. What should have been a trifle has become the subject of a whole episode, and the contrast with the previous chapter emphasises that this disproportion occurs because Yorick has replaced *neutrality* of reading by *directionality* of reading. There is the same incongruity in Yorick's dwelling on, and solidification of, the moment's feeling, as there is in his reading and interpretation of the world. Yorick takes words and feelings and uses them as separate units or counters, instead of considering them in their passing flux and flow.

His search for sentimental behaviour can perhaps be said to be incongruous in a similar way. As Stedmond says, he goes off in search of an ideal, his own image of The Good Man. He wants to 'learn better manners as I go along',[17] he wants 'knowledge and improvements',[18] standards by which to act, and he wants to get all these things from people (the French) who he thinks have got them already. If he were not forever trying to attain this ideal, he would not fall short of it so consistently. Instead of trying to produce actions which are in proportion with his immediate circumstances, he aims for something nobler. Again the incongruity is between flux and system, the contingency of a world and the selective drive of a vision of that world. Yorick's search, in short, is based on a particular reading of the world: and Yorick's reading is often to be felt as a misreading by the reader who (to use Goethe's phrase) has not been primed for his explosion; been preconditioned to want to respond as Yorick responds.

The alerted reader may laugh at Yorick for his strenuous, quixotic search after truth, or may condemn him for his demonstrable moral failings—for his continual sly confusion of the ethical, material and sexual regions, for instance: the Holy Grail of ideal behaviour will keep reverting back into a 'purse' for Yorick to put his 'crown' in. But if the reader does this he is claiming, by implication, a higher moral vision than

Yorick has, and claiming that Yorick could have succeeded in his search. Such a response is the equivalent of those passages in Cervantes where, to his gratification, the Don finds that the world has fallen in with him and is giving proof to those around him that his visions—or his reality—are real.[19]

Several incidents in the early part of the *Journey* emphasise the connections between these various incongruities, by making small chains of cause-and-effect which tie them all together. For instance, in the first of the three chapters called IN THE STREET—CALAIS, Yorick begins the process by examining an emotion (suspicion) he finds engendered in himself. He crystallises it out and fixes it: as he describes his suspicions of Mons. Dessein to the reader, the emotion itself rises up and controls not only Yorick but the text of the book. The power of words then rises up in its turn. Yorick bursts into a vocal harangue against his own feelings, of which he feels ashamed. The spoken word overwhelms him: he is inebriated with the exuberance of his own verbosity. Finally, in the best traditions of the quixotic, the power of verbosity overwhelms the 'real' dramatic world of the book, as the lady with black silk gloves responds seriously to Yorick's address to his own emotions: 'base, ungentle passion! thy hand is against every man, and every man's hand against thee—heaven forbid! said she'.[20] In the last of the three chapters headed THE REMISE DOOR—CALAIS, Yorick's parading and naming of his own emotions once again saturates the text and replaces the dramatic world. He runs through the various reactions of AVARICE, CAUTION, COWARDICE and so on, to the proposition that he should offer the lady with the gloves a seat in his chaise as far as Amiens. Finishing his soliloquy, he turns to the lady—'But she had glided off unperceived',[21] leaving Yorick without the courage to run after her.

These same incongruities, the disproportion of action depending on a disproportion of reading, are commented on in the second of these three chapters. Here the relationship between 'text' (the drama in the real world) and 'commentary' (the reading or interpretation of that drama) is for once happy, but only because it is the lady who does the commenting. Yorick himself, and not the world he is interrogating, is the source of the 'text'.

The scene begins with Yorick getting text and commentary into their usual unusual proportions. He is making heavy weather of being left alone with the lady while Mons. Dessein goes back to get the right key for the remise door. He is, we may conjecture, embarrassed. By prolonging his remarks about how 'Fortune's whimsical doings' have left the two of them alone together, he shows his embarrassment—not to the reader but to the lady, who remarks on it. What she finds most noteworthy, however, is not his embarrassment but the evidence he gives of it, the 'reflection', the stream of words from him which puts the passing moment under the microscope: 'who but an English philosopher', she wonders aloud, would be making such a deal of business out of a trivial event?—and she disengages her hand from Yorick's with a look which he 'thought a sufficient commentary upon the text'.[22] Exactly: the commentary is no more than a look, but it speaks volumes to Yorick.

The fact that the descriptive words 'text' and 'commentary' are applied to this process also reminds the reader that Yorick is a priest, who has set out to find real-life texts to give his secular sermons on. The commentary on a Biblical text is usually much longer than the text itself, the verse from the Bible. But in real life the proportions are different.

Almost always, the French people Yorick comes across in the course of his adventures act *well*. The monk is modest; the lady reserved; Mons. Dessein helpful; le Count de B**** sympathetic (if credulous); the peasants in THE SUPPER, near the end of the book, hospitable; the Piedmontese lady delicate; even the beggars at Montriul organise their begging and control the scene decorously; the officer in the box at the Paris theatre relieves the distress of the dwarf. But their acting well never involves any attempt at conscious benevolence or sentiment. It means acting as the situation demands, responding in tune to specific stimuli rather than to anything more general—rather than to the 'great SENSORIUM of the world',[23] or to any preconceived ideal of behaviour.

As a concomitant of this, these people tend to be able to control words, and thus events, where Yorick cannot. The 'little French *debonaire* captain',[24] in IN THE STREET—CALAIS, demonstrates how to make words serve things and thoughts—by not stopping to worry about those words. He accosts the lady with the gloves, interrogates her, ascertains that she is from Brussels, and passes a few inconsequential remarks about that city. If one looks closely at his remarks they (and he) become foolish—telling the lady how finely situated for a siege is Brussels, and how nicely the inhabitants of her home town surrendered when he assisted at that event in the last war. But as passing remarks, chat, they merely hold the lady's attention as complimentary titbits. She makes a curtsey, and allows him to effect his own introduction. He asks the lady's name—whether she is married—without offence—and his intention is accomplished. All of this is pointedly in contradistinction to Yorick, who watches the exchange in an admiring, if rather patronising, English silence.

The French officer in the box at the theatre represents a culmination of all these French pragmatists, and is even allowed to express their unassuming viewpoint. One could almost say that he puts forward the Brobdingnagian viewpoint in Yorick's search for the Houyhnhnms. '*Le* POUR, *et le* CONTRE *se trouvent en chaque nation*; there is a balance, said he, of good and bad everywhere.'[25] If there is any vision at the bottom of *A Sentimental Journey*, this is it. Like Swift's it is a highly traditional, almost reactionary vision of proportionate, balanced and harmonic life and activity, and like Swift's it has to be inferred from the need for a presence to counter extreme elements in the world presented by the text, elements which the protagonist-narrator appears to endorse, and which the reader is thus encouraged also to endorse.

When he has managed to overcome his old prejudice against the monk's Catholicism, Yorick begins his more purely sentimental quest. He searches for the good in the world, seeks to 'cultivate the fruits it offers'.[26] He reads the lady with the gloves; she is widowed, and 'disquieted',[27] and in general in need of some benevolence—in short, she is a sentimental object. She isn't. She can take care of herself much better than Yorick: she knows how to cope with his gauchenesses. Yorick sees in her what he wants to see. He also tries to make us see what he himself sees in the scene in THE SNUFF-BOX—CALAIS, the sentimental exchange of snuff-boxes between Yorick and the monk. There is his reading (that it is a sentimental scene), but there is a counter-reading available (that Yorick offers the monk his snuff-box in order to impress the lady, who is watching, with his own generosity; and that the monk, who blushes, blushes at the transparency of Yorick's motives). What kind of scene it really was depends on the reader himself. There is only one scene in the book which is definitely and certainly sentimental—the scene at the inn at Nampont. It is the one time that Yorick takes no part in the action. He remains sitting in the post-coach while the peasant mourns his dead ass, and reports on a visible, external response to the sentimental object—the peasant—rather than recording the object itself: 'Every body who stood about, heard the poor fellow with concern.'[28] This time the sentimental data is unequivocal; it does not need reading. Every other sentimental scene is open to the POUR and CONTRE of conflicting interpretations.

An important stage in the *Journey* is where Yorick chooses to insert a 'Fragment' into the text. This is a digression in praise of the powers of love over the profligate and 'coxcomb' elements in man's nature. It takes the form of a description of the beneficial effects of a staging of the *Andromeda*, a play by Euripides, on the vicious and corrupt inhabitants of the town of Abdera. (The word 'Fragment' refers to the line Yorick quotes from the play, but the chapter is also headed A FRAGMENT.) Yorick intends this digression as a commentary on the 'text' of La Fleur's character, which, in the previous scene, has been described to him by the innkeeper at Montriul—'He is always in love', says the innkeeper, as La Fleur takes his leave of a selection of young ladies. Yorick is glad of this, thinking that if it is true there is no danger that La Fleur will want to steal from him—''twill save me the trouble every night of putting my breeches under my head'.[29] So in grateful praise of the positive powers of love, he inserts his Fragment.

But the Fragment, as Yorick presents it, is not so much about the power of love as about the power of theatrical representation, and particularly of one fine speech. The Abderites do not owe their new gentility and pastoral amicability to love, but to their enthusiastic reception of Euripides' play. And their enthusiastic interpretation of Euripides looks very like Yorick's own continual enthusiastic interpretation of his world. It emerges that Yorick is having his old trouble again, reading events solely in terms of his own preoccupations.

In particular, Yorick chooses to misread, to misrepresent, the inhabitants of Abdera. These folk are (or were) traditionally notorious not for their viciousness but for their *stupidity*. The article on Abdera in the 1910–11 edition of the *Encyclopaedia Britannica* says that 'The air of Abdera was proverbial as causing stupidity'.[30] In view of what follows, it is interesting that this is attributed to a kind of contagion, to something in the air.

If it were not Yorick who was telling this story, the Abderites' response to '*O Cupid, prince of God and men*, & c.'[31] might be seen as merely symptomatic of their behaviour, of their foolishness, and not a reformation of it at all. What would the laughing philosopher of Abdera, Democritus, say, faced with a city whose inhabitants were so foolish as to let words overwhelm reality and dictate their conduct?

This is Yorick's first interpretation of a real (i.e. literary) text. He is made to speak against himself in just the same way as he did at Calais, where he made his rather transparently naive statements dissociating himself from the idea of mechanism. The phrasing he chooses illustrates the essentially amoral nature of the response of any audience to a literary text. The Abderites' response is conveyed as a kind of emotional contagion—'The fire caught'. It is an instinctual, paramechanical sympathy, not a moral one. But Yorick interprets this response as being, *of necessity*, morally directional. He takes it for granted that this kind of sympathy will return the Abderites to paradise: 'Friendship and Virtue met together, and kiss'd each other in the street—the golden age return'd, and hung o'er the town of Abdera'.[32] He imports a foreign set of values, and translates the Abderites from passive fools into moral agents, first vicious then virtuous. On this process depends his partisan vision of love.

This episode is taken (as is Robert Burton's description of the same story in *The Anatomy of Melancholy*) from *Lucian*, from the beginning of the introductory letter to Philo in *The Way to Write History*. (This is in fact the only extant testimony to the existence of the *Andromeda*—so the single line that Lucian quotes is the only extant line of the play.) H. W. and F. G. Fowler translate as follows:

> My dear Philo,
>
> There is a story of a curious epidemic at Abdera, just after the accession of King Lysimachus. It began with the whole population exhibiting feverish symptoms, strongly marked and intermittent from the very first attack . . . The mental effects, however, were most ridiculous; they were all stage-struck, mouthing blank verse and ranting at the top of their voices. Their favourite recitation was the *Andromeda* of Euripides; one after another would go through the great speech of Perseus; the whole place was full of pale ghosts, who were our seventh-day tragedians vociferating
>
> 'O love, who lord'st it over Gods and men',
>
> and the rest of it. This continued for some time, till the coming of winter put an end to their madness.[33]

Lucian goes on to find a physical explanation of this—that it was a very hot day, that it was a real fever everyone caught, and that the stage-struckness was an effect or a symptom of this.

It will immediately be seen what Yorick has done with this story: his phrase 'the fire caught' is the only direct evidence of the original nature of Lucian's story.

Other writers in the eighteenth century also use the story of Abdera. There is for instance a very attractive one-act French playlet-in-verse called *Les Abdérites*,[34] which dates from 1737. This piece takes the form of a love-story set in Abdera, which is interrupted towards the end by the girl's father coming home from the staging of the *Andromeda* with his anger at his daughter's fiancé changed to complete acceptance and a gooey romanticism which even the lovers have qualms about. Being mad, madly angry, madly in love and in love with the theatrical conventions of love, provides a fine confusion. The elegant 'Vaudeville' at the end sums it all up:

CHORUS: Non rien ne plait si constamment
Que de jouer la Comédie . . .
Pour les sots, peut-on faire mieux
Que de jouer la Comédie?
CARITE (*in love*): Ah que d'aimer bien tendrement
Est une douce Comédie.

The most difficult section of the *Journey* to read, as well as one of the most interesting, is where Yorick, in Amiens, writes a letter to Madame de L***, the lady with the gloves. The problem is that although there is one set of implications which seems to offer a 'right' reading, this is heavily disguised and very difficult to reach. A great deal has been written out of this scene, in order that the reader should be confused.

These are the main points:

Madame de L*** has written Yorick a very neutral letter, in which all she says is that she would like to tell him her 'story' (she promised this story once before, but, à la *Tristram Shandy*, we never hear it) and he is to deliver, if he would be so good, a letter from her to Madame R. in Paris.

It is, in short, a faintly friendly letter, making use of a chance acquaintance to get a letter delivered. Now—

La Fleur does not know that it is this kind of a letter. This is the first twist of the plot. He runs to Yorick from his interview with Madame de L***, convinced that his master is engaged in amorous correspondence with the lady, and that he must instantly write a letter in reply to hers, which he has inexplicably omitted to do. La Fleur knows she has sent Yorick a letter—he was there when it arrived—but he does not know what was in it, because he left to go drinking with the servant who delivered it.

So he reads his own preoccupations ('he is always in love') into the situation, just as Yorick so often does. Yorick, knowing himself ignorant of the exotic and miraculous ways of the French, accepts La Fleur's misreading of the situation, because—and this is the second twist—he is not aware of La Fleur's ignorance of the contents of Madame de L***'s letter. He just accepts that La Fleur knows what is correct etiquette, and sits down to write a suitably vague letter in reply. Not having anything very much to say, he cannot compose. La Fleur springs to his aid, offering him a specimen of what will be acceptable, namely a letter arranging an amorous assignation. Oh really? thinks Yorick, continuing to accept La Fleur's misreading: he writes his paraphrase and sends it off in holy simplicity, back to Madame de L***. Madame de L*** thus receives an invitation to commit adultery, in reply to a request that Yorick should deliver a letter for her. What is more, it is possible that the gaucheries in the letter La Fleur gives Yorick do not strike Yorick as being gauche, and are incorporated into his own version. '*Chacun a son tour*'[35] says the letter hopefully, 'Everybody gets a go', which does tend to give the beloved something of the status of a coconut shy. Perhaps it is not surprising that no more is heard from Madame de L***.

The peculiar texture of this episode is due to the fact that no direct reference is made to the elements of the plot, to Yorick's and La Fleur's misreading of the situation. Instead the text concentrates resolutely on events, on physical detail and on the minutiae of the scene between La Fleur and Yorick over the letter. It is thus very easy to misread the scene, and even to take Yorick's letter seriously, as a congruous and acceptable response. Brissenden for instance has a whole page of analysis of the two lines

> L'amour n'est *rien* sans sentiment
> Et le sentiment est encore *moins* sans amour.[36]

This strikes me as being just the kind of alley up which Sterne would like the reader to go. As this diversion of the reader has been achieved by a conscious control of the methods of prose fiction—the careful disguise of the devices, the 'plot'—one can only presume that it is an intentional effect, that the reader is invited to a misreading.

In the chapter called THE WIG—PARIS, the barber indulges in a piece of Gallic hyperbole, in praise of the buckle on the wig he has made for Yorick: 'You may immerge it, replied he, into the ocean, and it will stand'.[37] He puts the favourable interpretation on his wig. Yorick is very interested in the barber's words and tells the reader he approves of such language, which he calls 'the French sublime'. In the course of this, he reveals his own peculiarly innocent attitude towards language in general, and also towards this interpretative movement of mind: 'In honest truth, and upon a more candid revision of the matter, *The French expression professes more than it performs.*'[38] Yorick makes the mistake of taking the barber's hyperbole half-seriously, of feeling a need to dismiss his claim: 'Paris being so far inland, it was not likely I should run post a hundred miles out of it to try the experiment—the Parisian barber meant nothing.'[39] Certainly he meant nothing: but as Yorick halts the flow of the barber's words, snips out the interesting phrase and holds it up to the analytic light of his own mind, he makes it appear that the barber did in fact mean something—that his comparison was of permanent and intrinsic worth. Looking this minutely at what is really only a tiny gambit in language-as-game ruins the effect of that gambit. It is a quite different thing from the barber's very causal hyperbolic saturation of the wig. The barber is a Frenchman, and as such knows how to keep things in proper proportion.

A Sentimental Journey, although presented in two volumes, divides into three roughly equal sections. Before he reaches Paris, Yorick is learning how to cope with and live up to what he conceives of as French 'manners'; when he is in Paris he tries to use what he has learnt—tries to be more French than the French, in effect—and after he leaves the city, the book tends to the rustic: Yorick is in reaction against the civility, smoothness and polish that Paris society has brought out in him, and which he thinks he has found in Parisian society itself.

The material in the second of these sections is divided between Volumes I and II. Sterne seems to have designed the two parts of this segment of the book to stand as counter-weights to each other, for the purpose of qualifying Yorick's apparent final disgust with Paris life.

In the scenes in the Paris shop in Volume I (THE PULSE—THE HUSBAND: PARIS—THE GLOVES) things go very well for Yorick. The beautiful Grisset is so complaisant that the episode has the air of a fantasy: as if in a dream, Yorick finds himself feeling her pulse. Everything that could have gone wrong, goes right. It all reeks of wish-fulfilment. When the Grisset's husband comes in, far from objecting to Yorick's holding his wife's hand, he thanks him for his trouble and goes out again without a second thought.

While he is caught up in this mood, and in the course of explaining to the reader the difference between the roles of the sexes in London and Paris, Yorick uses an analogy with physical friction. The women in Paris, he explains, do the work and run the shop, and

> by a continual higgling with customers of all ranks and sizes from morning to night, like so many rough pebbles shook

> long together in a bag, by amicable collisions, they have worn down their asperities and rough angles, and not only become round and smooth, but will receive, some of them, a polish like a brilliant.[40]

Only good things, it seems, can come of this sort of social rubbing: the evidence for this is in the character of the Grisset, who has been treating Yorick so smilingly.

But in the scenes in Volume II (THE PASSPORT—VERSAILLES and CHARACTER—VERSAILLES) which have to do with Yorick's passport (or the lack of it) things go very badly for him. His situation engenders purely negative emotions in him. He is worried, and digresses into various appropriate stories—when he fears that he will be sent to the Bastille, he writes the history of the caged starling. Everything is as generally unfavourable as the first scenes were favourable. He is in a tricky situation, which he gets out of only after a long wait, and thanks to the Count de B***'s mistake over his identity. And when the Count asks his opinion of the French, Yorick once more picks up that analogy, this time using coins as an example: 'by jingling and ribbing one against another for seventy years together in one body's pocket or another's, they are become so much alike, you can scarce distinguish one shilling from another'.[41] Yorick is about to draw the analogy between such faceless coins and the polished French character, when he seems to realise that this might be offensive, and stops himself. The image is almost precisely the same as before, but it is used to contradict the first. In each case the same thing happens: Yorick begins with a basically neutral, physical image and reads his own preoccupations into it. As his own internal and external states vary, so his words and opinions vary. One partisan positive and one partisan negative do tend to cancel each other out.

It is not exactly that Yorick has been responding mechanically; this would be putting it much too strongly. But as in the scene with the monk at Calais, he gets mixed up in the *idea* of mechanism. At Calais this happened through his claiming that he could not possibly be a machine, while simultaneously failing to take account of his being a physical creature, full of instinctive or conditioned reflexes. Here it happens because the nature of the image he chooses points up the fact that he is writing 'to the moment' and producing figurative language directly out of his emotions, without any abstract reflection.

In view of the relationship between the *Journey* and its background which the final part of this chapter will try to consolidate, it is of some importance to know that the first of these two analogies is taken from Shaftesbury, from the essay on 'The Freedom of Wit and Humour':

> All Politeness is owing to Liberty. We polish one another, and rub off our Corners and rough Sides by a sort of *amicable Collision*. To restrain this, is inevitably to bring a Rust upon Men's Understandings.[42]

It is interesting that the particular phrase Yorick reproduces, 'amicable collisions', contains the seed of that confusion or insouciant juxtaposition of the human and mechanical orders which has been remarked several times in Yorick.

The Count de B***'s belief that Yorick is the king's jester in *Hamlet*, and the fact that it is this belief which means that Yorick finally gets his passport, is another fine example of the real world become quixotic, sharing or confirming Yorick's confusion of real and verbal, or real and fictional realms. Sterne lets Yorick perpetrate one or two more small ironies with Shakespeare in Volume II. He lets him validate the book's title (*A Sentimental Journey through France and Italy*) by picking up a copy of *Much Ado About Nothing* (in itself an interesting title, given the nature of Yorick's interpretations) and transporting himself instantly 'to Messina in Sicily'. It is also interesting that Yorick should remember, at the start of Volume II, Polonius's advice to Laertes. It would be too much to expect him actually to quote.

> Give thy thoughts no tongue,
> Nor any unproportion'd thought his act . . .
> do not dull thy palm with entertainment
> Of each new hatch'd, unfledg'd courage.[43]

Yorick's happier moments in the *Journey*—and his more strenuously defensive moments also—are often accompanied by rhapsodic flights of language. The most extended of these outbursts is the apostrophe to Sensibility near the end of the book. He has left Paris, a little weary of flattering the nobility, and his relief at being once more surrounded by genuine and natural emotion leads him to write this panegyric on fine feelings. In fact the tone of the apostrophe is in harmony with quite a long stretch of the book, as it is carried over into the next few pages, into the scene where, depending on your reading, Yorick either barges into or is invited into the supper of the peasantry.

Although this curious and subtle piece of writing brings the philosophical concerns of the book to a head, it is hard to draw final conclusions from it. Yorick after all does not give arguments, he externalises, outers, his feelings, and he does so in an intense and very persuasive way. What he says is attractive. Yet what he says contains, as usual, evidence of its own inadequacy. Both the attractiveness and the inadequacy will be found to be identical to qualities in the background to the book. The reading of the passage given here tends to be partisan in the sense of concentrating on the inadequacies.

It is Yorick's meeting with Maria of Moulines which occasions the apostrophe; the powerful emotions born in him by this encounter have to find a more general vent than their specific object, Maria. When he is looking for her, he makes a very revealing comment. He compares himself to Don Quixote without noticing how good a comparison this is (he did the same thing once before, in the Preface). Out of this comparison comes another parallel with the concerns of the book's first few pages. He begins to talk about his *soul*, and about how searching for sentiment, for good feelings, makes him feel that he possesses such an item:

> 'Tis going, I own, like the Knight of the Woeful Countenance, in quest of melancholy adventures—but I know not how it is, but I am never so perfectly conscious of the existence of a soul within me, as when I am entangled in them.[44]

From this he manages to get back to his old theme of how he cannot possibly be a machine, cannot be accounted for by materialist hypotheses: he is wiping away Maria's tears, and his own, with his handkerchief, and

> as I did it, I felt such undescribable emotions within me, as I am sure could not be accounted for from any combinations of matter and motion.
>
> I am positive I have a soul; nor can all the books with which materialists have pester'd the world ever convince me of the contrary.[45]

When he did this at Calais, Yorick immediately contradicted himself, insofar as he was forced by his prejudices into a quasi-mechanical response to the monk. This gives a clue as to how the apostrophe might be read.

First, though, it might be interesting to hark back for a moment to the parallel scene in *Tristram Shandy*, to where Tristram comes across Maria in Volume IX, Chapter 24. Yorick in the *Journey* is preconditioned to sentiment: he is bringing half the entertainment along with him, as Toby would say. So is Tristram; but Tristram lets the reader into the secret rather more than Yorick does:

> For my uncle Toby's amours running all the way in my head, they had the same effect upon me as if they had been my own—I was in the most perfect state of bounty and good will; and I felt the kindliest harmony vibrating within me, with every oscillation of the chaise alike; so that whether the roads were rough or smooth, it made no difference; every thing I saw, or had to do with, touch'd upon some secret spring either of sentiment or rapture.[46]

So that as soon as he hears Maria's pipes, '—They were the sweetest notes I ever heard'. Tristram recollects the scene, and invokes the spirit of Cervantes (earlier in the same chapter) as standing over it: Yorick writes to the moment, and compares himself to Don Quixote.

But the strongest links are between the scene in the *Journey* and the sermon-scene in *Tristram Shandy*. They are both worked by the same device. The claim Yorick makes in the apostrophe, that his system of sentiment is ruled over by a higher power, is qualified or disvalued in the very process of making the claim. In *Tristram Shandy* the effect was achieved through chronicling the emotional audience reaction to the sermon's ostensibly 'classical' values; in the *Journey* it is all done with delicate phrasing.

At first Yorick addresses himself directly to 'Sensibility', to the quality in man which makes him a feeling being. Sensibility is called the 'source' of man's emotions, and by choosing his words carefully—'all that's precious in our joys, or costly in our sorrows'[47]—he manages to make it clear that he is ascribing to sensibility the positive value inherent in emotions. His phrasing demonstrates his assumption that man's emotions of joy or sorrow are natural forces for good.

At this point Yorick finds that he cannot make do with 'Sensibility'. In order to support his assumption that emotions have some inherent value, some positive direction about them, he has to assume the presence of another, higher, independent ordering principle. Negative and unsentimental emotions, he says, are not real emotions because they are not in tune with the universal vibrations:

> and this is thy divinity which stirs within me—not, that in some sad and sickening moments, *'my soul shrinks back upon herself, and startles at destruction'*—mere pomp of words!—but that I feel some generous joys and generous cares beyond myself—all comes from thee, great—great SENSORIUM of the world! which vibrates, if a hair of our heads but falls upon the ground, in the remotest desert of thy creation.[48]

So has Yorick changed his tune? Is he now saying that the source of man's rich emotions is not within him but comes from without? It does seem, as the passage continues, that he is not applauding anything in man, but an abstraction.

Is this abstraction *God*? The history of Yorick's reference to the SENSORIUM appears to confirm that he has God in mind. As Cash notes,[49] it was originally Isaac Newton, in a passage of the *Opticks*, who referred to space as the sensory organs of God—'His boundless uniform sensorium', in which He makes the heavenly bodies move according to the universal laws of motion. And Addison, in the *Spectator* no. 565, uses the concept approvingly, as if it were no more than a modern restatement of the ancient idea that God is a being whose centre is everywhere and whose circumference is nowhere.

So for the educated eighteenth-century reader, there is a natural association between a 'great—great SENSORIUM' and Godhead.

But on closer inspection this association begins to appear unwarranted.

The passage begins as an apostrophe to 'Sensibility'. Yorick addresses Sensibility as 'thou', and refers to 'thy divinity'. So two qualities of Godhead, the personal pronoun and the word 'divinity', have been used up before the SENSORIUM is mentioned. When he reaches it, Yorick switches the personal pronoun to the SENSORIUM, thus giving the reader the impression that he is talking about Sensibility in figurative language and that Sensibility, the SENSORIUM and divinity are all happily mixed up together. But he also applies an impersonal pronoun to it ('*which* vibrates')—and he does not directly invoke divinity. At the same time as he gives the SENSORIUM first place in the causal chain his language slips, and the precise status of his higher power vanishes into ambiguity. The first half of the sentence makes the SENSORIUM an active causal power—'all comes from thee, great—great SENSORIUM'[50]—and the second makes it both impersonal and passive.

This impersonality comes back later in the passage in a worrying way: 'Thou giv'st a portion of it sometimes to the roughest peasant'.[51] 'Thou', it seems, refers to the divine SENSORIUM, which gives some Sensibility to the peasant—but Sensibility has not previously been called 'it', but consistently 'thou'—it has had five or six personal pronouns applied to it. The only quality or force to have an impersonal pronoun applied to it is the SENSORIUM itself.

So who is 'thou'? And what is 'it'? It cannot be Sensibility giving a portion of the divine SENSORIUM to the peasant: the connection or analogy made between man's faculties of perception and those of the cosmic force is a very direct one, and needs no help from intermediaries.

Cash, in his reference to this passage, points out that the SENSORIUM being made to *vibrate* shows that Yorick is treating a Newtonian idea in the light of post-Newtonian sciences: Cash refers to 'the vibration theory of the nerves' (some practitioners of which, Cheyne, Morgan, Whytt, etc., have been mentioned in earlier chapters). In this tradition the nervous system of man tends to vibrate

1. in reflex harmony with the physical macrocosm
2. thanks to the presence of the design-argument, in har-

mony with the divine emanations which provide the physical harmonies of the cosmos.

But Yorick is saying that the SENSORIUM vibrates, that it is nervous-sensitive: if this analogy with vibration-theory is taken to be anything like precise, this means that the SENSORIUM is in turn dependent for its motion upon the emanations of man. The phrasing seems designed to support this reading: 'which vibrates, if a hair of our heads but falls upon the ground, in the remotest desert of thy creation'.[52] The SENSORIUM's vibration is passive, reflex and preconditioned. It depends on action in the mundane sphere, depends on stimulation, like man's nerves and not like God. It becomes very difficult to say whether the emanations which control the motion of the SENSORIUM are God's or man's. Evidence of the existence of a godhead in the universe is turned, by unsuspecting sleight of hand, into mere anthropomorphism.

There remains the question of why Yorick feels he has to engage with this higher power. He does so in order to justify his own assumption of the natural and necessary goodness of man. This bias is at its clearest at the end of the apostrophe: the peasant, touched with sensibility (or whatever it is) is 'gentle', 'generous' and 'happy',[53] and lives in the gingerbread land of Pastoral. He responds in sympathy with the bleeding lamb he finds—'his gentle heart bleeds with it'; but this not quite the independent sympathy of sentiment. Because of that reference to the SENSORIUM it also takes on overtones of reflex response, involuntary rather than positive. Yorick's vision is once more dependent on his reading, his selection of positive data—the fact that the shepherd is 'gentle'; that he too is primed for a response.

There also remains the question of what has happened to *God*, in *A Sentimental Journey*. He is conspicuous by His absence, except as everyone's favourite ejaculation—'Good God!' is Yorick's favourite—'Mon Dieu!'—'God help her!'—'My God!'—'God knows how'—'for the love of God'—'Just God!'—and, on the last page, from Yorick, 'O my God!'.

It is a nice touch on Sterne's part that the only God present in the *Journey* of Yorick, a clergyman, is the God of the Abderites: 'Twas only in the power, says the Fragment, of the

God whose empire extendeth from heaven to earth, and even to the depths of the sea, to have done this.'[54] And the power of this God is nothing but the power of *words*. He demonstrates His omnipotence through no directional force, but through the agency of the fictive emotion itself, the suspension of disbelief.

II BACKGROUND

A Sentimental Journey mocks the response Sterne knows it will create. The text appears continually to demand an enthusiastic attitude in the reader and, historically speaking, it certainly got this. It can hardly help creating this mood in the eighteenth-century reader, for it has as its narrator a man whose beliefs are firmly rooted in the dangerous and quixotic idealisms which form the background or the preliminary to the phenomenon of literary sentimentalism. These idealisms are of course very attractive, and very laudable, but they are none the less dangerous in their historical context, because they contain elements of a kind of philosophy which they would claim to abhor. They have a dual character, just as Yorick has.

Yorick belongs to an older generation than Tristram. The *Journey* is really an anachronism—Yorick (in *Tristram Shandy*) was in his prime before Tristram was born in 1718; yet here he is in 1768 writing an apparently contemporary book. This isn't poor chronology on Sterne's part, but a way of implying a certain perspective on Yorick. It seems safe to suggest that Yorick, although publishing his book in the 1760s, is actually a representative of the 1720s, and is seen through Sterne's more modern eyes with a retrospective and rather knowing gaze.

There is one figure from the sentimental background who is present in the *Journey* in a very real and immediate sense. This is Anthony Ashley Cooper, Third Earl of Shaftesbury. There are points in the *Journey* where Sterne seems to want Yorick to remind the reader not merely of a general background of thought, but of Shaftesbury in particular. The phrase taken from 'The Freedom of Wit and Humour' has already been noted. The apostrophe to Sensibility is designed to recall an idea central to both Shaftesbury and his Platonist ancestors, that human virtue is a reproduction, within the microcosm of the individual, of the proportion so manifest in the greater world: that the balanced personality reflects inwardly the harmony and order of the cosmos. As R. L. Brett puts it,

> By regulating his passions the virtuous man attunes himself to the harmony of the larger system . . . Everything . . . has its own particular place in the universe and is organised in a great chain of being, which stretches from the meanest of beings up to God.[55]

Probably the most that can be said about the other surface similarities is that Yorick tends to express opinions and attitudes rather like Shaftesbury's in a prose which is rather like Shaftesbury's. For instance, the most plausible stylistic progenitors of Yorick's rhapsodic upliftments of language are the astonishing outbursts of Theocles in 'The Moralists'. When Theocles looks with as much favour upon Nature as Yorick looks upon Sensibility with, his approbation is expressed in similar glowing terms:

> O GLORIOUS *Nature*! supremely Fair and sovereignly Good! All-loving and All-lovely, All-divine! whose Looks are so becoming and of such infinite Grace; whose Study brings such Wisdom, and whose Contemplation such Delight . . .[56]

and so on, at some length. When he is not indulging in rhapsody, Yorick's self-complacency about his own values leads him to express his sentimental enthusiasm in a relaxed and chatty style—assuming that spectres can be laid 'much more effectively by banter than by zeal',[57] as Basil Willey says of Shaftesbury and Addison.

It is interesting that Sterne should pick Shaftesbury out as a partial model for Yorick. Shaftesbury is the eighteenth century's second most popular philosopher after Locke—eleven editions of the *Characteristicks* between 1711 and 1790 (there are approximately nineteen editions of Locke's *Essay* in the century after 1690). It may well be that as well as these similarities of content and style between Yorick and Shaftesbury, Yorick is to Shaftesbury as uncle Toby was to Locke. The analogy between Yorick and Shaftesbury, when pressed further, hints at another side of Shaftesbury's authorial personality—in something of the same way as Locke was drawn into the Shandean web at the beginning of Volume II of *Tristram Shandy.* It emerges that the relations between Shaftesbury and his world have the same problematic and quixotic quality as the relation between Yorick and his.

One of the things that I hope the examination of the text of the *Journey* made clear is that although Yorick is confident that he and the external world get on well together, this is not really the case. He makes the dramatic illusion convincing: the scenes and events are ordered and accessible. Yet there is always evidence that the reality he portrays is not an objective, external thing but a figment of his own mind. Yorick shows himself to be a true solipsist: the true solipsism being, not knowing that you are in a state of solipsism. This problem is echoed in the apostrophe to Sensibility. Yorick tries to reveal another external world—a higher order controlling or presiding over the lower world of the quotidian (or dramatic) reality—but this revelation turns into another unconscious demonstration of the illusory nature of those external worlds.

Much of the same trouble is found in Shaftesbury's writings. When reading the *Characteristicks*, one quickly realises that the recognition and acceptance of an absolute external reality is an essential part of Shaftesbury's Platonism. This is the higher spiritual reality of which, in Platonist cosmologies, the physical world is a mere copy or imitation. All of Shaftesbury's moral and aesthetic doctrines centre on the idea of an absent perfection, the greater nature which it is 'natural' for man to try to attain, 'right' for him to strive towards. His Platonist outlook finds expression in his constant setting-up of absolute standards of virtue and of taste. J. M. Robertson, in his introduction to the *Characteristicks*, says that

> The gist of Shaftesbury's doctrine of morals, later systematized by Hutcheson, lies in his claim that it is self-evident 'that in the very nature of things there must of necessity be the foundation of a wrong and a right taste, relish or choice, as well in respect of inward characters and features as of outward person, behaviour and action'.[58]

The Platonic Ideal Model exists as a 'right model of perfection'; it can be actively sought and learnt. 'One who aspires to the Character of a Man of Breeding and Politeness is careful to form his Judgment of Arts and Sciences upon right Models of *Perfection*.'[59] Man is a creature who has fallen from grace, so he cannot be expected to have immediate access to this higher reality; but by means of a proper education, any English gentleman of fashion may be accommodated with an appreciation of those proportions and harmonies which constitute the divine presence in the mundane world. This once done, there would be no more disputing about taste; the right models would be acknowledged. Beauty and taste are enlisted on the side of the angels. Whatever is beautiful is, by definition, properly designed and proportionate, and is thus in tune with the higher reality; whatever is not beautiful, is out of tune: 'For nothing is ridiculous except what is deform'd; nor is any thing proof against *Raillery* except what is handsom and just'.[60] Beauty is thus the equivalent of virtue or 'moral truth':

> And thus, after all, the most natural Beauty in the World is *Honesty*, and moral *Truth*. For all *Beauty* is TRUTH. *True* Features make the Beauty of a Face; and true Proportions the Beauty of Architecture; as *true* Measures that of Harmony and Music. In Poetry, which is all Fable, *Truth* is still the Perfection.[61]

The foundation of morality and of right behaviour is a cosmic aesthetic vision: in proportion as man's taste (or as Hutcheson later called it, his 'internal sense' or 'moral sense') is 'right', he will appreciate what is beautiful, and what virtuous. Man is a social animal and naturally seeks good; therefore it is natural that he should have this sense.

It would be easy to apply wide-ranging criticisms to such doctrines. They look like ethnocentricity disguised as Platonism—Shaftesbury keeps his personal opinions about specific works of art and nature out of the *Characteristicks*, but this only postpones the question of how one can tell a right model of perfection from a wrong one, and how we are to tell whether or not we are in tune with the divine vibrations if our 'breeding and politeness' are not yet up to Shaftesbury's own—may we assume we are, or do we have to ask Shaftesbury? The problem is the same as is found with Yorick's Abderites. If people are convinced that they are in harmony with divine vibrations, there is no end to the foolishness they may feel themselves sanctioned to indulge in.

But rather than making these criticisms, I would like to examine the places where Shaftesbury tries to answer them. In the 'Letter Concerning Enthusiasm' and the essay on 'The Freedom of Wit and Humour' he comes face to face with the question of how the individual is to know his own condition, and how he is to interpret the data he observes in the world around him. In each case his answer reveals a short-circuit of thought, an unconscious solipsism. Like Yorick in the apostrophe to Sensibility, he cannot quite reconcile the individual with the higher authority that he needs to govern his system of moral sentimentalism.

Shaftesbury spends most of his time in the 'Letter Concerning Enthusiasm' being very sensible, accommodating and unsystematic about his subject. The underlying doctrine of the 'Letter' is that the power of 'true' enthusiasm can be used for good—that it can be a positive virtue if we can see and select those enthusiasms which are genuinely God-given. But Shaftesbury also takes pains to acknowledge the demonic and irrational aspects of enthusiasm—in Section II of the 'Letter', for instance, he describes the original Panic, the mob hysteria of a group of people who encountered the god Pan, and goes on to say

> One may with good reason call every Passion *Panick* which is raised in a Multitude and conveyed by Aspect, or, as it were, by Contact of Sympathy. Thus popular Fury may be called *Panick* when the Rage of the People, as we have sometimes known, has put them beyond themselves; especially where Religion has to do. And in this state, their very Looks are infectious. The Fury flies from Face to Face; and the Disease is no sooner seen than caught . . . Such force has Society in ill as well as in good Passions; and so much stronger any Affection is for being *social* and communicative.[62]

At the beginning of Section VII, his summing-up of the examples he has given is similarly balanced, realistic and understated:

> The only thing . . . I would infer from all this is, that ENTHUSIASM is wonderfully powerful and extensive; that it is a matter of nice Judgment, and the hardest thing in the world to know fully and distinctly . . . Nor can Divine Inspiration, by its outward Marks, be easily distinguished from it.[63]

So how is he going to reconcile this equivocal data with his directional doctrine?

He falls back on the assumption that man naturally has access to an objective reality, in terms of which he can judge his own nature:

> For *to judge the Spirits whether they are of God*, we must antecedently *judge our own Spirit*, whether it be of Reason and *sound Sense*; whether it be free to *judge* at all, by being sedate, cool, and impartial, free from every biassing Passion, every giddy Vapour, or melancholy Fume. This is our first Knowledge and previous Judgment: 'To understand *ourselves*, and know *what Spirit we are of*'. Afterwards we may judge the *Spirit* in others, consider what their personal Merit is . . . By this means we may prepare ourselves with some *Antidote* against Enthusiasm.[64]

It is instructive to contrast this with its apparent source, Locke's chapter 'On Enthusiasm' in the *Essay*. Locke takes pains to stress that '*Reason* must be our last Judge and Guide in every Thing',[65] and this means that nothing can be achieved by an individual by himself:

> It is not the strength of our private perswasion within our selves that can warrant it to be a Light or a Motion from Heaven: Nothing can do that but the written Word of GOD without us, or that Standard of Reason which is common to us with all Men.[66]

Shaftesbury does not set up this dialectic between rationality and irrationality. In his system, the only quality required for self-awareness and self-knowledge is 'good nature'. So where Locke says that you have got to decide for yourself—but with the benefit of other people's standards—about the nature of your own enthusiasms, about the nature of the light that arrives in your mind, Shaftesbury says that you must *know yourself*, that you yourself must judge whether you are fit to judge yourself.

—But how exactly do you judge whether or not you are fit to judge yourself?—

That is what every man must decide for himself.

Shaftesbury's 'Essay on the Freedom of Wit and Humour' reveals a very similar problem. The thesis of this essay is that, as all truth is above criticism and above ridicule, the truth of any statement or position may be tested by exposing it to satire. Wit and judgment, opines Shaftesbury, are not incompatible—indeed, wit may be used as an alternative or supportive to judgment. The right-thinking man, the man of good taste, will be naturally unable to bear ridicule of the truth: ridicule may thus act as an emotional winnow of intellectual wheat and chaff, separating the true from the false.

But as J. M. Robertson points out,

> his humane prescription led him subtly into a position not tenable without paralogism . . . No right-thinking man can endure ridicule of the truth. But the right-thinking person, who thus admittedly apprehends the truth without the help of ridicule, has nothing to do with the case; since the business in hand is to enlighten the wrong-thinking, the enthusiast who takes error for truth. And as this person errs about what is truth, he can obviously err about the rightness of ridicule; so that for him it is no test; while the other man, in the terms of the case, does not need this test in particular.[67]

The same thing could be said of the 'Letter': the man who is competent to judge will be doing so already, the man who is not will probably be convinced that he is competent to judge, and will also be doing so. Shaftesbury's assumption that he need only talk about the individual in his relation to the higher Platonic reality means that it is very hard for him to deal with the relations between the mundane world and the individual who finds he has to cope with it. Shaftesbury's optimism and humanity seem to relate only to his own private world, and not to the real one. In this lies his quixotism, and also his similarity to Yorick.

Another of Yorick's problems in the *Journey* seems to have been designed to suggest a difficulty which arises when Shaftesbury is considered in his historical context rather than for his own sake.

Yorick had trouble with the principles of materialism and mechanism. At Calais, and again in the scene before the apostrophe to Sensibility, he declares his opposition to the mechanistic view of the world while at the same time managing to ally himself with it. As was the case with his presentation of the world of the book, his claims and his actions do not quite match.

Shaftesbury is also a great scorner of materialism. He is so fond of his own viewpoint that he is forever making a *prise de position* out of it, telling everyone what he is not, and what he sees as pernicious. Stanley Grean describes this as follows:

> Unlike the Baconian empiricists . . . Shaftesbury follows the Platonic tradition, seeking to understand the order of Nature for its own sake . . . The inner reality of Nature will not be discovered by mechanistic analysis, but only by aesthetic intuition . . .
>
> In all his writings, Shaftesbury attacks the ancient materialists, Epicurus and Democritus, and their modern followers. The 'modern hypothesis' that the universe is an eternal system of self-regulating matter cannot stand up under analysis. For one thing, Shaftesbury shares the popular opinion of his age that mechanistic materialism could not account for the marvellous adaptation to environment by plant or animal organisms. And had not the great Newton even conceded that the organisation of the solar system could not be explained entirely in terms of mechanical causation? The universe may be analogous to a machine but, if so, Shaftesbury argues that it is intelligible only as a 'God-governed machine'.[68]

Unfortunately, this is not much of an opposition. Grean almost admits the problem when he refers to the more occult, less scientific side of Newton's cosmology. Newton himself would not be at all averse to calling the universe a 'God-governed machine'. His materialist physics is not incompatible with Platonism.

Shaftesbury's real target in this attack on materialism is not Newton, but the earlier writers such as Hobbes and Descartes, who for several decades had been the subject of attacks from Cambridge Platonists such as Ralph Cudworth. In 1678 Cudworth complained that the writings of such men

> make God to be nothing else in the world, but an idle spectator of the various results of the fortuitous and necessary motions of bodies . . . They make a kind of dead and wooden world, as it were a carved statue, that hath nothing neither vital nor magical at all in it.[69]

Yet it is Newton, not Hobbes or Descartes, who is the model for such a large amount of eighteenth-century mental activity; and Newton's science was, at first, rejected by true materialist thinkers as being far too vital and magical to be sensible. Like Cudworth, Newton can describe his viewed cosmos as a 'System', something 'above the power of mere machinery', and this spurning of mechanism as a guiding concept is also fashionable among the post-Newtonian scientists. It is easy and tempting to take the notion of the divine plan and stand it behind one's own purely physical system.

Towards the end of his study of Shaftesbury, R. L. Brett tries to separate out these two 'contrary' concepts of Nature, the Platonic and the scientific. Yet even as he does so, he has to stress their similarity:-

> Broadly speaking, there were two meanings that were assigned to the concept at this time: the first of these was the mathematical and mechanical order given to nature by physical science; the other was the harmonious order with which contemporary Platonism endowed nature. The two were often confused, for both interpretations stressed what seemed to be the same things and, superficially, they were in agreement. But fundamentally they were quite different. The one conceived the order to be precise, mechanical and immutable; the other regarded it as evolving and organic, and a revelation of the divine order to which it only approximated.[70]

This difference was not acknowledged at the time; instead,

the similarities were exploited: 'Materialism itself could scarce dispense with a divine hypothesis . . . the Great Machine presupposed the Divine Mechanic.'[71] Such a context is not the best of times to deliver Platonic broadsides against materialism. When Shaftesbury bases a fashionable, attractive, idealistic, popular philosophy on the principle of Platonic analogy, he does not sanction Platonism so much as license the use of argument by analogy, and the misappropriation of the design-argument by anyone who cares to use it.

In a sense, analogy was already the mode of religious and scientific perception and argument: Leibnitz, Spinoza, Hobbes, Descartes, all believe in the application of the 'geometrical' method of reasoning to the other arts and sciences. As they see it, all reasoning can ultimately be reduced to a universal mathematical science. At the same time, the religious philosophers of the age are also prone to express their beliefs in mathematical language—and this includes men in the Platonist tradition such as Samuel Clarke. But there is a difference between the applications of this way of thinking in the seventeenth and the eighteenth centuries. In the eighteenth century it comes to be used much more widely, by the new sciences which arise to examine questions about human behaviour, and in particular questions about the nature of virtue and morality. When Shaftesbury argues from the natural proportion, decorum and design of the physical universe to the equally fixed and immutable standards of virtue and of taste, he provides a licence for the application of mathematical scientific models to discussions of ethics and aesthetics.

Shaftesbury's offspring are not at all what one might expect. He would have been very surprised and probably disconcerted at the uses to which his thought was put. For instance, the spirit of this argument from the ratios of musical harmony to the absolute standard of virtue—

> 'Tis the same case where *Life* and MANNERS are concerned. *Virtue* has the same fixed Standard. The same *Numbers, Harmony* and *Proportion* will have place in MORALS; and are discoverable in the *Characters* and *Affections* of Mankind; in which are laid the just Foundations of an Art and Science, superior to every other of human Practice and Comprehension[72]

—is very different from Hutcheson's treatment of the notion of Perfect Virtue in the following decade:

> Since then *Benevolence*, or *Virtue* in any *Agent*, is as M/A, or as M + 1/A, and no *Being* can act above his *natural Ability; that* must be the Perfection of *Virtue* where M = A, or when the *Being* acts to the utmost of his Power for the *publick Good*; and hence the Perfection of *Virtue* in this case, or M/A, is as Unity.[73]

Yet Hutcheson's argument is only a logical extension of Shaftesbury's attitude—and Hutcheson is convinced that he is a protégé of Shaftesbury. He refers admiringly to him in the Preface to the 'Enquiry'. 'To recommend the Lord *Shaftesbury's* Writings to the world is a very needless Attempt. They will be esteemed while any Reflection remains among Men.'[74] And Hutcheson's similar vision of a '*calm, universal Benevolence*'[75] is attained by a similar optimistic moral positivism.

Shaftesbury and Newton each seem to contribute a great deal to the thought of this period, and to be equally available as models. Louis Bredvold says, apropos the optimism of the early eighteenth century, 'the hope of a millenium through exact science', 'The Utopianism of the age might be defined as the aspiration of every radical thinker to be the Newton of Ethics or the Newton of Politics'.[76] For, to quote Elie Halévy,

> What is known as Utilitarianism, or Philosophical Radicalism, can be defined as nothing but an attempt to apply the principles of Newton to the affairs of politics and morals. In this moral Newtonianism the principle of the association of ideas and the principle of utility takes the place of the principle of universal attraction.[77]

Yet the acknowledged father of the Utilitarian movement, Hutcheson, sees himself as Shaftesbury's child. Shaftesbury is forced by history into a position like Yorick's, scorning and at the same time embodying the principle of mechanism. All the points at which Yorick's sentimentalism leads him into difficulties and self-contradictions seem to have their counterpart in Shaftesbury's writings or in the tradition to which he belongs.

—But how exactly does it come about that the problems of Yorick, a representative of the thought of the early eighteenth century, can be felt to be of relevance at the date of the publication of the *Journey* in 1768? Does Sterne design his character as an historical curiosity, or are the problems created by Shaftesbury and Newton still lingering on in contemporary culture in some way?—

It seems to be the case that a great many of the mid-century writers on aesthetics do have some trouble with the legacies of thought bequeathed to them by previous decades. (I should explain that eighteenth-century aesthetics is not an autonomous area of thought, but an extension of the sciences of psychology, motivation and behaviour. An Enquiry into the concept of 'the beautiful', for instance, will not be about what is beautiful and what is not, but about what it is in man that makes him prefer or *choose* one object before another. Such problems tend, in the eighteenth century, to be explored through such questions as whether or not there is in any situation a choice which is naturally right. Shaftesbury's assumption of a naturally correct *taste* is a way of coming to a conclusion about this problem, as is Gay's assumption of potential perfect choice based on association in the preliminary dissertation to King's *Essay on the Origin of Evil*.) Many writers who seem at first to be upholding the values of sentiment, of human feeling, have to do so under the cover of classical science. This is well expressed in Gilbert and Kuhn's *History of Aesthetics*:

> after allowing for all the variety of utterances and definite notes of rebellion in the new British school against the 'rules', one is forced to admit that the kinship of the 'taste' they found on inner sense, sentiment, passion or intuition is more with Boileau's neo-classic rules than with Ogier's relativity of time and place . . . In tracing the aesthetic treatises of the British school of this period, one observes again and again that what seems to be a limited empirical function, a sense or a sentiment, is dilated or bent outward at need to include a mathematical law, conformity with the dominant moral ideal, or an abstract idea.[78]

It may be that when Sterne makes Yorick take overt refuge in the idea of a higher power controlling his system of sentiment, he is endowing him with a kind of contemporary honesty, making visible a problem which usually remains invisible. Some of the more extreme Romantic statements in the literature of the late eighteenth century still carry within them the legacy of a neoclassical attitude. When Rousseau's Savoyard Vicar says 'what I feel to be right is right, what I feel to be wrong is wrong; conscience is the best casuist',[79] this could only be accepted as a felt truth if it were supported by an unstated belief in the natural correspondence between 'right' emotions and an equally 'right', and thus divinely directed, cosmos. Were this belief not present, such a statement would be felt as anarchic, destructive of the individual rather than supportive. The classical 'sympathy', the harmony between the levels of a proportionate, designed universe, lies for a while behind the Romantic ideals of sympathy and sentiment (in the apostrophe to Sensibility, it is sensed in the reference to vibration theory). When the Vicar, a few pages later, says

> Although all our ideas come from without, the feelings by which they are weighed are within us, and it is by these feelings alone that we perceive fitness or unfitness of things in relation to ourselves, which leads us to seek or shun these things,[80]

the case is exactly the same. The neoclassical supposition that 'right' things can be sought, that some things were made right in order that man should be right in following them, lies behind the statement.

—But how exactly is Sterne's making Yorick a quixote—quixotic about words rather than primarily about sentiment—relevant to this situation? If Yorick were as sophisticated about words as, say, Tristram Shandy, how might this make a difference to his sentimentalism?—

It might make him understand something about the nature of sympathy. It might make him able to distinguish between the two different kinds of sympathy which he so often confuses, the cognitive and the contagious, the positive and the neutral. Equally, it might lead him to reflect that it cannot be the job of a literary artist to portray what seems to him to be an absolute external reality, whether this be his own dramatic, sensory world or a higher, controlling world. He could have learnt that most basic of Romantic truths, that art is communication from mind to mind.

He could have learnt these lessons simply by reading Edmund Burke. The work in which an argument about words is used as a counter to the classical legacies of thought is Burke's *Philosophical Enquiry into the Origin of our Ideas of the Sublime and Beautiful* (1758). There are other aesthetic treatises of the 1750s and 1760s which come close to using a similar approach to this problem—the chapter called 'Emotions Caused by Fiction' in Kames's *Elements of Criticism* (1761),[81] for instance—but the argument is placed in a more interesting and provocative way in the *Enquiry*.

Most of the *Enquiry* actually inclines to a kind of classicism—a scientific rather than a religious or aesthetic classicism: J. T. Boulton calls it

> A prize example of Newtonian experimental methods applied to aesthetics . . . The conclusion that Burke reaches—that taste operates by fixed principles in all men—illustrates the eighteenth-century inclination to discover immutable laws governing human life and activities. In the Newtonian tradition Burke looks for—and finds—immutable laws governing taste.[82]

Newtonian, because the laws he finds are the laws of the physical universe. He feels able to do without the design-arguments and the Platonic higher reality to which writers on aesthetics have, in the recent past, had recourse. He is a sensationist: all he needs to make his arguments work are minds and objects. Beauty, he says, is not a matter of a higher reality visible in the mundane world and apprehended by an internal sense, it is a force or quality in objects themselves: 'Beauty is, for the greater part, some quality in bodies, acting mechanically upon the human mind by the intervention of the senses',[83] meaning, in this case, the physical senses. However his scientific methods only lead him back, in the end, to conclusions he could have reached with the old methods: that there exist objective standards of beauty and taste which are founded on the regular and ordered laws of an external world—that the 'internal sense' is pleased or displeased 'from the same principle on which the sense is pleased or displeased with the realities'.[84] But then in the final section of the *Enquiry* (Part V), Burke proceeds to put into perspective everything he has said so far. He begins by restating the belief which has ruled everything he has said:

> Natural objects affect us, by the laws of that connexion, which Providence hath established between certain motions and configurations of bodies, and certain consequent feelings in our minds.[85]

Having said this very clearly, he then says that words are not things, and seem to him to belong to an entirely different case from natural objects—even from the representational arts which deal not with words but with things: 'But as to words; they seem to me to affect us in a manner very different from that in which we are affected by natural objects, or by painting or architecture.'[86] They affect by 'sympathy' rather than 'imitation'. Burke talked about sympathy and imitation in Part I, elevating them to the status of the two social passions, the forces in man which make him a social being. His sympathy is a neutral rather than a positive force: Burke makes no claims for its innate virtue or usefulness, but simply says that 'sympathy must be considered as a kind of substitution, by which we are put into the place of another man, and affected in many respects as he is affected'.[87] Other arts cannot be said to work by sympathy:

> In reality poetry and rhetoric do not succeed in exact description so well as painting does; their business is to affect by sympathy rather than by imitation; to display the effect of things on the mind of the speaker, than to present a clear idea of the things themselves.[88]

What he stresses is the intensity of the literary emotion, and not its moral or physical directionality. He acknowledges language as a separate level of reality in its own right. In so doing, he dissolves the notion that such levels are 'higher' or external to man, or in the control of any power except that of man's own limited and conditioned mind:

> by the contagion of our passions, we catch a fire already kindled in another, which might probably never have been struck out by the object described . . . Words . . . [are] able to affect us as strongly as the things they represent, and sometimes much more strongly.[89]

To read is to lay oneself open, like the Abderites, to 'contagion'. The sympathy of reading is like the sympathy of sentiment—like the sympathy of sentiment when it is not seen through the rosy filter of the design-argument:

> Sensibility . . . is for the greater part a quality of the nerves, and a result of individual bodily temperament . . . in its mere self . . . it proves little more than the coincidence or contagion of pleasurable or painful sensations in different persons,[90]

said Coleridge in 1825.

As has already been said, Burke's clearest expression of the influence of 'things' on our minds is virtually a paraphrase of the motto from Epictetus which stands on the title-page of *Tristram Shandy*: but there is a crucial addition:

> Certain it is, that the influence of most things on our passions is not so much from the things themselves, as from our opinions concerning them; and these again depend very much on the opinions of other men, conveyable for the most part by words only.[91]

This is something that Tristram understands very clearly: that fiction illuminates the writer's mind for the reader quite as much as it displays the writer's world. The world as it appears in novels is essentially a figment of the writer's imagination, however plausible the illusion of reality. The writer knows he is writing his mind, his 'Opinions', the only real. Readers, on the other hand, are persuaded of the reality of the written world.

If Yorick had been a writer, he too could have understood this. If he had, then his unquestioning belief in the reality of the world presented to him by his good-nature would vanish, and he would no longer be able to transmit that world to the reader unadulterated by any other standards. The unadulterated reading itself, the sentimentality, would also go. But of course the point of the book is that Yorick is a reader, a natural quixote preconditioned to sentiment by his environment. To wonder why he cannot discover his own failings, cannot see his similarity to Lucian's Abderites, is like wondering why Don Quixote cannot see the windmills. 'We don't know', says Howard Gossage, 'who it was discovered water, but we're pretty sure it wasn't a fish.'[92] This brings us to the central paradox or comedy of the *Journey*, for Yorick actually *embodies* the belief that art is communication from mind to mind. He writes his own feelings so that others may feel them too. But he believes in his feelings to such an extent that, rather than having them complement the other worlds of the book, the physical and the higher controlling worlds, he identifies his feelings with them. He lives out and records his subjective beliefs with such conviction that they turn into their opposite. His belief in his feelings and their natural worth leads him to assume that the world those feelings present to him is real. From purely Romantic premises he writes a classically-ordered book about a classically-ordered world. In this curious paradox might be found some explanation of the doubleness of vision which Gardner Stout found in Yorick: although it should be said that this double vision is not really in Yorick but in his readers; his good, careful readers who are alert to the two contradictory readings which Sterne carefully lets Yorick's book allow.

Notes and References

INTRODUCTION

1. Martin C. Battestin, '*Tom Jones*: The Argument of Design', in *The Augustan Milieu, Essays Presented to Louis A. Landa*, ed. H. K. Miller, E. Rothstein, G. S. Rousseau (Oxford, 1970), pp. 289–319. Later as 'Fielding: the Argument of Design' in *The Providence of Wit: Aspects of Form in Augustan Literature and the Arts* (Oxford, 1974), pp. 141–63.
2. Samuel Taylor Coleridge, 'Table Talk', 5 July 1834. *Specimens of the Table Talk of the late Samuel Taylor Coleridge*, ed. Thomas Middleton Raysor (1936), p. 437.
3. Dorothy Van Ghent, 'On *Tom Jones*', in *The English Novel: Form and Function* (New York, 1953, rpt. New York and Evanston, 1961), p. 80.
4. William Empson, '*Tom Jones*', *Kenyon Review*, 20 (1958), 217–49.
5. Battestin, op. cit., p. 296.
6. Ibid., p. 293 n. 2.
7. Ibid., p. 313.
8. Ibid., pp. 295, 297.
9. Ibid., p. 302.
10. e.g. Tzvetan Todorov, 'The Structural Analysis of Literature: The Tales of Henry James', in *Structuralism, An Introduction*, ed. David Robey, Wolfson College Lectures 1972 (Oxford, 1973), pp. 73–103, especially p. 93—'Art therefore is not the reproduction of a given "reality", nor is it created through the imitation of such a reality . . . In the realm of art there is nothing preliminary to the work, nothing which constitutes its origin. It is the work of art itself that is original; the secondary becomes primary.'
11. Victor Borisovich Shklovsky, '*Tristram Shandy*' *Sternea i Teorija Romana* (Petrograd, 1921), later as 'Parodijnyj Roman' in *O Teorii Prozy* (Moscow and Leningrad, 1925); quoted and translated by Victor Erlich, *Russian Formalism: History-Doctrine* ('S-Gravenhage, 1955), p. 165.
12. Frank R. Leavis, *The Great Tradition: George Eliot, Henry James, Joseph Conrad* (1948), p. 29.

CHAPTER 1: STERNE AND THE FORM OF THE NOVEL

1. Joyce M. S. Tomkins, *The Popular Novel in England, 1770–1800* (1932), p. 1.
2. John Northouck, Article in *Monthly Review*, OS 39, 2 (July 1768), 84.

3. Walter Allen, *The English Novel* (1954), p. 81.
4. Charles Lamb, 'Detached Thoughts on Books and Reading', *London Magazine* (July 1822); rpt. in *The Life, Letters and Writings of Charles Lamb*, ed. Percy Fitzgerald (1876), III, 401.
5. Charlotte Lennox, *The Female Quixote; or, The Adventures of Arabella* (1752). Richard Graves, *The Spiritual Quixote; or, The Summer's Ramble of Mr. Geoffry Wildgoose: A Comic Romance* (1773). *The Philosophical Quixote; or, Memoirs of Mr. David Wilkins* (1782). The City Quixote (1785). *The Amicable Quixote; or, The Enthusiasm of Friendship* (1788). *William Thornborough, The Benevolent Quixote* (1791). *The History of Sir George Warrington; or, The Political Quixote* (1797). Charles Lucas, *The Infernal Quixote* (1801).
6. George Colman the elder and David Garrick, *The Clandestine Marriage* (1766), Act I Scene ii. In *Bell's British Theatre* Vol. 20 (1792), p. 19.
7. Archibald Shepperson, *The Novel in Motley* (Cambridge, Mass., 1936), p. 114.
8. Courtney Melmoth, *Family Secrets* (1797).
9. Richard Brinsley Sheridan, *The Rivals, A Comedy* (1775), 'Prolog by the Author, spoken on the 10th night by Mrs. Bulkley', 11. 22–3, in *Plays*, ed. Cecil Price (Oxford, 1973), p. 74.
10. Ibid., 11. 28–30, *Plays*, p. 74.
11. Sheridan, *The Critic: or, A Tragedy Rehearsed* (1781), Act I Scene i, *Plays*, p. 504.
12. Wayne C. Booth, 'The Self-Conscious Narrator in Comic Fiction before *Tristram Shandy*', *PMLA* 67 (1952), 163–85.
13. R. F. Brissenden, *Virtue in Distress: Studies in the Novel of Sentiment from Richardson to de Sade* (1974), p. 205. (Hereafter cited as *Virtue in Distress*.)
14. e.g. *A Letter from the Rev. George Whitfield to the Rev. Laurence Sterne, the supposed author of a book entitled 'The Life and Opinions of Tristram Shandy, Gentleman'* (1760), p. 20—'one would think the author had a cloven foot'. S. T. Coleridge, in 'Table Talk', 18 August 1833, says that *Tristram Shandy* is 'scarce readable by women' (*Coleridge's Miscellaneous Criticism*, ed. Raysor, 1936, p. 427).
15. *TS*, p. 49.
16. Ian Watt, 'The Comic Syntax of *Tristram Shandy*', in *Studies in Criticism and Aesthetics 1660–1800, Essays in Honour of Samuel Holt Monk*, ed. H. Anderson and J. S. Shea (Minneapolis, 1967), pp. 315–31. (Hereafter cited as 'The Comic Syntax of *Tristram Shandy*'.)
17. John Traugott, *Tristram Shandy's World: Sterne's Philosophical Rhetoric* (Berkeley and LA, 1954).
18. E. N. Dilworth, *The Unsentimental Journey of Laurence Sterne* (Morningside Heights, NY, 1948).
19. Melvyn New, *Laurence Sterne as Satirist: A Reading of 'Tristram Shandy'* (Gainsville, Florida, 1969).
20. Gardner Stout, 'Yorick's "Sentimental Journey": A Comic "Pilgrim's Progress" for the Man of Feeling', *ELH*, 30 (1963), 395–412.
21. Brissenden, op. cit., p. 90.
22. J. A. Work, Introduction to *TS*, p. lx.
23. John M. Stedmond, *The Comic Art of Laurence Sterne: Convention and*

Innovation in 'Tristram Shandy' and 'A Sentimental Journey' (Toronto, 1967), p. 3. (Hereafter cited as *The Comic Art of Laurence Sterne*.)

24. Ronald H. Paulson, *Satire and the Novel in Eighteenth-Century England* (New Haven, 1967), p. 249.
25. D. W. Jefferson, '*Tristram Shandy* and the Tradition of Learned Wit', *EC*, 1 (1951), 225–48.
26. Northrop Frye, *Anatomy of Criticism: Four Essays* (Princeton, NJ, 1957), p. 312.
27. Traugott, op. cit., Introduction p. xiii—'a rhetorician and not a novelist'.
28. Allen, op. cit., p. 72.
29. Paulson, op. cit., p. 262.
30. Ronald Saul Hafter, 'Sterne's Affective Art and Eighteenth-Century Psychology' (PhD Dissertation, Brandeis, 1970), p. 58.
31. *TS*, p. 218.
32. Hafter, op. cit., pp. 59–60.
33. Henri Fluchère, *Laurence Sterne: de l'Homme à l'Oeuvre; Biographie Critique et Essai d'Interprétation de 'Tristram Shandy'* (Paris, 1961), p. 235.
34. Watt, op. cit., 326–7.
35. Ibid., 327.
36. Sterne's letter to Dr John Eustace, *Letters of Laurence Sterne*, ed. Lewis P. Curtis (Oxford, 1935), No. 224, p. 411.
37. *TS*, p. 559.
38. Victor Erlich, *Russian Formalism: History-Doctrine* ('S-Gravenhage, 1955) p. 166.
39. Ibid., p. 123, and Yuri Tynianov, 'Literaturnoe Segodnja', *Ruskii Sovremennik* 1 (1924), p. 293, quoted and translated by Erlich, op. cit., pp. 123–4.
40. Victor Borisovich Shklovsky, *Sentimental'noe Puteshestvie, Vospominaniya 1917–22* (Moscow-Berlin, 1923), trans. Richard Sheldon (Ithaca, NY, 1970), as *A Sentimental Journey.*
41. Sheldon, ibid., Introduction pp. xv-xvi.
42. Victor Borisovich Shklovsky, 'On the Connection between Devices of Syuzhet Construction and General Stylistic Devices', 'Potebnya', *Poetika* (Petrograd, 1919), included in O Teorii Prozy (Moscow, 1925), trans. Jane Knox in *Russian Formalism*, ed. Stephen Bann and John E. Bowlt (Edinburgh, 1973), pp. 48–72.
43. S. T. Coleridge's notes for a lecture on 'Wit and Humour', delivered at the rooms of the Philosophical Society in Fetter Lane, 24 February 1818, in *Coleridge's Miscellaneous Criticism*, ed Raysor, pp. 117–26.
44. Shklovsky, 'On the Connection . . .', in *Russian Formalism*, ed. Bann and Bowlt, op. cit., pp. 56, 71.
45. Shklovsky, 'Sterne's *Tristram Shandy*: Stylistic Commentary', in *Russian Formalist Criticism*, trans. and intro. Lee T. Lemon and Marion J. Reis (Lincoln, Nebraska, 1965), pp. 25–57. This is the monograph that Erlich calls '*Tristram Shandy' Sternea i Teorija Romana* (see Introduction, note 11). Shklovsky called it this too: Lemon and Reis use a translation of the title on the first page of the text of Shklovsky's monograph, which they refer to as '*Tristram Shandy' Sterna: Stilistichesky Kommentary.*

46. Ibid., p. 57.
47. Ibid., p. 40.
48. Sheldon, op. cit., p. xx.
49. Ibid., p. xx.
50. Shklovsky, *A Sentimental Journey*, op. cit., p. 183.
51. Christopher Ricks, Introduction to *Tristram Shandy*, ed. Graham Petrie (Harmondsworth, 1967), pp. 26–7.
52. Sheldon, op. cit., p. xvii.
53. Wilfred Owen, *Poems* (1920), Preface, p. ix.
54. Gertrude Stein, sub-heading to 'Sentences and Paragraphs' in *How To Write* (Paris, 1931), p. 23.
55. H. W. Hewett-Thayer, *Laurence Sterne in Germany*, Columbia University Germanic Studies, Vol. 2, I (NY, 1905), p. 2.
56. Ronald H. Paulson, *Theme and Structure in Swift's 'A Tale of A Tub'*, Yale Studies in English, 143 (New Haven, 1960), p. 178, n. 1.
57. Information in this paragraph is from W. R. R. Pinger, *Laurence Sterne and Goethe*, University of California Publications in Modern Philology, Vol. 10, I (Berkeley, Cal., 1920). See Chapter 6, 'Imitators of Sterne' (pp. 112–55), and pp. 28, 84–9.
58. *The Life and Memoirs of Mr. Ephraim Tristram Bates, commonly called Corporal Bates, a broken-hearted Soldier, Printed by Malachi for E. Bates, relict. etc.* (1756), p. 214.
59. Ibid., p. 238.
60. *TS*, p. 32.
61. Hewett-Thayer, op. cit., p. 98, quoting A. D. Coleridge's translation of Johann Wolfgang von Goethe's letter to C. F. Zelter, Weimar, 25 December 1829; originally in *Werke*, 129+ vols. (Weimar, 1877 ff), IV, 46, 193–4.
62. Goethe, 'Maximen und Reflexionen über Literatur und Ethik', Einzelnes, III. Written 14–18 June 1826; in *Werke*, I, 42 (2), 160, quoted by Pinger, op. cit., p. 29: 'Die sentimentalität der Engländer ist humoristisch und zart, dar Franzosen populär und wienerlich, der Deutschen naiv und realistich'.
63. Goethe, 'Tagebuch', 20 December 1829, in *Werke*, III, 12, 169, quoted by Pinger, op. cit., p. 41.
64. Goethe, letter to Zelter, 25 December 1829, quoted by Pinger, op. cit., p. 42.
65. Goethe, *Aus Meinem Leben: Dichtung und Wahrheit*, Book XIII (1814), Trans. John Oxenford as *The Autobiography of Goethe. Truth and Poetry: From My Own Life* (1881), Vol. I, p. 513.

CHAPTER 2: PLOT AND CHARACTER IN *TRISTRAM SHANDY*

1. Tony Tanner, *City of Words: American Fiction 1950–1970* (1971), p. 156.
2. Alan D. McKillop, *The Early Masters of English Fiction* (Lawrence, Kansas, 1956), p. 210.

3. Ibid., p. 210.
4. Frank Brady, '*Tristram Shandy*: Sexuality, Morality and Sensibility', *Eighteenth-Century Studies*, 4 (1970), 41–56.
5. *TS*, p. 462.
6. Desiderius Erasmus, 'De Captandis Sacerdotiis', in *Familiarium Colloquiorum Formulae* (Basle, 1519), trans: Nathan Bailey as *All the Familiar Colloquies of Desiderius Erasmus* (1725), pp. 26–7.
7. Alexander Pope, *Epistle to Cobham* (1734), *Poems*, one-volume edition of the Twickenham text, ed. John Butt (1963, 5th printing 1973), pp. 549–59.
8. Michael V. Deporte, 'Digressions and Madness in *A Tale of A Tub* and *Tristram Shandy*', *Huntingdon Library Quarterly*, 34 (1970), 43–57.
9. *TS*, p. 584.
10. William Battie, *A Treatise on Madness* (1758), p. 85, rpt. with John Monro, *Remarks on Dr. Battie's Treatise on Madness* (1758), in Psychiatric Monograph Series, 3, Intro. Richard Hunter and Ida Macalpine (1962).
11. Walter Scott, Introductory Epistle to *The Fortunes of Nigel* (Edinburgh, 1822). Centenary Edition of Scott (Edinburgh, 1886), p. 16.
12. *TS*, p. 298.
13. Brady, op. cit., p. 47, quoting from McKillop, op. cit., p. 198.
14. Gabriel Josipovici, *The World and the Book: A Study of Modern Fiction* (1971), pp. 299–300.
15. Stephen Werner, *Diderot's Great Scroll: Narrative Art in 'Jacques le Fataliste'* (Banbury, Oxon., 1975), p. 96, n. 13.
16. *TS*, p. 10.
17. Ibid., pp. 6–7.
18. Ibid., p. 6.
19. Ibid., p. 4.
20. Ibid., p. 9.
21. Ibid., p. 9.
22. Ian Watt, 'The Comic Syntax of *Tristram Shandy*' (Minneapolis, 1967), p. 328.
23. R. F. Brissenden, *Virtue in Distress* (1974), p. 199.
24. Thomas Hardy, *The Life and Death of the Mayor of Casterbridge* (1886), Chapter 17: ' "Character is Fate", says Novalis', and George Eliot, though in a different mood, in *The Mill on The Floss* (1860), VI, 6: ' "Character," says Novalis, in one of his questionable aphorisms, "character is destiny." '
25. Tobias Smollett, *The Adventures of Roderick Random* (1748), rpt. Folio Society (1961), p. 25.
26. *TS*, p. 10.
27. Robert Alter, 'The Picaroon as Fortune's Plaything', an essay mostly on Smollett (from whom the essay's title is derived), in *Essays on the Eighteenth-Century Novel*, ed. R. Spector (Bloomington, Indiana, 1965), pp. 131–53.
28. Werner, op. cit., pp. 36–7.
29. Fred Gettings, *The Book of the Hand: An Illustrated History of Palmistry* (1965), p. 39. See also pp. 41, 54, 64, 72 for a discussion of early humour-theory.

30. *TS*, p. 10.
31. Ibid., p. 10.
32. Ibid., p. 80.
33. Ibid., p. 13. The other explanation, given in A. H. Cash's *Laurence Sterne: The Early and Middle Years* (1975), p. 295, is that Sterne's 'brief satirical jab was read as a reference to Mead's keeping in his house a young married woman for the pleasures of dalliance even when he had become impotent'. But I think Cash acknowledges that Mead could well have been recognised from the particular leisure activity mentioned in *Tristram Shandy*.
34. *TS*, p. 27.
35. Ibid., p. 13.
36. Ibid., pp. 13–14.
37. Ibid., p. 31.
38. Ibid., p. 298.
39. Ibid., p. 31.
40. John M. Stedmond, *The Comic Art of Laurence Sterne* (Toronto, 1967), p. 20.
41. Ibid., p. 28, quoting B. H. Lehman, 'Of Time, Personality and the Author: A Study of *Tristram Shandy*', *University of California Publications in English*, 8 (1941), 233–50.
42. *TS*, p. 41.
43. Ibid., p. 154.
44. Ibid., p. 50.
45. Ibid., p. 53.
46. W. J. Farrell, 'Nature versus Art as a Comic Principle in *Tristram Shandy*', *ELH*, 30 (1963), 16–35.
47. *TS*, p. 52.
48. Ibid., p. 55.
49. Ibid., p. 4, and John Traugott, *Tristram Shandy's World: Sterne's Philosophical Rhetoric* (Berkeley and LA, 1954), p. 135.
50. *TS*, p. 69.
51. Ibid., p. 63.
52. Ibid., p. 63.
53. Ibid., pp. 75–6.
54. Ibid., p. 75.
55. Earl R. Wasserman, *The Subtler Language: Critical Readings of Neoclassical and Romantic Poems* (Baltimore, 1959), p. 169.
56. Gustave Lanson, *Etudes d'Histoire Littéraire: Réunies et Publiécs par ses Collègues, ses Elèves et ses Amis* (Paris, 1929), p. 92.
57. It may even be wrong to say that novelists do 'use' philosophy directly. See Duke Maskell, 'Locke and Sterne, or, Can Philosophy Influence Literature?', *EC*, 23 (1973), 22–39.
58. *TS*, p. 336.
59. Ibid., p. 242.
60. Ibid., p. 68.
61. Ibid., p. 72.
62. Ibid., p. 73.
63. Ibid., p. 475. Work has a question-mark after GRAVITATION which

is not in the first edition of *Tristram Shandy* in the British Library, shelf-mark C.70. aa.28. First edition preferred.

64. Ian Donaldson, 'The Clockwork Novel: Three Notes on an Eighteenth-Century Analogy', *Review of English Studies*, NS 21 (1970), 14–22.
65. Bob Dylan, 'Idiot Wind', CBS LP 69097 *Blood on the Tracks* (CBS Inc., 1974).
66. Sigurd Burkhardt, 'Tristram Shandy's Law of Gravity', *ELH*, 28 (1961), 70–88.
67. Ibid., p. 76.
68. Ibid., p. 80.
69. Ibid., p. 87.
70. Ibid., p. 81.
71. With a narrator and central character as ingenious as Tristram and Walter, *Tristram Shandy* is a book that cries out to be theorised about. My own favourite Theory about the book is the 'Guy Fawkes' theory, which is designed to explain why Tristram is so specific about his date of birth: 5 November. The answer is that the central action of the book is a very good allegory of the Gunpowder Plot. *Upstairs* Mrs Shandy gives birth to a new son and heir: James I in the Houses of Parliament, the new dynasty. *Downstairs* in the parlour (the cellars of the House) a train of events is set in motion which will end with a *Catholic* (Dr Slop) doing irreparable damage to the new-born child—a Catholic who has been teased and made fun of over his religion ever since he entered the house, and whose state of mind cannot be particularly pacific . . . and of course all the events are *blown up* out of all proportion to their real significance.

    If the reader should, unaccountably, be sceptical of this theory, I would remind him that Guy Fawkes was and is something of a local legend in York, Sterne's cathedral city. Guy Fawkes was born there, and educated at a well-known school in the town. Sterne may well have begun his book with some idea of writing it for a York audience, and making it another *Political Romance*. The allegory never really gets used, of course, because the Shandys become interesting in their own right. But it makes a nice Theory.
72. Traugott, op. cit., p. 7.
73. Simon Stevin, *Beghinselen der Weeghconst* (Leyden, 1586), describes the experiment: see Edouard Jan Dijksterhuis, *The Mechanization of the World-Picture* (Oxford, 1961), translated from the Dutch *De Mechanisering van het Wereldbeeld* (Amsterdam, 1950) by C. Dikshoorn, p. 329. Galileo's working life started *c.* 1605.
74. *TS*, p. 117.
75. W. W. Rouse Ball, *A Short Account of the History of Mathematics* (1888, 3rd ed, 1901), p. 254.
76. *TS*, p. 186.
77. Dijksterhuis, op. cit., pp. 179–80. Material in the preceding paragraph is from Dijksterhuis, pp. 176–85, 'On Falling Bodies'.
78. Ibid., p. 180.
79. John Ferriar, *Illustrations of Sterne* (1798), p. 182.

CHAPTER 3: STERNE AND THE SCIENTIFIC STUDY OF MAN

1. Isaac Newton, *Philosophiae Naturalis Principia Mathematica* (1687, 3rd ed. 1726), 'De Mundi Systemate', Liber Tertius, Regula 1: 'Causes rerum naturalium non plures admitti debere, quam quae et verae sint et earum phaenomenis explicandis sufficiant'.
2. Thomas S. Kuhn, *The Structure of Scientific Revolutions* (Chicago and London, 1962, 2nd impr. 1963), p. 104.
3. Christiaan Huygens, *Discours de la Cause de la Pesanteur* (Leyden, 1690), *Oeuvres Complètes de Christiaan Huygens, publiées par la Société Hollandaise des Sciences*, 22 vols. (La Haye, 1888–1950), XXI, 471, quoted by Dijksterhuis, *the Mechanization of the World-Picture* (trans. C. Dikshoorn, Oxford, 1961), p. 480.
4. Leibniz, letter to Huygens, 20 March 1693, Huygens, *Oeuvres* X, 428, quoted by Dijksterhuis, op. cit., p. 480.
5. George Berkeley, *A Treatise Concerning the Principles of Human Knowledge* (1710), Section 103, ed. and intro. G. J. Warnock (London and Glasgow, 1962), 6th impr. October 1972, p. 116.
6. Ibid., Section 107, p. 117.
7. John Locke, *An Essay Concerning Human Understanding* (1690), Book 2, Chapter 33 ('Concerning the Association of Ideas'), of the 4th and subsequent editions of the *Essay*, ed. P. H. Nidditch, Clarendon edition of the Works of John Locke, Vol. I (Oxford, 1975), pp. 394–401. (Hereafter cited as *Essay*.)
8. The list of twenty Locke-invoking critics is given by R. S. Hafter, 'Sterne's Affective Art and Eighteenth-Century Psychology' (PhD Dissertation, Brandeis, 1970), p. 72. Other recent examples could be added to his list, e.g. Helene Moglen, *The Philosophical Irony of Laurence Sterne* (Florida, 1975). Hume's three categories of association are mentioned by Hafter, pp. 156–7; they are from Hume's *A Treatise of Human Nature* (1739–40), Book I, Part 1, Section 4, 'Of the Connection or Association of Ideas', Everyman edition (London and NY, 1911), rpt. 1974, ed. and intro. A. D. Lindsay, 2 vols., Vol. I, p. 19. (Hereafter cited as *Treatise*.
9. Hume, *Treatise*, I, 1, 4; Vol. I, p. 21.
10. Ibid., II, 1, 5; Vol. II, p. 15.
11. John Passmore, *Hume's Intentions* (Cambridge, 1952), revised ed. 1968, p. 108.
12. David Hartley, *Observations on Man: his Frame, his Duty, and his Expectations* (1749), Part II, Chapter 2 (Proposition 28), p. 146: 'Association, i.e. Analogy, perfect and imperfect, is the only Foundation upon which we in fact do, or can, or ought to assent'. Hartley is using the word Analogy in its sense of argument by example, rather than by proportion.
13. Fred Gettings, *The Book of the Hand: An Illustrated History of Palmistry* (1965), p. 178, paraphrasing Paracelsus.
14. Kenelm Digby, *A Late Discourse Made in a Solemne Assembly of Nobles and Learned Men at Montpellier . . . Touching the Cure of WOUNDS by the*

Powder of Sympathy, Rendred faithfully out of French into English by R. White (1658), p. 3.
15. Ephraim Chambers, *Cyclopaedia* (1713), article on 'The Powder of Sympathy'.
16. Kenelm Digby, op. cit., p. 151.
17. Ibid., p. 76.
18. Tobias Smollett, *The Expedition of Humphry Clinker* (1771), ed. Lewis M. Knapp (1966), p. 18. The Doctor finds relief not from bad breath but from low spirits.
19. Richard Mead, *A Mechanical Account of Poisons in Several Essays* (1702), p. 15. Newton is referred to on p. 14 with reference to Bellini's cohesion, 'which is indeed, tho' express'd in other words, the very same thing with the *Attraction* of the Particles one to another; This Mr. *Newton* has demonstrated to be the great Principle of Action in the Universe'.
20. Ibid., Preface, n. pag.
21. Ibid.
22. Samuel Bowden, Introductory poem ('To Dr. Morgan') to Thomas Morgan's *Philosophical Principles of Medicine* (1726), pp. xlv–xlvi.
23. Thomas Morgan, *Philosophical Principles of Medicine*, Proposition 28 ('To explain the Origination and Mechanism of the *Passions*, with regard to their different Modifications, and Impressions of Pleasure and Pain'), pp. 365–95.
24. Thomas Morgan, *Physico-Theology* (1741), p. 72.
25. Ibid., p. 72.
26. Ibid., p. 112.
27. Ibid., p. 113.
28. Alexander Pope, *An Essay on Man* (1733–4) Epistle I, 11. 289–93, *Poems*, ed. John Butt (1963), 5th printing 1973, p. 515.
29. Abraham Cowley, annotation to the 'Davideis', Davideis 1 in Works (1668) p. 36.
30. George Cheyne, *An Essay of Health and Long Life* (1724), Chapter vi, prop. 4, p. 149.
31. William King, *An Essay on the Origin of Evil . . . To which is prefix'd A Dissertation Concerning the Fundamental Principle and Immediate Criterion of Virtue* [by J. Gay] (1739). This is not John Gay the dramatist, but John Gay, Fellow of Sidney Sussex College, Cambridge.
32. Ibid., Chapter v, Section iii, pp. 222–5.
33. Gay, op. cit., p. xxxi.
34. Ibid., p. xiv.
35. Locke, op. cit., Book II, Chapter xxxiii, p. 395.
36. Richard A. Lanham, in *'Tristram Shandy': The Games of Pleasure* (Berkeley, LA, and London, 1973) p. 57.
37. *TS*, p. 352.
38. King, op. cit., Chapter v, p. 218.
39. Hartley, op. cit., Part II, p. 27.
40. P. McReynolds, Introduction to *Four Early Works on Motivation*, ed. McReynolds (Gainsville, Florida, 1969), p. xvii. The reference is to Locke's *Essay*, Book II, Chapter xxi ('Of Power'), paras. 31 and 40.

41. *TS*, p. 517.
42. Ibid., p. 518. Work has '*Wales*'. First edition preferred.
43. Ibid., p. 383.
44. Ibid., p. 386.
45. Hartley, op. cit., Part I, p. 5.
46. Ibid., Part I, p. 83.
47. Ibid., Part I, p. 82.
48. S. T. Coleridge, *Biographia Literaria* (1817), ed. J. Shawcross (Oxford, 1907), pp. 82, 92.
49. Earl R. Wasserman, 'Nature Moralized: The Divine Analogy in the Eighteenth Century,' *ELH*, 20 (1953), 39–76.

CHAPTER 4: BREAKING PATTERNS: ANALOGY AND PROPORTION

1. *TS*, p. 146. Work has 'minute holes'. First edition preferred.
2. Ibid., p. 145.
3. Ibid., p. 145. Apart from the two examples where the 'larger world' does just appear, there is also the abortive discussion on 'analogy' in Volume II, Chapter 8. Of all the conversations which do not happen in *Tristram Shandy*, this is easily the most interesting.
4. *Concise Oxford Dictionary of Current English*, ed. H. W. and F. G. Fowler (Oxford, 1951), 4th ed., rpt. 1959, p. 1201.
5. *TS*, p. 208.
6. Ibid., p. 236.
7. Ibid., p. 240.
8. Ibid., p. 240.
9. Ibid., pp. 277–8.
10. Ibid., p. 145.
11. Ibid., p. 149.
12. John Locke, *Essay* (1690, ed. Nidditch, Oxford, 1975), Book II, ch. xi, p. 161.
13. George Cheyne, *The English Malady, or, A Treatise of Nervous Diseases of all Kinds* (1731), 2nd ed., 1734, Introduction pp. 4–5.
14. *TS*, p. 160.
15. Ibid., p. 160.
16. Ibid., pp. 414–15.
17. Ibid., p. 415.
18. Ibid., p. 415.
19. Richard Lanham, '*Tristram Shandy*': *The Games of Pleasure* (Berkeley, LA, and London, 1973), pp. 30–31.
20. *TS*, p. 75. Work has 'wrapt' for 'warpt'. First edition preferred.
21. Ibid., p. 443.
22. Ibid., p. 301.
23. Ibid., p. 293.
24. Ibid., p. 432.
25. Ibid., pp. 431–2.
26. Ibid., p. 426.

27. Gilbert Ryle, *The Concept of Mind* (1949), p. 20.
28. Stephen Werner, *Diderot's Great Scroll: Narrative Art in 'Jacques le Fataliste'* (Banbury Oxon., 1975), p. 97.
29. *TS*, p. 1: Work translates as 'It is not actions themselves, but opinions concerning actions, which disturb men'. Michel de Montaigne, *Essays* (1580), trans. in three books by C. Cotton, *Essays of Michael Seigneur de Montaigne* (1693), p. 401. The epigram is from Epictetus's *Encheiridion*, Chapter 5. It appears in *TS* in Greek.
30. Edmund Burke, *A Philosophical Enquiry into the Origin of our Ideas of the Sublime and Beautiful* (1758: 2nd ed. 1759), Part V, Section iii, p. 335.
31. *TS*, pp. 13–14.
32. W. V. Holtz, *Image and Immortality: A Study of 'Tristram Shandy'* (Providence, R I, 1970).
33. William Freedman, '*Tristram Shandy*: The Art of Literary Counterpoint', *MLQ*, 32 (1971), 268–80.
34. *TS*, p. 16.
35. Ibid., p. 16.
36. Ibid., p. 122.
37. Ibid., p. 181.
38. Ibid., p. 315.
39. Ibid., pp. 515–16.
40. William Hogarth, A Harlot's Progress (1730–32). Ronald Paulson, *The Art of Hogarth* (1975), plates 23–28 (n. pag.).
41. Hogarth, *The March to Finchley* (1749–50). Paulson, *The Art of Hogarth* (1975), plates 102–3 (n. pag.).
42. C. B. MacPherson, 'The Social Bearings of Locke's Political Philosophy', *Western Political Quarterly*, 7 (1954), 1–22. Ian Watt's discussion of individualism is in *The Rise of the Novel* (1957), Chapter 3.
43. *TS*, p. 269.
44. Ibid., p. 348.
45. David Hume, *Treatise* (1739–40, ed. Lindsay, 1911), III, iii, i: Vol. II, p. 272.
46. *TS*, pp. 371–2.
47. Alexander Pope, *An Essay on Man*, (1733–4) Epistle III, 11. 313–18, *Poems*, ed. John Butt (1963), 5th printing 1973, p. 535.
48. *TS*, pp. 597–8.
49. Ibid., p. 598, adapting Pope, *Essay on Man*, Epistle I, 11. 99–112.
50. Ibid., p. 474.
51. Ibid., p. 474.
52. Ibid., p. 474.
53. Ibid., p. 342.
54. Ibid., p. 456.
55. Ibid., p. 336.
56. Ibid., p. 157.
57. Ibid., p. 157.
58. Ibid., p. 167.
59. Ibid., p. 159.
60. Ibid., pp. 162–3.

61. Ibid., p. 69: 'a nonsense song ridiculing the Irish Papists, which was extremely popular in England', says Work.
62. Ibid., p. 169.
63. Ibid., p. 169.
64. Ibid., p. 183.
65. Ibid., p. 182.
66. Ibid., p. 183.
67. Ibid., pp. 182–3.
68. Ibid., p. 182.
69. Douglas Brooks, *Number and Pattern in the Eighteenth-Century Novel* (London and Boston, 1973), p. 178.

CHAPTER 5: STERNE AND LOCKE

1. Francis Doherty, 'Sterne and Hume: A Bicentenary Essay', *Essays and Studies*, NS 22 (1969), pp. 71–87.
2. Kenneth Maclean, *John Locke and the English Literature of the Eighteenth Century* (New Haven, 1936). Preface, p. v: Maclean says the *Essay* was 'The book that had most influence in the eighteenth century, the Bible excepted'. Arthur Cash, *Laurence Sterne: The Early and Middle Years* (1975), pp. 43, 51 mentions the importance attached to the study of Newton and Locke at Cambridge in this period.
3. Maclean, op. cit., p. 2.
4. Oliver Goldsmith, *An Enquiry into the Present State of Polite Learning in Europe* (1759), pp. 102–3.
5. *TS*, p. 87.
6. Ibid., p. 86.
7. John Traugott, *Tristram Shandy's World: Sterne's Philosophical Rhetoric* (Berkeley and LA, 1954), p. 58.
8. John Locke, *Essay* (1690, ed. Nidditch, Oxford, 1975), Book II, Chapter xxix, pp. 363–4.
9. *TS*, p. 86.
10. Locke, op. cit., Book III, Chapter ix, 'Of the Imperfection of Words', pp. 475–90.
11. *TS*, p. 85.
12. Locke, op. cit., Book III, Chapter x, para. xxxiv: p. 508, where Locke describes metaphor as 'perfect cheat', and then ends the paragraph with: 'Eloquence, like the fair Sex, has too prevailing Beauties in it to suffer itself ever to be spoken against. And it is vain to find fault with those Arts of Deceiving wherein Men find Pleasure to be deceived'.
13. Ibid., Book IV, Chapter xiv, para. 3: p. 652, where he defines judgment (or rather the probability of true knowledge which judgment lets man attain) through metaphor, the manifestation of *wit*. One faculty is described by its opposite: 'Therefore, as God has set some Things in Broad day-light; as he has given us some certain Knowledge . . . So, in the greater part of our Concernment, he has afforded us only the twilight, as I may so say, of *Probability*'.
14. *TS*, p. 90.

15. Carol Kyle, 'A Note on Laurence Sterne and the Cannon-Bullet of John Locke', *PQ*, 50 (1971) 672–4.
16. *TS*, p. 577.
17. Ibid., p. 577.
18. Ibid., p. 619.
19. Locke, op. cit., 'Epistle to the Reader', p. 6.
20. *TS*, p. 92.
21. Locke, 'The Second Treatise of Government', *Two Treatises of Government* (1690), ed. P. Laslett (Cambridge, 1960), rpt. with corrections 1964, p. 341. Should it be objected that Tristram's phrasing is actually *un*Lockean, in the sense that it appears to admit the concept of ideas which are innate to the mind, I would point out that an idea is neither a 'desire' (Tristram) nor a 'power'; what Locke says here is that 'Man being born . . . with a Title to perfect Freedom and an uncontrouled enjoyment of all the Rights and Priviledges of the Law of Nature, equally with any other Man . . . in the World, hath by Nature a Power, not only to preserve his Property, that is, his Life, Liberty and Estate, against the Injuries and Attempts of other Men; but . . .'.
22. *TS*, p. 93.
23. Maclean, op. cit., p. 39.
24. Ibid., p. 45.
25. Locke, *Essay*, op. cit., 'Epistle to the Reader', p. 6.
26. Locke, 'The Second Treatise of Government', op. cit., para. xl, p. 314.
27. Ivan Petrovich Pavlov, *Lectures on Conditioned Reflex*, ed. and trans. W. Horsley Gantt, 2 vols. (Vol. I, 1928; Vol. II, 1941), 5th printing 1963: Vol. I, pp. 276–7.
28. Ibid., Vol. II, p. 162.
29. W. Horsley Gantt, Introduction to Pavlov's *Lectures*, op. cit., Vol. II, p. 19.
30. Robert Whytt, *An Essay on the Vital and Other Involuntary Motions of Animals* (1751), 2nd ed. 1763, pp. 280, 283.
31. Robert Whytt, *Observations on the Nature, Causes, and Cure of those Disorders . . . commonly called Nervous, Hypochondriac or Hysteric: To which are prefixed some Remarks on the Sympathy of the Nerves* (1761), 2nd ed., Edinburgh, 1765. (Hereafter cited as *Observations on those Disorders*.)
32. Whytt, *Essay on the Vital Motions*, op. cit., p. 3.
33. Arthur Cash, 'The Lockean Psychology of *Tristram Shandy*', *ELH*, 22 (1955), 125–35.
34. *TS*, p. 540.
35. Robert Alter, '*Tristram Shandy* and the Game of Love', *American Scholar*, 37 (1967–8), 316–23.
36. Ibid., 317.
37. Locke, *Essay*, op. cit., Book II, Chapter xi, pp. 156–7.
38. *TS*, p. 200.
39. Ibid., p. 202.
40. Ibid., p. 200.
41. Ibid., p. 193.
42. Ibid., p. 202.

43. Locke, *Essay*, op. cit., Book III, Chapter x, p. 508.
44. Ibid.
45. *TS*, p. 202.
46. Ibid., p. 202.
47. Locke, *Essay*, op. cit., Book IV, Chapter xiv, p. 653.
48. Ibid., Book II, Chapter xxxiii, p. 395.
49. Ibid., Book IV, Chapter xiv, p. 652.
50. *TS*, p. 195.
51. Ibid., p. 198.
52. Locke, *Essay*, op. cit., Book IV, Chapter xiv, p. 652.
53. *TS*, p. 197.
54. Ibid., p. 197.
55. 'The Wisdom of Solomon', Chapter 11 Verse 20 in *The Apochrypha of the Old Testament*, ed. Bruce M. Metzger (New York, NY, 1965), p. 115.

CHAPTER 6: SYMPATHY AND SENTIMENT

1. R. F. Brissenden, *Virtue in Distress* (1974), p. 189.
2. John Traugott, ed. and intro., *Laurence Sterne: A Collection of Critical Essays* (Englewood Cliffs, NJ, 1968), p. 4.
3. Ibid., p. 15.
4. Brissenden, op. cit., p. 195.
5. Traugott, op. cit., pp. 4–5.
6. Robert Whytt, *Observations on those Disorders* (1761; 2nd ed. Edinburgh, 1765), pp. 9–10.
7. Ibid., p. 219.
8. David Hume, *Treatise* (1739–40, ed. Lindsay, 1911), Book II, Part i; Volume II, p. 15.
9. Ibid., p. 9.
10. David Mercer, *Sympathy and Ethics* (Oxford, 1972), p. 36.
11. David Hume, letter to Adam Smith, 28 July, 1759, in *Letters*, ed. J. Y. T. Greig (Oxford, 1932), I, 313.
12. David Garrick, *Occasional Prologue on Quitting the Theatre* (1776).
13. Jean-Jacques Rousseau, *Discours Sur L'Origine et les Fondements de L'Inégalité parmi les Hommes* (Amsterdam, 1755), in *Great Books of the Western World* Vol. XXXVIII, Montesquieu/Rousseau, ed. R. M. Hutchins, trans. G. D. H. Cole as *On the Origin of Inequality* (Chicago, 1952), pp. 344–5.
14. R. B. Sheridan, *The Rivals, A Comedy* (1775), Act II Scene i: *Plays*, ed. Cecil Price (Oxford, 1973), p. 94.
15. *The Life and Opinions of Miss Sukey Shandy, of Bow Street, Gentlewoman. In a series of Letters to her Dear Brother, Tristram Shandy, Gent.* (1760), Letter 2, p. 10.
16. *TS*, p. 140.
17. Arthur Cash, 'The Sermon in *Tristram Shandy*', *ELH*, 31 (1964), 395–417.
18. John Milton, *Paradise Lost* (1667), Book III, 11. 195–8. *Poetical Works*, ed. D. Bush (1966), p. 261.

19. Joseph Conrad, 'Henry James: An Appreciation', *North American Review*, 180 (1905), 102–8.
20. Samuel Johnson, *A Dictionary of the English Language* (1755), 2 vols. Item on 'Conscience', Vol. I.
21. Brissenden, op. cit., p. 215.
22. W. J. Farrell, 'Nature versus Art as a Comic Principle in *Tristram Shandy*', *ELH*, 30 (1963), 16–35.
23. *TS*, p. 122.
24. Ibid, p. 122.
25. Ibid., p. 140.
26. Brissenden, op. cit., p. 215.
27. *TS*, p. 109.
28. Ibid., p. 108.
29. Eugène Jolas, 'My Friend James Joyce', in *James Joyce: Two Decades of Criticism* ed. Seon Givens (New York, NY, 1948), rpt. 1963, pp. 3–18.

CHAPTER 7: *A SENTIMENTAL JOURNEY*

1. Edwin Muir, 'Laurence Sterne', in *Essays on Literature and Society* (London and Toronto, 1949), 2nd ed. 1965, pp. 50–57.
2. Arthur Cash, *Sterne's Comedy of Moral Sentiments: the Ethical Dimension of the Journey* (Pittsburgh, 1966); p. 34.
3. J. M. Stedmond, *The Comic Art of Laurence Sterne* (Toronto, 1967), p. 150.
4. Gardner Stout, 'Yorick's "Sentimental Journey": A Comic "Pilgrim's Progress" for the Man of Feeling', *ELH*, 30 (1963), 395–412.
5. R. S. Crane, 'Suggestions Towards a Genealogy of the Man of Feeling', *ELH*, 1 (1934), 205–30.
6. John Laird, *Philosophical Incursions into English Literature* Cambridge, 1946), pp. 90–91.
7. Sterne, Sermon 43, *Works*, ed. W. L. Cross (NY, 1904), V, 344–5.
8. Q. D. Leavis, *Fiction and the Reading Public* (1932), rpt. 1965, p. 135.
9. W. M. Thackeray, *English Humourists of the Eighteenth Century* (1853) rpt. in *Henry Esmond, The English Humourists, The Four Georges*, ed. George Saintsbury, (London, New York & Toronto, n.d.), p. 666.
10. *SJ*, p. 3.
11. Ibid., p. 4.
12. Ibid., p. 5.
13. Ibid., p. 5.
14. Ibid., p. 5.
15. Ibid., p. 6.
16. Ibid., p. 7.
17. Ibid., p. 8.
18. Ibid., P. 12.
19. For instance, *Don Quixote*, Part II, Chapters xii–xv, the episode of the 'Knight of the Mirrors', *DQ* trans. Motteux/Ozell, intro. H. Brickell (1934), pp. 515–35.
20. *SJ*, p. 15.

21. Ibid., p. 22.
22. Ibid., p. 18.
23. Ibid., p. 117.
24. Ibid., p. 24.
25. Ibid., p. 62.
26. Ibid., p. 28.
27. Ibid, p. 17.
28. Ibid., p. 40.
29. Ibid., p. 34.
30. *Encyclopaedia Britannica*, 11th ed. 1910–11, Article on 'Abdera'.
31. *SJ*, p. 34.
32. Ibid., p. 35.
33. Lucian, *Works*, ed. H. W. and F. G. Fowler (Oxford, 1905), II, 109. See August Nauck, *Tragicorum Graecorum Fragmenta* (Lipsiae, 1856), ed. B. Snell (Gottingen, 1971), p. 18, for reference to Lucian's line as the only one extant from the *Andromeda*.
34. F. A. Paradis de Moncrif, 'Les Abdérites', in *Nouveau Receuil Choisi et Mêlé des Meilleurs Pièces de Théâtre François et Italien* (La Haye 1733–50), Vol. IV, 1737.
35. *SJ*, p. 47.
36. Brissenden, *Virtue in Distress* (1974), pp. 222–3, and *S J*, p. 47.
37. *SJ*, p. 50.
38. Ibid., p. 50.
39. Ibid., p. 50.
40. Ibid., p. 54.
41. Ibid., p. 90. Jack has 'rubbing' for 'ribbing' but notes that the first edition of the *Journey* has 'ribbing': Jack, p. xxi. Apart from this, quotations used are identical in Jack and in the first edition in the Cambridge University Library, Catalogue no. CCD. 5. 139–.
42. Anthony Ashley Cooper, Third Earl of Shaftesbury, '*Sensus Communis*; An Essay on the Freedom of Wit and Humour', Section ii, I, 64–5. References to Shaftesbury are to essays in *Characteristicks of Men, Manners, Opinions, Times* (1711, 4th ed. 1728), 3 vols.
43. 'Hamlet, Prince of Denmark', Act I Scene iii, *Complete Plays of William Shakespeare*, ed. P. Alexander (1951), p. 1034.
44. *SJ*, p. 113.
45. Ibid., p. 114.
46. Ibid., p. 629.
47. Ibid., p. 117.
48. Ibid., p. 117.
49. Cash, op. cit., p. 94.
50. *SJ*, p. 117.
51. Ibid., p. 117.
52. Ibid., p. 117.
53. Ibid., p. 117.
54. Ibid., p. 35.
55. R. L. Brett, *The Third Earl of Shaftesbury: A Study in Eighteenth-Century Literary Theory* (1971) p. 75, Fn. ref.
56. Shaftesbury, 'The Moralists, A Philosophical Rhapsody', II, 345.

57. Basil Willey, *The Eighteenth-Century Background* (1940), p. 74.
58. Shaftesbury, *Characteristicks*, ed. J. R. Robertson (1900), editor's introduction p. xxxvii.
59. Shaftesbury, 'Soliloquy, or, Advice to an Author', Chapter iii, Section iii, I, 338.
60. Shaftesbury, 'The Freedom of Wit and Humour', Chapter iv, Section i, I, 128.
61. Ibid., I, 142.
62. Shaftesbury, 'A Letter Concerning Enthusiasm to my Lord *******', Section ii, I, 15–16.
63. Ibid., Section vii, I, 52–3.
64. Ibid., I, 54–5.
65. Locke, *Essay* (1690, ed. Nidditch, Oxford, 1975), Book IV, ch. xix, p. 704.
66. Ibid., p. 705.
67. Shaftesbury, *Characteristicks*, ed. J. M. Robertson, op. cit., editor's introduction p. xxii.
68. Stanley Grean, *Shaftesbury's Philosophy of Religion and Ethics* (Ohio, 1967), pp. 50, 57–8.
69. Ralph Cudworth, *The True Intellectual System of the World* (1678), ed. J. Harrison (1845), I, 220–21.
70. Brett, op. cit., p. 199.
71. Willey, op. cit., p. 5.
72. Shaftesbury, 'Soliloquy', Chapter iii, Section iii, I, 353.
73. Francis Hutcheson, *An Enquiry into the Original of our Ideas of Beauty and Virtue: in Two Treatises* (1725), Part II, Section iii, p. 172. To be fair to Hutcheson, these mathematical expressions were removed from the 4th ed.
74. Ibid., (3rd ed. 1742), Preface p. xxi. The 1st ed. only mentions Hutcheson's 'Obligations to a certain LORD'. Preface p. ix.
75. Hutcheson, *An Essay on the Nature and Conduct of the Passions and Affections: with Illustrations on the Moral Sense.* (1728), Treatise I, Section VI, p. 167.
76. Louis Bredvold, 'The Invention of the Ethical Calculus' in *The Seventeenth Century: Studies in the History of English Thought and Literature from Bacon to Pope*, ed. Richard Foster Jones (Stanford, 1951), pp. 165–80.
77. Elie Halévy, *La Formation du Radicalisme Philosophique* (Paris, 1901–4), trans. M. Morris as *The Growth of Philosophic Radicalism* (1928), 3rd ed. 1952, p. 6.
78. K. E. Gilbert and H. Kuhn, *A History of Aesthetics* (1956), p. 234.
79. Jean-Jacques Rousseau, *Emile, ou de l'Education* (1762), trans. Barbara Foxley (1911), pp. 249–50.
80. Ibid., p. 253.
81. Henry Home, Lord Kames, *Elements of Criticism* (1762, 3rd ed. Edinburgh, 1765), Chapter ii, Part I, Section vi, pp. 79–96.
82. Edmund Burke, *A Philosophical Enquiry into the Origin of our Ideas of the Sublime and Beautiful* (1758, 2nd ed. 1759), ed. and intro. J. T. Boulton (1958), editor's introduction p. xxviii.

83. Ibid., 2nd ed. 1759, p. 210.
84. Ibid., Introduction ('On Taste'), p. 17.
85. Ibid., p. 311.
86. Ibid., p. 312.
87. Ibid., p. 70.
88. Ibid., p. 332.
89. Ibid., pp. 340, 342.
90. S. T. Coleridge, 'Aids to Reflection in the Formation of a Manly Character' (1825), *Inquiring Spirit*, ed. Kathleen Coburn (1951), p. 394.
91. Burke, *Enquiry*, p. 335.
92. Attributed to John Culkin S J by Howard Luck Gossage, *McLuhan: Hot and Cool* (Harmondsworth, 1968), ed. G. E. Stearn, p. 32. Yorick is in fact unlike Don Quixote in the completeness of his immersion in his own imagined world. There is no point in the *Journey* where Yorick establishes the exact quality of his beliefs in the way that the Don can when he chooses his verbs so well, in reply to Sancho's asking him whether he really does think that the muscular village girl Aldonza Lorenzo is the Lady Dulcinea del Toboso: 'I am quite satisfied . . . to imagine and believe that the good Aldonza Lorenzo is lovely and virtuous . . . I think of her as the greatest princess in the world'. (*Don Quixote* Part I, Chapter xxv.)

Select Bibliography

Sterne, Laurence, *The Life and Opinions of Tristram Shandy, Gentleman* (York and London, 1760–67). Ed. J. A. Work (New York, 1940).

——, *A Sentimental Journey through France and Italy* (1768). Ed. Ian Jack (1968).

——, *A Political Romance* (York, 1759). Ed. Ian Jack (1968).

——, *The Sermons of Mr. Yorick* (1760–69). *Works*, ed. W. L. Cross (New York and London, 1904), Vol. 5.

——, 'The Journal to Eliza', written 1767. Ed. Ian Jack (1968).

——, *Letters of Laurence Sterne*. Ed. Lewis P. Curtis (Oxford, 1935).

PRIMARY SOURCES

Amory, Thomas, *The Life of John Buncle* (1756).

Anon, *A Supplement to the Life and Opinions of Tristram Shandy* (1760).

——, *Argal; or, The Silver Devil, being the Adventures of an Evil Spirit . . . Related by Himself* (Dublin, 1794).

——, *The Amicable Quixote; or, The Enthusiasm of Friendship* (1788).

——, *The City Quixote* (1785).

——, *The History of Sir George Warrington; or, The Political Quixote* (1797).

——, *The Life and Memoirs of Mr Ephraim Tristram Bates, commonly called Corporal Bates, a broken-hearted Soldier, Printed by Malachi for E. Bates, relict. etc.* (1756).

——, *The Life and Opinions of Miss Sukey Shandy, of Bow Street, Gentlewoman. In a series of Letters to her Dear Brother, Tristram Shandy, Gent.* (1760).

——, *The Philosphical Quixote; or, Memoirs of Mr. David Wilkins* (1782).

——, *The Slave of Passion; or, The Fruits of Werther* (1802).

——, *William Thornborough, The Benevolent Quixote* (1791).

Barton, Richard, *The Analogy of Divine Wisdom* (1737).

——, *Farrago* (1739).

Battie, William, *A Treatise on Madness* (1758). Printed with Monro, John, *Remarks on Dr. Battie's Treatise on Madness* (1758), Psychiatric Monograph Series, 3, intro. Richard Hunter and Ida Macalpine (1962).

Berkeley, George, *A Treatise Concerning the Principles of Human Knowledge* (1710), ed. G. J. Warnock (London and Glasgow, 1962; 6th impr. 1972).

Bowden, Samuel, Introductory poem, 'To Dr. Morgan', to Thomas Morgan's *Philosophical Principles of Medicine* (1726).

Burke, Edmund, *A Philosophical Enquiry into the Origin of our Ideas of the Sublime and Beautiful* (1758, 2nd ed. 1759).

Burton, Robert, *The Anatomy of Melancholy: What it is, with all the Kindes, Causes, Symptomes, Prognosticks, and Seurall Cures of it . . . With a Satyricall Preface, Conducing to the Following Discourse* (Oxford, 1621).

Butler, Joseph, *The Analogy of Religion, Natural and Revealed, to the Constitution and Course of Nature* (1736).

Cervantes Saavedra, Miguel de, *El Ingenioso Hidalgo Don Quixote de la Mancha* (Valencia, 1605). *Don Quixote . . . Ozell's Revision of the translation of Peter Motteux,* intro. H. Brickell (1934).

Chambers, Ephraim, *Cyclopaedia: An Universal Dictionary of Arts and Sciences* (1713).

Chambers, William, *A Treatise on the Decorative Part of Civil Architecture* (1759).

Cheyne, George, *An Essay of Health and Long Life* (1724).

——, *The English Malady: or, A Treatise of Nervous Diseases of all Kinds* (1731, 2nd ed. 1734).

Coleridge, S. T., 'Table Talk', *Specimens of the Table Talk of the late Samuel Taylor Coleridge*, ed. H. N. Coleridge (1835).

——, *Biographia Literaria* (1817), ed. J. Shawcross (Oxford, 1907, rpt. with corrections, 1962).

——, *Aids to Reflection in the Formation of a Manly Character* (1825).

Colman, George and Garrick, David, *The Clandestine Marriage* (1766).

Conrad, Joseph, *Chance: A Tale in Two Parts* (1913).

Cooper, Anthony Ashley, 3rd Earl of Shaftesbury, *Characteristicks of Men, Manners, Opinions, Times* (1711, 4th ed. 1728), 3 vols.

Cowley, Abraham, 'Davideis'. *Poems* (1656).

Cudworth, Ralph, *The True Intellectual System of the World* (1678), ed. J. Harrison (1845).

Diderot, Denis, *Paradoxe sur le Comédien* (Paris, 1757).

——, *Jacques le Fataliste et son Maître* (1796 [written 1773], rpt. Geneva, 1956).

Digby, Kenelm, *A Late Discourse Made in A Solemne Assembly of Nobles and Learned Men at Montpellier . . . Touching the Cure of WOUNDS by the Powder of Sympathy, Rendred faithfully out of French into English by R. White* (1658).

Dylan, Bob, 'Idiot Wind', CBS LP 69097, *Blood on the Tracks* (CBS Inc., 1974).

Erasmus, Desiderius, *Familiarium Colloquiorum Formulae* (Basle, 1519). Trans. N. Bailey as *All the Familiar Colloquies of Desiderius Erasmus . . . translated into English* (1725).

Fielding, Henry, *The History of Tom Jones, a Foundling* (1749).

——, *The History of the Adventures of Joseph Andrews, and of his friend Mr. Abraham Adams* (1742).

——, *Don Quixote in England* (1734).

Fontenelle, Bernard Le Bovier de, *Entretiens sur la Pluralité des Mondes* (Amsterdam, 1686).

Garrick, David, *Occasional Prologue on Quitting the Theatre* (1776).

Gerard, Alexander, *An Essay on Taste* (1759).

Goethe, Johann Wolfgang von, Letter to C. F. Zelter, Weimar, 25 December 1829; *Werke*, 129+ vols. (Weimar, 1887 ff), IV, 46, 193–4.

——, 'Maximen und Reflexionen über Literatur and Ethik', written 14–18 June 1826; *Werke*, I, 42 (2), 160.

——, 'Tagebuch', 20 December 1829, *Werke*, III, 12, 169.

——, *Aus Meinem Leben: Dichtung und Wahrheit* (1814). Trans. John Oxenford as *The Autobiography of Goethe. Truth and Poetry: From My Own Life* (1881).

Goldsmith, Oliver, *An Enquiry into the Present State of Polite Learning in Europe* (1759).

——, *The Good-Natur'd Man: A Comedy* (1768).

Graves, Richard, *The Spiritual Quixote: or, The Summer's Ramble of Mr. Geoffry Wildgoose. A Comic Romance* (1773).

Hardy, Thomas, *The Life and Death of the Mayor of Casterbridge* (1886).

Hartley, David, *Observations on Man: his Frame, his Duty, and his Expectations* (1749).

Hobbes, Thomas, *Leviathan: or, The Matter, Forme and Power of a Commonwealth Ecclestiasticall and Civill* (1651).

Hogarth, William, *A Harlot's Progress* (1730–32). Ronald Paulson, *The Art of Hogarth* (1975), Pl. 23–8.

——, *The March to Finchley* (1749–50) Paulson, *The Art of Hogarth*, Pl. 102–3.

——, *The Analysis of Beauty* (1753).

Home, Henry, Lord Kames, *Elements of Criticism* (1762, 3rd ed. Edinburgh, 1765).

Hume, David, *A Treatise of Human Nature* (1739–40), Ed. A. D. Lindsay, 2 vols. (1911, rpt. 1974).

——, Letter to Adam Smith, 28 July 1759, *Letters* (ed.) J. Y. T. Greig (Oxford, 1932), I, 313.

——, *Dialogues Concerning Natural Religion* (1779).

Hutcheson, Francis, *An Enquiry into the Original of our Ideas of Beauty and Virtue: in Two Treatises* (1725).

——, *An Essay on the Nature and Conduct of the Passions and Affections: with Illustrations on the Moral Sense* (1728).

Huygens, Christiaan, *Discours de la Cause de la Pesanteur* (Leyden, 1690) *Oeuvres Complètes de Christiaan Huygens, publiées par la Société Hollandaise des Sciences* 22 vols. (La Haye, 1888–1950), XXI.

Jameson, William, *An Essay on Virtue and Harmony* (Edinburgh, 1749).

Johnson, Samuel, *A Dictionary of the English Language* (1755).

Joyce, James, *Finnegans Wake* (1939).

——, *Ulysses* (London and Paris, 1922).

King, William and Gay, John, *An Essay on the Origin of Evil . . . To which is Prefix'd A Dissertation Concerning the Fundamental Principle and Immediate Criterion of Virtue* (1739).

La Mettrie, J. O. de, *L'Homme Machine* (Leyden, 1747).

Lennox, Charlotte *The Female Quixote; or, The Adventures of Arabella* (1752).

Locke, John, *An Essay Concerning Human Understanding* (1690), ed. P. H. Nidditch (Oxford, 1975).

——, 'The Second Treatise of Government' (1690) *Two Treatises of Government* (1690) ed. P. Laslett (Cambridge,

1960, rpt. with corrections, 1964).

Long, James, *An Enquiry into the Origin of the Human Appetites and Affections* (Lincoln, 1747).

Lucas, Charles, *The Infernal Quixote* (1801).

Lucian of Samosata, *The Works of Lucian of Samosata* trans. H. W. and F. G. Fowler (Oxford, 1905).

Mackenzie, Henry, *The Man of Feeling* (1771).

Maclaurin, Colin, *An Account of Sir Isaac Newton's Philosphical Discoveries* (1748).

Mead, Richard, *A Mechanical Account of Poisons in Several Essays* (1702).

Melmoth, Courtney, *Family Secrets* (1797).

Milton, John, *Paradise Lost* (1667). *Poetical Works*, ed. Douglas Bush (1966).

Moncrif, F. A. Paradis de, 'Les Abdérites', *Nouveau Receuil Choisi et Mêlé des Meilleurs Pièces de Théâtre François et Italien*, Vol. IV (La Haye, 1737).

Montaigne, Michel de, *Essais* (1580), trans. C. Cotton as *Essays of Michael Seigneur de Montaigne* (1693).

Morgan, Thomas, *Philosophical Principles of Medicine* (1726).

——, *Physico-Theology: or, A Philosophico-Moral Disquisition Concerning Human Nature. Free Agency, Moral Government, and Divine Providence* (1741).

Newton, Isaac, *Philosophiae Naturalis Principia Mathematica* (1687, 3rd ed. 1726).

Owen, Wilfred, *Poems* (1920).

Pavlov, Ivan Petrovich, *Lectures on Conditioned Reflex*, ed. and trans. W. Horsley Gantt, 2 vols (Vol. I, 1928, Vol. II, 1941), 5th printing 1963.

Piles, Roger de, *Cours de Peinture par Principes* (Paris, 1708).

Pope, Alexander, *Moral Essays, Epistle One. To Richard Temple, Viscount Cobham* (1734). *Poems*, ed. John Butt (1963), pp. 549–59.

——, *An Essay on Man: or, The first Book of Ethics. Epistle to H. St. John Bolingbroke* (1733–4). *Poems*, Butt, pp. 501–47.

Pynchon, Thomas, *Gravity's Rainbow* (1973).

Richardson, Samuel, *Clarissa: or, The History of a Young Lady* (1747–8).

Rousseau, Jean-Jacques, *Discours sur l'Origine et les Fondements de l'Inégalité parmi les Hommes* (Amsterdam, 1755), trans. G. D. H. Cole as *On the Origin of Inequality*, in *Great Books of the*

Western World, Vol. XXXVIII, Montesquieu/Rousseau, ed. R. M. Hutchins (Chicago, 1952).

——, *Emile, ou de l'Education* (1762) trans. Barbara Foxley (1911).

Ryle, Gilbert, *The Concept of Mind* (1949).

Scott, Walter, *The Fortunes of Nigel* (Edinburgh, 1822; Centenary Edition of Scott, Edinburgh, 1886).

Shakespeare, William, 'Timon of Athens', *Complete Plays*, ed. P. Alexander (1951), pp. 940–68.

——, 'Much Ado About Nothing', *Complete Plays*, Alexander, pp. 137–65.

——, 'Hamlet, Prince of Denmark', *Complete Plays*, Alexander, pp. 1028–72.

Sheridan, R. B., *The Critic: or, A Tragedy Rehearsed* (1781), *Plays,* ed. Cecil Price (Oxford, 1973), II, 494–550.

——, *The Rivals: A Comedy* (1775), *Plays*, ed. Price, I, 72–148.

Sherlock, William, *A Discourse Concerning the Divine Providence* (1694).

Shklovsky, Victor Borisovich, *Sentimental 'noe Puteshestvie: Vospominaniya 1917–22* (Moscow and Berlin, 1923), trans. Richard Sheldon as *A Sentimental Journey: Memoirs 1917–22* (Ithaca, NY, and London, 1970).

Smith, Adam, *The Theory of Moral Sentiments* (1759).

Smollett, Tobias, *The Adventures of Roderick Random* (1748, rpt. Folio Society, 1961).

——, *The Expedition of Humphry Clinker* (1771), ed. Lewis M. Knapp (1966).

——, *The Adventures of Sir Launcelot Greaves* (1762).

Stein, Gertrude, *How To Write* (Paris, 1931).

Swift, Jonathan, *A Tale of a Tub: Written for the Universal Improvement of Mankind. To which is added, An Account of a Battel between the Antient and Modern Books in St. James's Library* (1704), ed. A. C. Guthkelch and D. Nichol Smith (Oxford, 1920).

——, *Travels into Several Remote Nations of the World. In four parts. By Lemuel Gulliver* (1726), ed. H. Davis (Oxford, 1941).

Taylor, John, *An Examination of the Scheme of Morality, Advanced by Dr. Hutcheson* (1759).

Turnbull, George, *Principles of Moral Philosophy* (1740).

Warton, Joseph, *An Essay on the Genius and Writings of Pope* (Vol. I 1756: Vol. II, 1782).

Wezel, J. K., *Lebensgeschichte Tobias Knauts, des Weisen, sonst der Stammler gennant* (Leipzig, 1773–6).
Whitfield, George, *A Letter from the Rev. George Whitfield to the Rev. Laurence Sterne, the Supposed Author of a Book entitled 'The Life and Opinions of Tristram Shandy, Gentleman'* (1760).
Whytt, Robert, *An Essay on the Vital and Other Involuntary Motions of Animals* (1751, 2nd ed. 1763).
——, *Observations on the Nature, Causes, and Cure of those Disorders . . . commonly called Nervous, Hypochondriac or Hysteric: To which are Prefixed some Remarks on the Sympathy of the Nerves* (1761, 2nd ed. Edinburgh, 1765).
Woolf, Virginia, *Mrs. Dalloway* (1925).
Young, Edward, *Conjectures on Original Composition: in a Letter to the Author of Sir Charles Grandison* (1759).

SECONDARY SOURCES

Allen, Walter, *The English Novel* (1954).
Alter, Robert, 'The Picaroon as Fortune's Plaything', *Essays on the Eighteenth-Century Novel*, ed. R. Spector (Bloomington, Indiana, 1965) pp. 131–53.
——, '*Tristram Shandy* and the Game of Love', *American Scholar*, 37 (1967–8) 316–23.
Anderson, Howard, '*Tristram Shandy* and the Reader's Imagination', *PMLA*, 86 (1971), 966–73.
——, 'Answers to the Author of *Clarissa*; Theme and Narrative Technique in *Tom Jones* and *Tristram Shandy*', *PQ*, 51 (1972), 859–73.
——, 'Associationism and Wit in *Tristram Shandy*', *PQ*, 48 (1969), 27–41.
——, 'A Version of Pastoral: Class and Society in *Tristram Shandy*', *Studies in English Literature*, 7 (1967), 509–27.
Baird, Theodore, 'The Time-Scheme of *Tristram Shandy* and a Source', *PMLA*, 51 (1936), 803–20.
Ball, W. W. Rouse, *A Short Account of the History of Mathematics* (1888); 3rd ed. 1901.
Bann, Stephen, and Bowlt, John E., (eds), *Russian Formalism: A Collection of Articles and Texts in Translation* (Edinburgh, 1973).
Battestin, Martin C., '*Tom Jones*: The Argument of Design',

The Augustan Milieu: Essays Presented to Louis A. Landa, ed. H. K. Miller, E. Rothstein, G. S. Rousseau (Oxford, 1970) pp. 289–319. Later as 'Fielding: The Argument of Design', *The Providence of Wit: Aspects of Form in Augustan Literature and the Arts* (Oxford, 1974), pp. 141–63.

Birkhead, Edith, 'Sentiment and Sensibility in the Eighteenth-Century Novel', *Essays and Studies*, OS 11 (1925), 92–116.

Booth, Wayne C. 'The Self-Conscious Narrator in Comic Fiction before *Tristram Shandy*', *PMLA*, 67 (1952), 163–85.

——, *The Rhetoric of Fiction* (Chicago, 1961).

Boulton, J. T., Introduction to Burke's *Philosophical Enquiry into . . . the Sublime and Beautiful*, ed. J. T. Boulton (1958).

Brady, Frank, '*Tristram Shandy*: Sexuality, Morality and Sensibility', *Eighteenth-Century Studies*, 4 (1970), 41–56.

Braudy, Leo, *Narrative Form in History and Fiction: Hume, Fielding and Gibbon* (Princeton, NJ, 1970).

Bredvold, Louis, 'The Invention of the Ethical Calculus', *The Seventeenth Century: Studies in the History of English Thought and Literature from Bacon to Pope*, ed. R. F. Jones (Stanford, 1951), pp. 165–80.

Brett, R. L., *The Third Earl of Shaftesbury: A Study in Eighteenth-Century Literary Theory* (1971).

Brissenden, R. F., *Virtue in Distress: Studies in the Novel of Sentiment from Richardson to de Sade* (1974).

Brooks, Douglas, *Number and Pattern in the Eighteenth-Century Novel* (London and Boston, 1973).

Burkhardt, Sigurd, '*Tristram Shandy's Law of Gravity*', *ELH*, 28 (1961), 70–88.

Canguilhem, Georges, *L'Histoire du Concepte de Réflexe aux XVIIe et XVIIIe Siècles* (Paris, 1955).

Cash, Arthur, 'The Lockean Psychology of *Tristram Shandy*', *ELH*, 22 (1955), 125–35.

——, 'The Sermon in *Tristram Shandy*', *ELH*, 31 (1964), 395–417.

——, *Sterne's Comedy of Moral Sentiments: The Ethical Dimension of the Journey*, Philological Series, VI, Duquesne Studies (Pittsburgh, 1966).

——, *Laurence Sterne: The Early and Middle Years* (1975).

Cassirer, Ernst, *Die Platonische Renaissance in England und die Schule von Cambridge* (Leipzig and Berlin, 1932), trans.

J. P. Pettegrove as *The Platonic Renaissance in England* (Edinburgh, 1953).

Coburn, Kathleen (ed.), *Inquiring Spirit: A New Presentation of Coleridge from his Published and Unpublished Prose Writings* (1951).

Conrad, Joseph, 'Henry James: An Appreciation', *North American Review*, 180 (1905), 102–8, rpt. *Notes on Life and Letters* (1921).

Crane, R. S., 'Suggestions Towards A Genealogy of the Man of Feeling', *ELH*, 1 (1934), 205–30.

Cross, Wilbur L., *The Life and Times of Laurence Sterne* (New York, 1909).

Deporte, Michael V., Digressions and Madness in *A Tale of A Tub* and *Tristram Shandy*', *Huntingdon Library Quarterly*, 34 (1970), 43–57.

Dijksterhuis, E. J., *De Mechanisering van het Wereldbeeld* (Amsterdam, 1950), trans. C. Dikshoorn as *The Mechanization of the World-Picture* (Oxford, 1961).

Dilworth, Ernest N. *The Unsentimental Journey of Laurence Sterne* (Morningside Heights, NY, 1948).

Doherty, Francis, 'Sterne and Hume: A Bicentennial Essay', *Essays and Studies*, NS 22 (1969), 71–87.

Donaldson, Ian, 'The Clockwork Novel: Three Notes on an Eighteenth-Century Analogy', *Review of English Studies*, NS 21 (1970), 14–22.

Empson, William, '*Tom Jones*', *Kenyon Review*, 20 (1958), 217–49.

Encyclopaedia Britannica, 11th ed., 1910–11. Article on 'Abdera'.

Erämetsa, Erik, 'A Study of the Word 'Sentimental' and of other Linguistic Characteristics of Eighteenth-Century Sentimentalism in England', Annales Acad. Scientiarum Fennicae, B 74, 1 (Helsinki, 1951).

Erlich, Victor, *Russian Formalism: History-Doctrine* ('S-Gravenhage, 1955).

Evans, James, 'Tristram as Critic: Momus' Glass vs. Hobby-Horse', *PQ*, 50 (1971), 669–71.

Farrell, W. J., 'Nature versus Art as a Comic Principle in *Tristram Shandy*', *ELH*, 30 (1963), 16–35.

Ferriar, John, *Illustrations of Sterne: with other Essays and Verses* (1798).

Fluchère, Henri, *Laurence Sterne: de l'Homme à l'Oeuvre; Biographie Critique et Essai d'Interprétation de 'Tristram Shandy'* (Paris, 1961).

Foster, James R., *The History of the Pre-Romantic Novel in England* (London and New York, 1949).

Fowler, Alistair (ed.), *Silent Poetry: Essays in Numerological Analysis* (1970).

Freedman, William, '*Tristram Shandy*: The Art of Literary Counterpoint', *MLQ*, 32 (1971), 268–80.

Frye, Northrop, *Anatomy of Criticism: Four Essays* (Princeton, NJ, 1957).

Gettings, Fred, *The Book of the Hand: An Illustrated History of Palmistry* (1965).

Gilbert, K. E., and Kuhn, H., *A History of Aesthetics* (1956).

Grean, Stanley, *Shaftesbury's Philosophy of Religion and Ethics* (Athens, Ohio, 1967).

Hafter, Ronald S., 'Sterne's Affective Art and Eighteenth-Century Psychology', PhD Dissertation, Brandeis, 1970).

Halévy, Elie, *La Formation du Radicalisme Philosophique* (Paris, 1901–4), trans. M. Morris as *The Growth of Philosophic Radicalism* (1928, rpt. with corrections 1952).

Hartley, Lodwick C., *Laurence Sterne in the Twentieth Century: An Essay and a Bibliography of Sternean Studies, 1900–65* (Chapel Hill, NC, 1965).

Hewett-Thayer, H. W., *Laurence Sterne in Germany*, Columbia University Germanic Studies, Vol. 2, I (New York, 1905).

Holtz, W. V., *Image and Immortality: A Study of 'Tristram Shandy'* (Providence, RI, 1970).

Howes, Alan B., *Yorick and the Critics: Sterne's Reputation in England, 1760–1868*, Yale Studies in English, No. 137 (New Haven, 1958).

Hurlbutt, R. H. III., *Hume, Newton, and the Design-Argument* (Lincoln, Nebraska, 1965).

James, Overton P., *The Relation of 'Tristram Shandy' to the Life of Sterne* (The Hague, 1966).

Jefferson, D. W., '*Tristram Shandy* and the Tradition of Learned Wit', *EC*, 1 (1951), 225–48.

Jolas, Eugène, 'My Friend James Joyce', *James Joyce: Two Decades of Criticism*, ed. Seon Givens (New York, 1948, rpt. 1963), pp. 3–18.

Josipovici, Gabriel, *The World and the Book: A Study of Modern Fiction* (1971).

Kallich, Martin, *The Association of Ideas and Critical Theory in Eigteenth-Century England: A History of a Psychological Method in English Criticism*, Studies in Eng. Lit., No. 55 (The Hague, 1970).

Kuhn, Thomas S., *The Structure of Scientific Revolutions* (Chicago and London, 1962; 2nd impr. 1963).

Kyle, Carol, 'A Note on Laurence Sterne and the Cannon-Bullet of John Locke', *PQ*, 50 (1971) 672–4.

Laird, John, *Philosophical Incursions into English Literature* (Cambridge, 1946).

Lamb, Charles, 'Detached Thoughts on Books and Reading', *London Magazine*, July 1822, rpt. *The Life, Letters and Writings of Charles Lamb*, ed. Percy Fitzgerald (1876).

Lamb, Jonathan, 'Language and Hartleian Associationism in *A Sentimental Journey*', *Eighteenth-Century Studies*, 5(1971), 243–55.

Lanham, Richard A., *'Tristram Shandy': The Games of Pleasure* (Berkeley, LA, and London, 1973).

Lanson, Gustave, *Etudes d'Histoire Littéraire: Réunies et Publiées par ses Collègues, ses Elèves et ses Amis* (Paris, 1929).

Leavis, Frank R., *The Great Tradition: George Eliot, Henry James, Joseph Conrad* (1948).

Lehmann, B. H., 'Of Time, Personality and the Author: A Study of *Tristram Shandy*', *University of California Publications in English*, 8 (1941) (Berkeley, Cal., 1941), pp. 233–50.

Maclean, Kenneth, *John Locke and the English Literature of the Eighteenth Century* (New Haven, 1936).

——, 'Imagination and Sympathy: Sterne and Adam Smith', *Journal of the History of Ideas*, 10 (1949), 399–410.

MacPherson, C. B., 'The Social Bearings of Locke's Political Philosophy', *Western Political Quarterly*, 7 (1954), 1–22.

Maskell, Duke, 'Locke and Sterne, or, Can Philosophy Influence Literature?' *EC*, 23 (1973), 22–39.

Mayo, R. D., *The English Novel in the Magazines, 1740–1815, with a Catalogue of 1735 Magazine Novels and Novelettes* (Evanston, Illinois and London, 1962).

Mayoux, Jean-Jacques, 'Diderot and the Technique of Modern Literature', *Modern Language Review*, 31 (1936), 518–31.

McKillop, Alan D., *The Early Masters of English Fiction* (Lawrence, Kansas, 1956).

McReynolds, P. (ed.), *Four Early Works on Motivation (1726–1815)* (Gainsville, Florida, 1969).

Mendilow, Adam A., *Time and the Novel* (1952).

Mercer, David, *Sympathy and Ethics: A Study of the Relationship between Sympathy and Morality, with special reference to Hume's 'Treatise'* (Oxford, 1972).

Metzger, Bruce M. (ed.), *The Apochrypha of the Old Testament: Revised Standard Version* (New York, 1965).

Moglen, Helee, *The Philosophical Irony of Laurence Sterne* (Florida, 1975).

Moore, Robert E., *Hogarth's Literary Relationships* (Minneapolis, 1948).

Muir, Edwin, 'Laurence Sterne', *Essays on Literature and Society* (London and Toronto, 1949; 2nd ed. 1965), pp. 50–57.

Nauck, August, *Tragicorum Graecorum Fragmenta* (Lipsiae, 1856), ed. B. Snell (Gottingen, 1971).

New, Melvyn, *Laurence Sterne as Satirist: A Reading of 'Tristram Shandy'* (Gainsville, Florida, 1969).

Northouck, John, Article in *Monthly Review*, OS 39, 2 (July, 1768) p. 84.

Ortega y Gasset, Jose, *La Deshumanizacion del Arte e Ideas sobre la Novela* (Madrid, 1923), trans. H. Weyl as *The Dehumanization of Art and Notes on the Novel* (Princeton, NJ, 1948).

Passmore, John, *Hume's Intentions* (Cambridge, 1952; revised ed. 1968).

Paulson, Ronald H., *Satire and the Novel in Eighteenth-Century England* (New Haven, 1967).

——, *Theme and Structure in Swift's 'A Tale of A Tub'*, Yale Studies in English, No. 143 (New Haven, 1960).

Petrie, Graham, 'Rhetoric as Fictional Technique in *Tristram Shandy*', *PQ*, 48 (1969), 479–94.

Pinger, W. R. R., *Laurence Sterne and Goethe*, University of California Publications in Modern Philology Vol. 10, I (Berkeley, Cal., 1920).

Platonov, K. I., *The Word as a Physiological and Therapeutic Factor: The Theory and Practice of Psychotherapy according to I. P. Pavlov*, trans. from the Russian 2nd ed. by D. A. Myshne (Moscow, 1959).

Preston, John, '*Tom Jones* and the *Pursuit of True Judgment*', *ELH*, 33 (1966), 315–26, rpt. *The Created Self: The Reader's Role in Eighteenth-Century Fiction* (1970).

Putney, Rufus, 'The Evolution of *A Sentimental Journey*', *PQ*, 19 (1940), 349–69.

Raysor, Thomas M. (ed.) *Coleridge's Miscellaneous Criticism* (1936).

Ricks, Christopher, Introduction to *Tristram Shandy*, ed. Graham Petrie (Harmondsworth, 1967).

Robertson, J. M. (ed.), Introduction to Shaftesbury's *Characteristicks* (1900).

Rothstein, Eric, *Systems of Order and Enquiry in Later Eighteenth-Century Fiction* (Berkeley, LA, and London, 1975).

Rousseau, G. S., 'Science and the Discovery of the Imagination in Enlightened England', *Eighteenth-Century Studies*, 3 (1969), 108–35.

Ruthven, K. K., 'Fielding, Square, and the Fitness of Things', *Eighteenth-Century Studies*, 5 (1971), 243–55.

Schwartz, Leon, '*Jacques le Fataliste* and Diderot's Equine Symbolism', *Diderot Studies*, 16 (Geneva, 1973), 241–51.

Shepperson, Archibald, *The Novel in Motley* (Cambridge, Mass., 1936).

Shklovsky, Victor B., '*Tristram Shandy' Sternea i Teorija Romana* (Petrograd, 1921). Later as 'Parodijnyj Roman' in *O Teorii Prozy* (Moscow, 1925), trans. Lee T. Lemon and Marion Reis, *Russian Formalist Criticism*, ed. Lemon and Reis (Lincoln, Nebraska, 1965), pp. 25–57.

——, 'On the Connection Between Devices of Syuzhet Construction and General Stylistic Devices', 'Potebnya', *Poetika* (Petrograd, 1919). Later in *O Teorii Prozy* (Moscow, 1925), trans. Jane Knox, *Russian Formalism*, ed. S. Bann and J. E. Bowlt (Edinburgh, 1975), pp. 48–72.

Simon, Ernest, 'Fatalism, the Hobby-Horse, and the Esthetics of the Novel', *Diderot Studies*, 16 (Geneva, 1973), 253–74.

Stedmond, John M., *The Comic Art of Laurence Sterne: Convention and Innovation in 'Tristram Shandy' and 'A Sentimental Journey'* (Toronto, 1967).

Stearn, G. E (ed.), *McLuhan: Hot and Cool* (USA, 1967, Harmondsworth, 1968).

Stewart, J. B., *The Moral and Political Philosophy of David Hume* (New York, 1963).

Stout, Gardner, 'Yorick's "Sentimental Journey": A Comic "Pilgrim's Progress" for the Man of Feeling', *ELH*, 30 (1963), 395–412.

Tanner, Tony, *City of Words: American Fiction 1950–1970* (1971).

Thackeray, W. M., *English Humourists of the Eighteenth Century* (1853) in *Henry Esmond, The English Humourists, The Four Georges*, ed. George Saintsbury (London, New York and Toronto, n.d.).

Todorov, Tzvetan, 'The Structural Analysis of Literature: The Tales of Henry James', *Structuralism: An Introduction*, ed. David Robey, Wolfson College Lectures 1972 (Oxford, 1973), pp. 73–103.

Tompkins, J. M. S., *The Popular Novel in England, 1770–1800* (1932).

Traugott, John, *Tristram Shandy's World: Sterne's Philosophical Rhetoric* (Berkeley and LA, 1954).

—— (ed.), *Laurence Sterne: A Collection of Critical Essays* (Englewood Cliffs, NJ, 1968).

Tynianov, Yuri, 'Literaturnoe Segodnja', *Ruskii Sovremennik*, 1 (1924).

van Ghent, Dorothy, 'On *Tom Jones*' in *The English Novel: Form and Function* (New York, 1953, rpt. New York and Evanston, 1961), pp. 65–81.

Vartanian, Aram, *La Mettrie, 'L'Homme Machine': A Study in the Origins of an Idea* (Princeton, NJ, 1960).

Wasserman, Earl R., *The Subtler Language: Critical Readings of Neoclassical and Romantic Poems* (Baltimore, 1959).

——, 'Nature Moralized: The Divine Analogy in the Eighteenth Century', *ELH*, 20 (1953), 39–76.

Watson, Wilfred, 'Sterne's Satire on Mechanism: A Study of *Tristram Shandy*'. (PhD Dissertation, Toronto, 1951).

Watt, Ian, 'The Comic Syntax of *Tristram Shandy*', *Studies in Criticism and Aesthetics 1660–1800: Essays in Honour of Samuel Holt Monk*, ed. H. Anderson and J. S. Shea (Minneapolis, 1967), pp. 315–31.

——, *The Rise of the Novel* (1957).

Wellek, Rene, and Warren, Austin, *The Theory of Literature* (New York and London, 1949).

Werner, Stephen, *Diderot's Great Scroll: Narrative Art in 'Jacques le Fataliste'*. Studies on Voltaire and the Eighteenth Century, No. CXXVIII (Banbury, Oxon., 1975).

Willey, Basil, *The Eighteenth-Century Background* (1940).

Wittkower, Rudolf, *Palladio and English Palladianism*, The Collected Essays of Rudolf Wittkower, Vol. I (1974).

Wormhoudt, Arthur, 'Newton's Natural Philosophy in the Behmenistic Works of William Law', *Journal of the History of Ideas*, 10 (1949), 411–29.

Index

One of the remnants of 'doctoralese' in this work is its habit of using other writers on Sterne as points of reference against which to define its own argument. For this reason I have included secondary references in the index in those cases where more than a few words of the critic are used in the text, or where the critic is used to further the argument.